Sheldon Pollock, General Editor

MIR TAQI MIR
REMEMBRANCES

MCLI 22

CONTENTS

INTRODUCTION

Remembrances (*Zikr-e Mīr*) is one of the very few autobiographical texts in the annals of Persian letters in South Asia. Its author, Mir Muhammad Taqi "Mir"—the first "Mir" indicates his claim to be a descendent of the prophet Muhammad; the second is his *takhallus,* the name he used in the "signature lines" of his poems—is commonly regarded as the most important Urdu poet of the eighteenth century and the most influential *ghazal* poet in the language. Mir was also the most prolific writer of his generation. His legacy in Urdu consists of six volumes of short lyrical poems (*ghazal*), the same number of long narrative poems (*masnawi*), and any number of quatrains, panegyrics, satires, and occasional poems of a great variety. Like many of his peers he also wrote in Persian, excelling in both quality and quantity. In addition to some five hundred *ghazals* and one short *masnawi,* he also left behind in Persian three works of prose: *Nikāt-al-Shuʻarā* (Subtleties of Poets), an account mainly of the significant Urdu poets of Delhi in his time; *Faiẓ-e Mīr* (Mir's Bounty), a short book of Sufistic anecdotes aimed at teaching Persian to his son; and the present book, an account of portions of his life and the political events he witnessed or learned about.

Born in Agra in A.H. 1135 (1723 C.E.), Mir belonged to a respectable family of Arab origins. His father's name was Muhammad ʻAli. While Mir's grandfather had been an employee of the state, Muhammad ʻAli, according to Mir, lived the life of a Sufi dervish. He may have also been engaged in the book trade. Muhammad 'Ali married twice. His first wife, with whom he had one son, Muhammad Hasan, was from a notable Sunni family of Gwalior and either a sister or a cousin of Sirajuddin 'Ali Khan "Arzu," the preeminent Persian litterateur and lexicographer of his age. His second wife was from a Shia family and bore him two sons, Muhammad Taqi and Muhammad Razi, and a daughter.

Mir tells us nothing about his mother. She was probably still alive when her husband died. Mir says he left his younger brother at home when he first went to Delhi at the age of eleven or twelve; when a few years later he leaves Agra for good, he makes no similar remark. Quite possibly, she too moved to Delhi, along with her younger son, and died there. She is not mentioned at the time Mir visits the grave of his father at Agra on his first return trip in more than two decades.

After moving to Delhi when he was about seventeen, Mir first stayed with Arzu, the eminent uncle of his half brother, but soon a conflict between them prompted him to set up his own household. It is possible that during those early years Mir not only studied some books with Arzu, and later on his own, but also learned calligraphy in order to pursue the occupation of bookselling of his father. But his exceptional talent in poetry soon attracted the attention of some notables of Delhi, who patronized him. The most significant was Raja Nagar Mal (d. 1774), a Jat nobleman who held various high ranks in the service of several Mughal emperors. Mir stayed in his service until late 1771. Then, after suffering almost a decade of misfortune and hardship, Mir moved to Lucknow in 1781, where he enjoyed the largesse of Nawab

Asaf-ud-Daula (d. 1797), the ruler of Awadh, who also held the rank of vizier to the Mughal emperor.

In all likelihood, Mir, like his father, married twice—the age difference between his two sons is too big to be accounted for differently. The first marriage took place in Delhi and produced two children: Mir Faiz 'Ali and a daughter, who was married to a cousin. Mir's first wife is believed to have died before he left Delhi; he then took a second wife in Lucknow, with whom he had a son, Mir Hasan 'Askari, aka Mir Kallu "'Arsh." Sadly, the second wife, the only daughter, and the first son, Faiz 'Ali, all predeceased Mir. By that time he had also lost the patronage of the new nawab, Sa'adat 'Ali Khan. As a result, Mir's final years were again spent in great mental and physical misery. The remaining son was not successful in life, and little is known of Mir's two grandsons except that, like their father, 'Arsh, they were insignificant poets. It is possible that Mir received some attention when the British were hiring experts in Urdu for work at the College of Fort William, but he could not have moved to Calcutta at his advanced age. He died in Lucknow on Sha'ban 21, A.H. 1225 (September 21, 1810 C.E.). The college, however, did publish a year later a meticulously prepared edition of his entire Urdu corpus that is yet to be surpassed in quality and care.

Contrary to the image created by Muhammad Husain Azad in Āb-e Ḥayāt (Water of Immortality), the most influential of all histories of Urdu poetry (1881), and his own frequent remarks in Remembrances, Mir was not always a dour recluse. In fact, on the evidence of many of his topical poems, he could be said to have been a man of appetites.

He could feel strongly for his friends and lovers and openly find pleasure in their company, just as he could launch scurrilous attacks against those who would enrage him for any reason. The poems he wrote about his patron Asaf-ud-Daula's hunting expeditions—they are thematically unique in Urdu poetry—display a keen appreciation of natural beauty and wildlife. He must have been quite fond of animals, for at various times he kept cats, dogs, and goats as pets, and wrote delightful little poems about them.

Mir's three substantial prose works are all in Persian. The practice of using Persian, rather than Urdu, for any serious composition in prose was not uncommon at the time. The earliest *tazkira*s (biographical dictionaries) of Urdu poets, authored by men who were accomplished poets in Urdu, were nevertheless in Persian. *Daryā-e Laṭāfat* (Ocean of Subtleties), the first book to deal with Urdu linguistics and poetics, completed in 1807, was written in Persian with Urdu examples. *Gharā'ib-al Lughāt* (Strange Words), a much earlier work and arguably the first dictionary of Urdu, was written in Persian. Mir's choice in language for his prose works, therefore, was in conformity with the practice at the time.

Mir's first venture in prose was *Nikāt-al-Shu'arā*, a *tazkira* compiled on the model of existing books on Persian poets. The extant text has been dated to 1752 on the basis of internal evidence. It contains brief notes on 103 poets, arranged mostly in chronological order, each followed by selected verses. Its contents, in particular Mir's nasty comments on some of his peers, caused an uproar, and a couple of his peers wrote rejoinders in similar works of their own. Concerning himself, Mir had only this to say: "This humble fakir, Mir Muhammad Taqi Mir, author of the book, belongs to Akbarabad (i.e., Agra), but driven by changing times presently resides in Shahjahanabad (i.e., Delhi)."

The second book, *Faiz-e Mīr*, is a short collection of five brief narratives about mystics, in which Mir often appears as a sympathetic interlocutor. The book's name refers to Faiz 'Ali, Mir's eldest son, for whom the book was written as a basic reader. Again, no date of composition is given in the text, but most likely it was written in 1761–1762, while Mir and his patron were at Kumher. We get little personal information about Mir, except that he could ride a horse but did not own one. The anecdotes give the impression of being eyewitness accounts, but the mystics mentioned in them, like those mentioned in *Remembrances,* are not identifiable in any available source on mystics of that time. Mir's fascination with them, however, is only too evident, as is their alleged willingness to let Mir get close to them on account of his innate disposition toward mystical thought. In language and style, however, *Faiz-e Mīr* is very close to *Remembrances.* Much of it is in delightful rhymed prose; more important, it too extensively exploits a particular lexicographical work by Arzu, discussed below.

At the beginning of *Remembrances,* Mir follows the established convention and explains why he wrote the book:

Now says this humble man, Mir Muhammad Taqi, whose *takhallus* is Mir, that being unemployed these days and confined to my solitary corner, I wrote down

my story, containing the events of my life, the incidents
of my times, and some other edifying and pleasing anecdotes. And I concluded this book, entitled *Zikr-e Mīr*
(Remembrances of Mir), with some witty tales.

The book actually contains a brief notice of Mir's ancestors; an extended section on Muhammad 'Ali, his beloved
friend Amanullah, and some mystics the two come to know;
followed by a fairly detailed narrative of the political events
of Mir's time, only some of which he personally witnessed.
Vignettes of Mir's personal life come in summary snatches;
he does not provide the details that are expected in an autobiography, not even his date of birth. He is similarly silent
concerning his literary life except for mentioning his patrons
and how he came to meet them. The book, surprisingly, ends
with several pages of jokes, some of them explicitly sexual.
All together, while it makes for a curious "autobiography,"
it has many attractions.

For one, it gives us a detailed awareness of the political
intrigues and betrayals that had become endemic among the
ruling elite in the declining years of the Mughal regime. Mir
moved to Delhi circa 1740, during the reign of the Emperor
Muhammad Shah, not long after parts of the city had been
ransacked by the soldiers of the Iranian invader Nadir Shah,
while the city's elite had been deprived of their wealth by the
emperor himself. But much wealth and joy still remained
in the city, as is evident from the eyewitness account of
Dargah Quli Khan in his memoirs now generally known as
Muraqqa'-e Dihlī. Moreover, Delhi still consisted of two
densely populated and fairly flourishing cities: the walled

city of Shahjahanabad—Mir referred to it as "the city" or "the New City"—and the vast urban sprawl south of it— Mir called it "the Old City"—that had existed and flourished for at least two hundred years. By the time Mir abandoned Delhi for Lucknow, only a misery-filled Shahjahanabad was left standing. The "Old" city no longer existed; it had been plundered several times, and even burned and razed. The Bishop of Calcutta, Reginald Heber, visiting Delhi in the winter of 1824 described it as "a very awful scene of desolation, ruins after ruins, tombs after tombs, fragments of brickwork, free stone, granite, and marble, scattered everywhere over a soil naturally rocky and barren, without cultivation, except in one or two small spots, and without a single tree... The ruins really extended as far as the eye could reach."[1] The bishop was riding an elephant at the time.

During the four decades of Mir's stay in Delhi, first in one city and then in the other, the Red Fort saw five occupants. Of them, Emperor Ahmad Shah was deposed by his nobles and blinded; 'Alamgir II was assassinated in a similar conspiracy; Shah Jahan III lasted only one year on the throne, though stayed alive in prison; and Shah 'Alam II gained the throne only after years of exile, and then was publicly humiliated, tortured, and blinded by a Rohilla marauder until the Marathas again came to his rescue. Mir provides us not only a detailed account of the political intrigues and betrayals that had become endemic among the elite of Delhi but also a better awareness of the plight and suffering of the ordinary people at the hands of the Jats, the Rohillas, the Sikhs, and the Marathas, who preyed on them, sometimes singly but often in various alliances.

Most significantly, given Mir's status in Urdu and Persian literatures in India, *Remembrances* discloses certain obsessions of his in a manner that no other source does. It may have been written during a time of enforced solitude, but it shows clear signs of being a deliberate enterprise, with certain specific goals in mind. First, while Mir's Shia faith is fully evident in his poetry and prose, *Remembrances* makes it clear that he was also keen to claim a sayyid lineage for himself, and that his father, despite his marrying into a prominent Sunni family, had also been a Shia. The claim to sayyidhood was questioned, even mocked, by some of Mir's peers, probably encouraged by the fact that the son of Mir's half brother made no such assertion.

Second, in addition to establishing Shia-sayyid credentials for his father, Mir goes to great efforts to represent him as a mystic, respected by the nobility and the masses alike and possessing strong transformative powers. So far, no independent source has been found to confirm either of the claims. Muhammad 'Ali, no doubt, belonged to a respectable family, otherwise he couldn't have married Arzu's sister. He was also much regarded by at least one prominent grandee of the time, from whom the orphaned Mir obtained a daily stipend. But the fact remains that even Mir had felt no need to mention his name when he described himself in his first book.

In view of the considerable lengths Mir goes to in *Remembrances* to make such assertions, one may justifiably speculate about motives. Could it be that he was positioning himself on an equal footing in social status with his peer Khwaja Mir Dard, who belonged to a prominent Sunni Sufi family and

who was also a sayyid on both sides of his lineage? Dard's
father, Khwaja Muhammad Nasir "'Andalib," had declared
himself the founder of a new spiritual tradition within the
Naqshbandi order, one of the four major Sufi traditions in
South Asia, and Dard had championed his father's claims in
copious writings. Mir knew both the father and the son quite
well, and mentions elsewhere that 'Andalib had once blessed
him and foretold his future greatness. Even if we disallow
envy as a motive, Dard's glorification of his own father may
arguably have suggested to Mir a way to similarly establish
a distinguished forebearer for himself, with the additional
gain of avoiding any reference to Arzu in the fulfillment of
a deep social and personal need—to be known as somebody
important's son instead of as Sirajuddin 'Ali Khan Arzu's
step-nephew.

Perhaps the most startling portions of *Remembrances* are
where Mir obsessively denigrates Arzu, whom he had earlier
described as his benefactor and mentor in his *tazkira*. Now
he charges Arzu with treating him so ill that it caused him,
Mir, to go insane for a while. He further minimizes Arzu
in connection with his studies in Delhi and his growth as
a poet, and asserts his own expertise in Persian language
by making inordinate use of the arcane words and idioms
included in Arzu's highly regarded dictionary, *Charāgh-e
Hidāyat* (Lamp of Guidance); he does the same in *Faiż-e
Mīr*, written around the same time, without once mentioning either the book or the author.

Mir's almost vengeful obsession with Arzu is yet to be
satisfactorily explained. Was it a sectarian conflict—Arzu
was Sunni; Mir was Shia; and Shia-Sunni conflict was much

present in Delhi at the time—as some scholars have said? Did it arise out of some family scandal—Mir fell in love with a cousin, a member of Arzu's household—as others have speculated? It was clearly an intense relationship of both admiration and hatred, for when a copy of Arzu's highly influential *tazkira, Majma'-al-Nafā'is* (A Gathering of Precious Beings), was prepared at Kumher for Mir's patron, Raja Nagar Mal—arguably under Mir's own supervision—a blatantly forged entry found its way into it, praising Mir in a most fulsome manner.

A major disappointment for Urdu lovers is Mir's total silence on his literary milieu. None of his peers finds any mention, not even Mirza Rafi' Sauda, his ablest peer and strongest rival. No books are discussed; no literary gathering or contestation gets an accounting, though we learn about many from other sources. Instead, we find Mir presenting himself as a man of the political world, as if his patron, Raja Nagar Mal, had taken him into his service not for his poetry but exclusively for his skills at diplomacy. In fact, according to *Remembrances,* Mir finally left the raja's service only because the latter ignored Mir's advice in a political matter and thus put him in an embarrassing position. That Mir could have performed diplomatic duties for the raja is perfectly acceptable, though it is more than likely that Mir's official duties involved taking care of the raja's library; but what one sorely misses is some glimpse into those long evening sessions they must have shared over almost seventeen years of Mir's employment.

The final feature of the book that requires comment is the inclusion of some fifty-five "witty" anecdotes at the end.

Their inclusion should surprise us, but their coarse language should not. The language of satirical poems in Urdu at the time was often quite rough. These jokes come as a corrective to the doleful image of Mir offered in almost all post-1857 writings about him. No print edition of *Zikr-e Mīr* has ever included them. The first editor, Maulvi Abdul Haq, wrote on the issue in 1928: "Mir Sahib has also put together some jokes at the end of the book ... But sadly some of them are so obscene that it is not possible to include or describe them. We learn from them the taste of those days, otherwise Mir Sahib's sobriety and refinement need no comment. For that reason, and also because they are quite irrelevant, we have left the jokes out."[2]

Contrary to modern editors, Mir obviously wished to share the jokes with his readers. He offers them with a simple statement: "Now the pen has on its tongue some witty tales, and lays them out for its friends' sake." It is as if by the end of *Remembrances* Mir was done with history and politics, even mysticism, and wished simply to conclude on an informal, happier note. The inclusion of the jokes also begins to make ample sense when we note the self-image that Mir had already projected in the preceding text—a man equally at home among otherworldly Sufis and this-worldly nobles—while making little or no mention of his prowess as a poet, taking that for granted. The jokes reassure us that Mir, in other moments, could also be a jovial fellow and excellent company.

Concerning the date of the composition of *Remembrances,* Mir avers that he undertook it at a time when he was "unemployed ... and confined to his solitary corner." But a comparison of the five manuscripts immediately shows that the text was not all written at one particular time, that additions were intermittently made over a number of years. He could have started during a period of unemployment in Delhi and before 1760, but the bulk of the core text was written after 1760 and elsewhere—in the Jat forts of Kumher and Dig, where Mir and his family, as well as his patron, Raja Nagar Mal, took shelter for almost eleven years—August 1760 to July or August 1771.

The period of exile from Delhi, despite its hardships, was doubtless also a period of relative peace for Mir, which he utilized by concentrating on Persian. Ghulam Hamdani Mushafi, a younger contemporary of Mir, reports being told by Mir in Lucknow that during a certain period of two years he stopped writing poetry in Urdu and wrote close to two thousand verses in Persian. That total abandonment of Urdu couldn't have been possible in Delhi with its many *musha'ira*s (formal poetry gatherings), in which a tacit challenge from Mir's many peers would have required Mir to present new Urdu verses. We should also recall Mir's obsession with Arzu and his extensive, and unacknowledged, use of Arzu's lexicon of rare Persian words and idioms in both *Faiz-e Mīr* and *Zikr-e Mīr*—it too required concentrated effort and ample time. Mir could afford both during those years; his patron, Raja Nagar Mal, was often away at other forts, and Mir did not always accompany him.

Mir finished the book he originally had in mind by March 1773, when he was back in Delhi but jobless, and when he had completed fifty lunar years of his life, as indicated in a chronogram at the end. The text consisted of two distinct parts: a long narrative that began as distinctly familial and autobiographical but gradually turned into political history; and a set of fifty-five jokes. I call this core book Narrative A. Mir continued to add to the historical section as he felt necessary—not only to complete the account of some specific event or person but also to postdate his devotion to his final patron, Nawab Asaf-ud-Daula—sometimes even at the cost of disturbing the linear chronology he had otherwise maintained. He also moved some of his more personal remarks around and deleted a small paragraph listing some of his minor patrons. All versions, however, retained the jokes; he did not reduce or change them in any fashion. A second redaction of the text apparently took place in 1783, as is indicated in the altered chronogram in a later manuscript, but the extended historical narrative concludes with some events of 1789. I call this expanded version Narrative B. Mir lived on for another twenty-one years but apparently made no further additions or changes.

NOTES

1 Heber 1843: v. 1, 302.
2 Mir 1928: xix.

NOTE ON THE TEXT
AND TRANSLATION

Mir's Persian text has come down to us in six manuscripts—
Etawah (1808), Calcutta (n.d.), Rampur (1830-31), Lucknow
(n.d.), Lahore (1816), and Gwalior (date unknown)—each
identified by the place where it was discovered. The first
two contain the expanded Narrative B. I was able to make
use of the first five; the one at Gwalior remained inaccessible.
The Etawah manuscript was edited and published in 1928 by
Maulvi Abdul Haq, who also made limited use of the Lahore
manuscript. He left out the jokes, however, labeling them
obscene. His text was superbly translated into Urdu by Nisar
Ahmad Faruqi in 1957; a revised edition came out in 1996,
containing also the Persian. He too, however, felt compelled
to leave out the jokes.

The text presented here is a "composite" of Narrative
A and Narrative B, based on the above-mentioned five
manuscripts. It contains in full the core book, including a
paragraph not found in two later manuscripts, and all the
additions that Mir made over the next ten years. Portions
of the concluding remarks in the "core" that were of the
conventional edifying nature have been moved—as, indeed,
Mir had done—to the very end after the jokes, together with
the chronogram Mir composed when he was sixty. I did not
change the order of the nonautobiographical additions he
made over a decade; they appear where Mir had placed them.
Nothing has been left out. The MCLI edition, accordingly,

is the first complete published text, based on all accessible manuscripts.

In preparing this edition of the translation, I have gone over my earlier version, referred to in the footnote below, and corrected errors of misreading and mistranslation. Additionally, in order to make it more readable for a nonspecialist, I have made it less literal than before. The translation of the biographical and historical portions, however, remains closer to the original language than is the case with the jokes, where I have taken greater liberty to retain their amusing effect. While matters demanding some elucidation have been handled in the endnotes, places and dates of important events are indicated in footnotes to help the reader with chronology. The latter are entirely based on the monumental work of Jadunath Sarkar.[1]

NOTES

1   Sarkar 1964. For more information on all aspects of the text as well as Mir's life and career as a poet, see Mir 1999.

Remembrances

بسم الله الرحمٰن الرحیم

١ حمد بیحد مر سخنوری را که یکه بیت یکتائی او بعالم دوید،
و ثنای لاتعد صنعت گری را که گوهر معنی در سلک نظم و نثر
کشید. قادرسخنی که هزار رنگ سخن را جلوه بر زبان میدهد،
تعلیم گری که هر فرد عاجزسخن را زبان میدهد. خالقی که خلق
عالم را نوازد، صانعی که خاک را آدمی سازد. دارندهٔ که بی لطف
او نگاهداشتن خود محال است، نگارندهٔ که صورت نویسی نقش
او کرا مجال است. علیمی که در احاطهٔ علم او و هر مرکب و بسیط
این جاست که «إنّ الله علی کل شئ محیط». حکیمی که دانای
رازهاست، قدیمی که هستی او را سزاست. رازقی که نان دهد،
مالکی که جان دهد. رحیمی که عذر گنهگار نیوشد، کریمی که
عطا پاشد و خطا پوشد. شمس یک ذرهٔ از ظهور او، قمر یک شمعهٔ
از نور او. چیزی نیست که بی نور او فرض کنی. غرض که «الله نور
السماوات والأرض».

٢ ناز او از بسکه نیاز را دوست میدارد، هرکه سر فرود می آرد
نومید نمیگذارد. آفرینندهٔ که چها آفرید و بینندهٔ که نهان همه
کس دید. هرچند چرخ کج رفتار با من کج بازد امّا چشم دارم که
روی مرا بر خاک نیندازد. زبانی نیست که نام او ازو نمی آید، جانی
نی که نغمهٔ وصف او نمی سراید. خبیری که از حال همه کس خبر
دارد، بصیری که همه را در نظر دارد. نیازی باید که گلهای ناز

"In the name of God, most Gracious, most Merciful."
Endless praises be to that Eloquent One alone, the word   1
of whose uniqueness resounds throughout the world; and
acclaimed beyond measure be that Master Craftsman who
placed pearls of meaning upon the thread of prose and verse.
The Master of Eloquence who makes known a thousand
different hues of speech; the Noble Teacher who provides a
tongue to those who cannot speak. The Creator who blessed
the world with creation; the Crafter who turned dust into
the human. The Bountiful, without whose bounty none can
survive; the Artist, to copy whose design no one may dare
to strive. The Knower who comprehends all that is elemen-
tal or complex; indeed, it has been said: "Allah has in his
grasp everything that exists."[1] He is the Wise who knows
even that which is hidden, who alone *is*, he, the Eternal One.
The Provider who gives nourishment to us; the Master who
bestows life upon us. The Merciful who listens to the excuses
of the sinners; the Benevolent who ignores and forgives our
errors. The sun is just a grain of his manifestation, and the
moon but a trace of his effulgence. Nothing can happen
outside his sight; for "Allah is, of the heavens and the earth,
the light."[2]

He is disdainful, but befriends those who are humble, for   2
he who goes before him bent in humility never comes back
empty-handed. What a Creator he is, and how wondrous
his creation! What a Seer he is, who can perceive what
lies hidden inside anyone. Though the ill-turning heavens conspire against me, I confidently hope that he will
not shame me. There is no tongue that does not speak his
name; and there is no soul that does not sing in acclaim.

او چیند، چشمی شاید که تازه کاری او بیند. فردیکه بفردانیت موصوف، احدیکه بوحدانیت معروف. رفیعی که بدرگاه او ملک نرود، سمیعی که الحاح هر عاجزی شنود. قلم دو زبان چه قدرت دارد که کمالات او یک یک برنگارد، مگر او خود را خود ستاید و از عهدهٔ کمالات خود برآید.

۳ و درود نامحدود بر فصیحی که گوی فصاحت از میان برده، و تحیات نامعدود بر بلیغی که بخدا رسید و بخود نسپرده. شاهی که از سر تا پا قدر و جلال است، ماهی که زنگ زدای کفر و ضلال است. پیشوائی که بی اقتدای او کاری نمیکشاید، رهنمائی که بی رهنمائی او راهی نمی نماید. امیری که فرمان او بجان و دل پذیریم، دستگیری که اگر دست دهد دنبال او گیریم. صبیحی که صباحت او روشنگر آئینهٔ عالم ، ملیحی که ملاحت او نمک رخسارهٔ آدم. نگاری که خاک زیر پای او بهای جانی، بهاری که سایه روِ علم سبز او جهانی. یاری گری که چشم محشریان بر شفاعت او، نی نی هر دو جهان را کار با عنایت او. صلی الله علیه و آله الطیبین الطاهرین، که هر یکی امام المؤمنین و شفیع المذنبین است.

He is informed of everyone's plight; nothing that happens here escapes his sight. Submit, that you may receive what he vouchsafes from his bounty; and cultivate an eye that can perceive his ever-new artistry. He is the Unique, only his uniqueness is beyond any doubt; he is the One whose Oneness is absolute. He resides so high, even the angels cannot reach the lowest threshold of his palace; and yet he hears the importunities that any human supplicant makes. No pen, even with its two tongues, can describe his each and every perfection;[3] it befits only him to speak in his own praise and do justice to his preeminence.

And may endless blessings be upon that eloquent person who surpassed everyone in eloquence; and may benedictions beyond count be upon that man of elegant words who reached God but did not show arrogance. He is the king who embodies power and eminence; he is the moon that dispels the darkness of impiety and ignorance. He is the exemplar we must follow to make our actions sound; he is the guide, without whose guidance no path can ever be found. He is the overlord whose command we must accept, heart and soul. He is the patron and protector to whom we must hold on, if such be our good fortune. He is that fair one who gives the mirror of the world its shine; and he is that dark-complexioned one who adds spice to Adam's tribe. Our lives are a ransom for the dust under his feet; he is that acme of beauty; and he is that season of glorious spring whose verdure gives shade and comfort to every entity. He is the intercessor we must look to for redemption on the Day of Judgment. Nay, there is nothing here and in the hereafter that is not due to his munificence. May God's blessings be upon him and upon

۴ بعد حمد خالق ودود و معبود کلّ موجود، و درود نامحدود و
ثنای نامعدود بران صاحب مقام محمود، میگوید فقیر میر محمد
تقی المتخلص بمیر که درین ایام بیکار بودم و در گوشهٔ تنهائی
بی یار. احوال خود را متضمن حالات و سوانح روزگار و حکایات و
نقلها نگاشتم، و بنای خاتمهٔ این نسخه موسوم به «ذکر میر» بر
لطائف گذاشتم. امید از یاران زمان آنست که اگر بر خطای اطلاع
یابند، چشم عنایت نپوشند و در اصلاح بکوشند.

۵ بزرگان من با دارودستهٔ خود از نامساعدت ایام، که صبح در
این اوقات شام می نماید، از حجاز رخت سفر بربسته بسرحد
دکن رسیدند. ناکشیدنیها کشیدند و نادیدنیها دیدند. از آنجا
وارد احمدآباد گجرات گشتند. بعضی فروکش کرده ازهم گذشتند
و بعضی همت برین گماشتند که پیشتر بیایند و بازوی تلاش
کشایند. چنانچه جدّ کلان من به مستقرالخلافت اکبرآباد توطن
اختیار کرد. اینجا از آب گردش بر بستر افتاد و جهان آب و گِل
را دعا گفت. ازو پسری باقی ماند که جدّ من باشد. او کمر همت
بربسته بتلاش روزگار برخواست. بعد از استخوان شکنی به
فوجداری گرد اکبرآباد سرافراز گشت. آدمیانه میزیست. چون
سن شریفش به پنجاه کشید مزاج از اعتدال منحرف شد. چند
روز بتبرید پرداخت. هنوز صحت کامل نشده بود که بگوالیار
رفت. بسبب حرکت عنیفی که در نقاهت سم است بجا افتاد و

his excellent and pure descendants, each one of whom is an "Imam of the Believers" and an "Intercessor of the Sinners."

After praising the Benevolent Creator, the Lord of All Existence, and offering endless blessings and praises to him who truly claims all praises, now says this humble man, Mir Muhammad Taqi, whose *takhallus* is Mir,[4] that being unemployed these days and confined to my solitary corner, I wrote down my story, containing the events of my life, the incidents of my times, and some other edifying and pleasing anecdotes. And I concluded this book, entitled *Zikr-e Mīr*, with some witty tales. I hope my friends would not deny me forgiveness should they notice any error therein, and only strive to set me right.

My ancestors, beset with hard times when even mornings appear dark as night, left the Hijaz with their wives and dependents and traveled to the border of the Deccan. After suffering what none should suffer and experiencing what none should experience, they moved to Ahmedabad, Gujarat, where some of them chose to settle down. Others, however, decided to be more resolute, and pressed on to seek their fortune elsewhere. And so my great-grandfather came to the capital, Akbarabad, and made it his home. The climate of the place did not suit him; he fell ill and eventually bade farewell to this world of dust and water. He left behind one son, who was my grandfather. Girding his loins, my grandfather set about looking for a job and after much struggle gained the honor of being appointed a *faujdār* in the neighborhood of Akbarabad.[5] He lived a decent life, but when he came to be fifty his disposition lost its balance. For some days he treated himself with cooling drinks, but before he could

4

5

7

جامه گذاشت. و او دو پسر داشت. کلانی خالی از خلل دماغ نبود،
جوان مُرد و حکایت او پسِ سر شد.

۶ پسر خورد که پدر من باشد ترک لباس کرد و پا بدامن کشید.
تحصیل علم ظاهر که بی آن بعالم معنی رسیدن دشوار است در
خدمت شاه کلیم الله اکبرآبادی که از کمّل اولیای آنجا بود کرد،
و از ریاضت شاقه پی به باطن برد. در سعی ترک و تجرید تصدیع
بیحد کشید، و برهنمائی آن بزرگ به سرخانهٔ درویشی رسید.

پس از خرابی بسیار دل بدست افتاد.

جوان صالحی عاشق پیشه بود. دل گرمی داشت، بخطاب علی
متقی امتیاز یافت.

۷ روزی در خدمت شیخ سوال کرد که بنده انچه عقاید خود
درست کرده ام بخدمت عالی واضح است، اما در حق حاکم شام
چه میفرمایند. فرمود، خواهم گفت. بعد مدتی آخر شب که هنوز
کاکل صبح پریشان نشده بود، در مسجد محرم خان خواجه سرای
شاهجهانی تشریف آورد. غلامان پدر من دویدند که برای وضوی
شیخ آب بهم رسانند. پدر خود برخاست و آفتابه بدست گرفت.
دست و دهن بآب کشیده، گفت که ای علی متقی، نام او در
مدت العمر بزبان من نیامده است، زبان ندارم که شکر این بجا
آرم. پدرم میگفت، الحمدلله که ازان باز نام او و من هم نگرفته ام.

8

Devotion and relationship to God is stressed

fully recover he traveled to Gwalior. The rigors of the journey were fatal to his weakened body; he collapsed and died. He had two sons. Of them the older was not without a disturbed mind; he died young, and that put an end to his story.

The younger son, i.e., my father, withdrew from the world. [6] He studied with Shah Kalimullah Akbarabadi—who was one of the most perfect men of God in that city—those mundane subjects that one must perforce learn to eventually gain access to the "world of meaning." My father strove hard to tread the path of inner knowledge and suffered a great deal in his pursuit of renunciation and abstinence, but under the guidance of that venerable master he eventually became a perfect dervish.

After much suffering the heart reached its goal.

He was a virtuous man, given to love and possessing a passionate heart, and soon people honored him by calling him 'Ali-e Muttaqi.[6]

Once my father said to his Master, "You well know how [7] this humble person has set aright his beliefs. But what is your verdict concerning the 'Ruler of Syria?'"[7] "I shall let you know," the Master replied. After some days, near the end of one night when dawn had not yet made its appearance, the Master came to the mosque of Mahram Khan, who had been a *khwāja sarā* at Shahjahan's court.[8] My father's servants hurried forward with water for him to use for his ablutions, but my father arose and grabbed the ewer himself. The Master washed his hands and rinsed his mouth, then said, "Listen, 'Ali-e Muttaqi, the name of that person has not

روز و شب بیاد الهی می پرداخت، حق تعالی روی او را بر خاک
نینداخت. چون دماغش میرسید میگفت که ای پسر عشق بورز.
عشق است که درین کارخانه متصرف است. اگر عشق نمی
بود، نظم کل صورت نمی بست. بی عشق زندگانی وبال است،
دل باختهٔ عشق بودن کمالست. عشق بسازد، عشق بسوزد. در
عالم هرچه هست ظهورعشق است. آتش سوز عشق است، باد
اضطراب عشق است، آب رفتار عشق است، خاک قرار عشق
است، باد اضطرار عشق است. موت مستئ عشق است، حیات
هشیاری عشق است. شب خواب عشق است، روز بیداری
عشق است. مسلم جمال عشق است، کافر جلال عشق است.
صلاح قرب عشق است، گناه بُعد عشق است. بهشت شوق
عشق است، دوزخ ذوق عشق است. مقام عشق از عبودیت
و عارفیت وز اهدیت و صدیقیت و خلوصیت و مشتاقیت و
خلیلیت و حبیبیت برتر است. جمعی برآنند که حرکت آسمانها
حرکت عشقی است، یعنی بمطلوب نمیرسند و سرگردانند.

بی عشق نباید بود، بی عشق نباید زیست
پیغـــمبر کنعـــانی، عشـــق پسری دارد

LOVE

crossed my lips all my life, and I cannot thank God enough for that favor." My father used to say: "Allah be praised! I too have never mentioned that name again."

My father remained busy day and night in the remem-brance of God, and God too did not forsake him. When my father would come out of that state of absorption, he would say to me: "Son, practice love, for it is love that holds sway over everything. Nothing would have taken shape here but for love. Without love, life is a burden. To give one's heart to love, that is perfection. Love creates and love consumes. Whatever exists in the world is a manifestation of love. Fire is love's ardor; wind is love's agitation. Water is the flow of love; earth is the repose of love. Death is love's inebriated state; life is love's sober state. Night is the sleep of love. Day is the wakefulness of love. The Muslim is love's comfort-ing beauty, the infidel its awesomeness. Virtue lies in love's proximity; sin arises from its separation. Paradise is having a fondness for love; hell is to have a true taste for it. The state of love is above the states of worship, gnostic know-ing, asceticism, companionship, sincerity, desirousness, and friendship—above even the state of being loved. All agree that the movement of the heavens is caused by love—they never reach what they desire and so keep going round and round.

> *Do not be without love, for one cannot live without love.*
> *Even the prophet Jacob is filled with love for his son."*

8

→ Mir's father on love

kind of beautiful

11

۹ روز حیران کار، شب زنده دار. اکثر روی نیاز بر خاک، مدام مست شوق و دامن پاک. چهرهٔ نورانیش رونق افزای بزم صبح خیزان، آفتابی بود اما از سایهٔ خود هم گریزان. هرگاه بخود آمدی، گفتی که ای پسر، عالم هنگامهٔ بیش نیست. باید که برین آستین بیفشانی و گرد علائق بر دامن خود ننشانی. عشق الهی را پیشهٔ خود کن، روزی در پیش است، اندیشهٔ خود کن. هرکه اهل است میداند که دنیا سهل است. زندگانی وهمی است. بنا بر وهم گذاشتن آب را با ریسمان بستن است، و در بند فسحت امل بودن مهتاب بگز پیمودن. انداز رفتنی داری، بی خبر آه نشوی، فکر زادی بکن تا خرج راه نشوی. رو بکسی آر که عالم را آئینهٔ او میگویند؛ اختیار خود بکسی سپار که او را در خود می جویند. اگرچه مقصود حاصل است اما طلب شرط است. هرچند همه اوست لیکن ادب شرط است. معیت حق با خلق چون معیت روح است با جسم. ترا بی او وجودی نه، و او را بی تو نمودی نه. عالم پیش از ظهور عین او بود و بعد از ظهور او عین عالم است:.

مشکل حکایتیست که هر ذره عین اوست
اما نـمـی تــــوان که اشـارت بـدو کنـد

My father was oblivious to one and all during the day, and 9
at night he remained awake, alert to his call. Much of the
time he would lie prostrate in submission; all the time he
was drunk with desire but pure and chaste. His glorious face
adorned the ranks of the devotees who rise at dawn; he was a
sun who avoided even his own light. When he was himself he
would say: "Son, this world is but a momentary excitement;
turn your back on it. Do not let any attachment to it soil your
hands. Engage yourself only with a love for God. A day awaits
you, so give yourself some thought. A worthy person knows
that the world is only a trifle, and life merely a conjecture.
To found something on a conjecture is like entrapping water
with a piece of rope. If one pursues the amplitude of worldly
boons, one is running with a yardstick after the moon. You
are a transient here. Do not ignore that fact; prepare well for
the journey that lies ahead, lest you come under attack. Turn
your face toward him whose mirror the universe is said to be,
and put yourself in the hands of him whom everyone seeks
within himself. Although the goal has already been reached,
it is still obligatory to continue seeking. Everything is him,
yet one must be proper and not speak of it. God is with his
creation, like soul is with body. You do not exist without
him, and he is not manifest without you. Before creation, the
world was his essence; and after creation, he is the world's
essence.

What a terrible paradox! Every particle is his essence,
But not one of them can dare disclose his presence."

lovely metaphor

۱۰ درویش درویش پرستی، شکسته دلی مشتاق شکستی. نیازمند
عجیبی، در وطن غریبی. وسیع المشرب، فقیر کامل، چون آب در
هر رنگ شامل. هرگاه مرا در بغل کشیدی و بنظر شفقت رنگ
کاهی مرا دیدی، گفتی که ای سرمایهٔ جان، این چه آتشیست که
در دلت نهانست، و چه سوزیست که ترا با جان است. من خنده
میکردم، او میگریست؛ قدر نشناختم تا میزیست. مردی بود
بحال خودی، کسی را بارِ دوشی نشدی.

۱۱ یکی بعد از نماز اشراق روی توجه بمن آورد و مرا سرگرم بازی
یافت. گفت، ای پسر، زمانه آن سیال است یعنی بسیار کم
فرصت. از تربیت خود غافل مشو؛ درین راه نشیب و فراز بسیار
است، دیده دیده برو:

نشـــان پای تو فرد حساب زندگیســـت
قدم شمرده درین کهنه خاکدان بردار

۱۲ این چه بازیست که اختیار کردهٔ و چه ناهمواریست که برخود
هموار ساختهٔ. محو کسی شو که بلاگردان رنگین رفتن او آسمانها؛
رفتهٔ آن باش که قربان هر آن او و دلها و جانها. عندلیب گلی باش که
همیشه بهار است، [...]آن سادهٔ شو که یک پرکار است. دورِ آسمانِ
دورنگ درنگ ندارد. بشتاب، فرصت غنیمت شمار و خود را دریاب.

14

My father was a dervish, and also devoted to dervishes. He   10
possessed a broken heart but was ever eager to suffer more.
A man of unusual humility, he lived like a stranger in his own
city. Free of prejudice, a perfect Sufi, he identified himself
with every hue of life, as water does with any color. At times
he would hold me in his embrace and, affectionately looking
at my pale countenance, say, "Treasure of my life, what fire
burns hidden in your heart? What passion has become your
life's integral part?" I would laugh, but he would shed tears.
I did not recognize his worth when he was here. A man lost
to his own self, he was never a burden to another person.

Once, after the late morning prayers, he looked for me   11
and found me engaged in some game. He said, "Son, time
flows very fast; it leaves you with little opportunity. So do
not neglect the task of improving yourself. This road is full
of ups and downs; tread it with extreme care.

Your footprints are an account of your life's progress—
So count every step you take in this ancient dust heap.

"What game is this that you have chosen for yourself, and   12
what impropriety is this that you have preferred for yourself? Devote yourself to the One to whom the heavens are
devoted, and give your heart to him whom every heart adores.
Be a nightingale to that rose whose spring never ends, and
adore only that simple beauty whose colorful ways are never
over. The ever-turning heavens tolerate no delay—hurry,
count this little time a boon and strive to discover yourself."

۱۳ صورت متبرکش معنی مجسم، در تمام عالم اجسام یک آدم. مؤقری که عنان اختیار از دست خود نداد، متقئی که چشم نامحرم بر دست و پای او نیفتاد. اگر میدیدی میگفتی که شاید ملک و این عزیز سر از یک گریبان برآورده اند، و رفتگان هم پای استقامت باین خوبی کم فشرده اند. متخلق باخلاق سنجیده، متصف باوصاف حمیده. طبعش مشکل پسند، جانش دردمند. مژگان نم، حال درهم.

۱۴ یک روز سرکن پرکن بخانه درآمد. کهنه داهی نشته بود. گفت، ای داه، امروز بسیار گرسنه ام. طاقت صبر ندارم، اگر پارهٔ نانی بهم رسد زنده میمانم. او گفت، فقدان اسباب است. باز گفت که گرسنه ام. داه برخاسته رفت و از بذال آرد و روغن آورد تا نان بپزد. این بار بی طاقتی بسیار کرد. داه بی دماغ شد و گفت که صاحب این فقیریست، اینجا ناز را دخلی نیست. گفت، ای داه، تو با دل جمع نان بپز، من برای دیدن درویشی به لاهور میروم. روماليكه از گریهٔ شبش لکهٔ ابر تری شده بود برداشت و پا براه گزاشت. چون داه دید بی مزه شده میرود، دویده و گریه کنان در دامن آویخت، هیچ فائده نکرد. ناچار آبی بر آئینه ریخت.

۱۵ هر جا که فرود می آمد رزاقیت خدای کریم کار میکرد. بعد از چندی به لاهور رسید وان درویش ریاکار را دید. بر کنار رودخانه که به راوی شهرت دارد نشسته می ماند و عالمی را

the model devotee in all ways ←

His graceful visage was embodied Truth. In the entire
world he was the one man who never for a moment lost
control over himself. A man so filled with piety that no one
ever cast a doubting glance upon him. Had you seen him, you
might have thought he was an angel. Even in the past, few
persons could have shown such steadfastness. He possessed
choicest virtues and worthiest qualities. He preferred to take
on hard tasks, but in his heart he was profoundly tender. His
eyes were constantly moist with tears, and in appearance he
was always distraught.   13

One day he came into the house highly agitated, and said
to the old maidservant, "I am starved and cannot bear it any
longer. Find me a piece of bread that I may live." She replied,
"There are no provisions in the house." "But I am hungry,"
he repeated. The maid got up, went out, and brought from
the market some flour and oil to make the bread. My father
went on complaining of his unbearable hunger. The maidservant got irritated and said, "Sir, that is how the life of a
fakir is—there is no place in it for vanity." He replied, "Go on,
make your bread in good time; I now leave for Lahore to see a
dervish." He picked up his kerchief—it was dripping wet like
a cloud from the tears of the preceding night—and immediately set out. When the maid saw that he was annoyed and
leaving, she ran crying after him and clung to his clothes to
stop him. But it was to no avail. Finally she gave up and bade
him good-bye.   14

Wherever my father stopped on that journey, his needs
were met by God's providence. Eventually he reached
Lahore and found that hypocrite of a dervish seated by the
river Ravi and busy deceiving people. The man was known   15

باب میراند. بنام خفشان نمود مشهور بود. چند الفاظ زبان دری بر زبان داشت، نافهمی چند که نمی فهمیدند پیش او خط به بینی میکشیدند. گفت که من تائید دین محمد علیه الصلاة و السلام میکنم؛ بی حقیقتان مرا مغوی میدانند. پدرم برآشفت و گفت که ای بی ته، دین پیغمبر ما محتاج تائید همچون توئی نیست. فهمیده بگو که اینجا شمشیر در میان است، مبادا که کشته شوی. آخر در اول ملاقات صحبت بی مزه شد. بترش روی تمامی از آنجا برخاسته در تکیۀ فقیری شب گزرانید. چون صبح سفید شد آن سیه گلیم از در معذرت درآمد. پدر من گفت که حالا سودی ندارد. دیروز سفید گفته ام امروز سفیدتر خواهم گفت. چون پرده از روی کار برخاست بی لطف است. برو سر خود گیر؛ نشود که بدهن ها افتی. هرچند از عرق خجلت ترآمد اما بسیار از آب بد برآمد.

وقتیکه آن مجلس بی لطف برشکست، دفعةً آنعزیز بار سفری که نداشت توکلت علی الله بربست، و در عرصۀ ده دوازده روز از کروراه به شاهجهان آباد دهلی رسید، و بخانۀ فخرالدین خان پسر شیخ عبدالعزیز عزت که دیوان صوبۀ بود و قرابت قریبه داشت رحل اقامت انداخت. عزیزان شهر هجوم آوردند و باعتقاد تمام آب بدستش ریختند. آن مرد که شراب عشق از هوش برده بود اگر نشستی بی خود نشستی و اگر برخاستی چون مست سرانداز

by the name of Khafshan Namud. He was in the habit of muttering some words in the Dari language, and ignorant people who could not understand him bowed before him in humble submission. He said to my father, "I confirm the religion of Muhammad, may he be blessed with praise and peace. But those who cannot see Truth think that I err." My father flared up and said, "Fool! The religion of my Prophet does not need confirmation from the likes of you. Think before you speak, for therein lies a sword between us—you may get killed." In short, in the very first meeting, my father found that man's company distasteful; he left in anger and spent the night at another fakir's retreat. When it was bright morning, that dark-robed wretch came to my father, full of apologies. My father said to him, "Your words serve no purpose now. Yesterday I spoke to you bluntly; today my words will be more blunt. It is futile to seek to cover up now that you have been exposed. Go and hide where you can, lest your reputation be completely destroyed." The more the man apologized, the worse he started to look. Finally that unpleasant meeting came to an end.

Then suddenly my father, even though he had no provisions for a journey, set out again, and placing his trust in God and taking a zigzag route reached Delhi in ten or twelve days. There he stayed at the house of Fakhruddin Khan, son of Shaikh 'Abdul 'Aziz 'Izzat, who had been the *dīwān* of a province and was also closely related to my father. The gentry of the city came in droves and with great devotion sought to serve my father, who remained intoxicated with the wine of love. When seated, he was like an enraptured person, and when standing, he appeared as if drunk. His speech was

16

19

somewhat of a prominent Sufi sheik

برخاستی. مستانه و بیخودانه حرف سرکردی، دم جانسوزش آتش شوق برکردی. بسیاری دست ارادت بدست او دادند. اکثری بتاثیر نگاهش از پا افتادند. غسالهٔ وضوی او از کمال رسوخ میگرفتند و به بیماران شهر میدادند، هرکه می خورد به می شد. از بس گریستی، گریه اش در گلو گره گشتی. نالهٔ که از دلش سر برزدی از آسمان گزشتی.

۱۷   آوازهٔ درافتاد که درویشی باین حالت وارد شهر است. امرا التماس ملاقات نمودند. قبول نکرد که من فقیر و شما امیر، میان من و شما نسبت نمی گنجد. امیر الامرا صمصام الدوله نظر بر حقوق سابق ناز آغاز کرد که مرا از دولت دیدار محروم نباید گذاشت، اگر از لطف اشاره رود این روسیاه داخل صحبت روسفیدان شود. تبسمی کرد و گفت، برای ملاقات مناسبت شرط است. امید که معذور داری و بحال خودم واگذاری. چون از کثرت خلق تنگ شد دل شب برخاست، و بعد از نماز تهجد از شهر بدر زد. هرچند در تلاشش نفس سوختند اما بگرد او نرسیدند، و نقش پای که نشان ازو دهد ندیدند. (المصنفه)

بپـا کان کار کی گیرد فلـک تنـگ
که عیسیٰ از سر سوزن برون شد

20

similarly inebriated, and his passionate breath set afire many an eager heart. People in great numbers placed their hands in his hand and became disciples, and many of them were transformed when his glance fell upon them. When he did his ablutions, people saved the water and gave it to the sick. Those who drank it became well. My father would weep so much that he would begin to choke, and when he would let out a cry it could pierce the heavens.

News spread throughout the city that a dervish of such eminence had arrived. Now even the nobles sought permission to visit him. My father refused: "I am a fakir and you are an emir—we have nothing in common." Amir-ul-Umara Samsam-ud-Daula,[9] on account of his previous claims on my father, persisted and said, "You should not deny me the boon of seeing your face. Be kind, and let this ignoble person join the company of those who are truly noble." My father smiled and sent back the following reply: "There must be something in common for two persons to meet. I hope you will accept my excuse and leave me alone." When the crowds began to bother him too much, he arose one night, and after performing the *tahajjud* prayers left the city. People tired themselves out looking, but none could find even a trace of him. (Author's verse:)

The heavens can't hold a pure person down; see
How easily Jesus passed through a needle's eye!

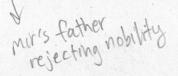

[Handwritten marginalia: "wow", "17", "true recluse", "mir's father rejecting nobility"]

١٨ در دو سه روز به بیانه که سه منزلی اکبرآباد شهریست قدیم و آبادی شرفاست غریبانه وارد شد و بیکسانه بر در مسجدی نشست. سید پسری، لاله رخساری خوش پرکاری، بنظر درآمد. چشمی چراند و از جذب کامل بسوی خود کشید. تغیری در احوال آن غیرت پری راه یافت. چون پریدار بی هوش افتاد و سر در پای این دیوانه وش نهاد. عزیزان فهمیدند که حال پسر که دگرگونست از تاثیر نظر درویش جگرخون است. گفتند که رحمی بر حال این جوان کن. دم آبی طلبید و دعای برو دمید. چون آب از گلو فرو ریخت آن پسر بخود آمد و معتقدانه زانو زده گفت، اگر چندی مهمان من باشند و قدمی که بردارند بر چشم نیازمند گذارند عین بنده نوازیست. وگرنه در عالمی که حضرت تشریف دارند ناز پیش نمی رود که آنجا بی نیازیست.

١٩ فرمود که در عالم دوستی مضایقه ندارد. اما من بسرپا نشسته ام. فرا رفتنی در پیش دارم. حاضران گفتند، ما تابع مزاجیم. مبالغه کردن سوء ادبست، لیکن این قدر هست که اگر بخانۀ این پسر تشریف شریف ارزانی فرمایند و چیزی تناول نمایند، دور از عنایتی نخواهد بود. چون پاس عزت اکابران آنجا منظور داشت، گفت، قبول است، اما خاطر فقیر گاهی شاد و گاهی ملول است، کسی متعرض احوال نشود. گفتند، چه یارا و کرا گوارا. اگر خلاف مزاج بظهور آید، این سعادت بشقاوت

22

In a couple of days my father reached Bayana, which is   18
an old town about three days' journey from Akbarabad and
inhabited by the gentry. He arrived there stranger-like, know-
ing no one, and sat down at the door of a mosque. A sayyid's
son, winsome and rosy cheeked, happened by. My father
let his eyes linger upon him, and with his perfect powers
drew the youth toward himself. A change happened in that
bewitching person: he himself became bewitched. Rushing
forward like someone mad, he fell down at my father's feet.
His relatives recognized that the youth's transformed state
was due to the glance cast by the dervish. They pleaded:
"Please show this young man some pity." My father sent for
some water and said a prayer over it. When the water went
down the youth's throat, he regained consciousness. Now,
sitting with folded knees like a respectful devotee, he said to
my father, "It would be an act of charity toward this humble
slave if you came to my house for a little while—treading
upon my eyes, as it were—for I know that in the world you
inhabit, blandishments only beget disdain."

My father replied, "It is all right to do so between friends,   19
but I sit here ready to leave at any moment." The people who
were present said, "We are obedient to your every wish, and
so it would be improper for us to insist. We merely submit
that if you were to grace the house of this young man with
your presence and taste a morsel or two there, it would be
nothing short of perfect kindness." My father did not wish
to show disrespect to the elders of that place, and so replied,
"I accept. But this humble person is sometimes happy and
sometimes sad—no one should bother him with questions."
The elders said, "Who would even dare to do that? We would

گرآید. غرضکه آن جماعت بخانهٔ پسر برد، و این مرد هم آنجا
چیزی خورد.

۲۰ اتفاقاً همان شب شب کدخدائی او بود. پارهٔ از شب گذشته،
با کدخدایان شهر پیش آمد و گفت، اگر حضرت هم قدم رنجه
فرمایند و رونق بزم عروسی افزایند، موجب سربلندیست. گفتا،
مبارکست، اما افسوس، کدخدائی مانع خدارسی است. ای عزیز
نمیدانی که لفظ داماد، مرکب است از دام و کلمهٔ آد که فارسیان
برای نسبت آرند، از عالم آباد و نوشاد. یعنی هرکه کدخدا شد،
گرفتار دام بلا شد. من مردی ام وارسته و چون برق ازین دامگه
جسته. مرا باین کارها چه کار. برو که آدم درین امر ناچار است.
بنده نیز در ابتدای جوانی از شراب عیش مست بودم، آخر غیر
از خمار که رنجیست حاصلی ندیدم. چون خدای عزوجل ازین
گرفتاری رهائیم داد، خود را بمسمار دوختم و بسان شمع بر سر
یک پا سوختم. اکنون تودهٔ خاکستری بیش نیستم. دل کجا که
هوس انگیزد، دماغ کو که فقیر بهر تماشا برخیزد. ازین مشعلها
که همراه تو اند بوی فتیله می آید. تو که غزالی عجب است که
رم نمی کنی. اگر فهم درستی داری، بکنه این نکته برس که «الله
بس، باقی هوس».

۲۱ الحاصل آن پسر بخانهٔ عروس درآمد و این فقیر لاأبالی از شهر
برآمد. در مدت یک و نیم روز به اکبرآباد رسید، و با دل جمع

not tolerate it. If something happened to displease you, it would only make us more wretched." In short, they took my father to that youth's house, and he partook of some food there.

It so happened that it was the night the young man was to get married. A few hours after dark, the young man, accompanied by the city's elders, returned to my father and said, "Sir, if you would come and grace the occasion, it would enable us to hold our heads high." My father replied, "May you be blessed! But marriage is an obstacle to reaching God. My dear, do you not know that the word *dāmād* for son-in-law is compounded from *dām,* noose, and *ād,* a word that the Persians use to indicate a qualifying relationship? In other words, he who gets married gets caught in the noose of affliction. I am a free man; like a flash of lightning I escaped that trap. Leave me alone, for I have nothing to do with such matters. A man is helpless in this regard. In my youth I too was drunk with the wine of pleasure, but in the end I was left with nothing but a painful hangover. When Almighty God released me from that prison, I guarded myself with utmost resolution. I stood firm like a candle and let myself be consumed. Now I am no more than a heap of ashes. I have no heart that lust can excite; I cannot care less for beguiling sights. These bright torches that are with you are like burning fuses of matchlocks. What a strange gazelle you are that you do not take flight. If you are rightly intelligent, seek to understand that 'God is enough; the rest is only lust.'"

Eventually, the young man went off to the bride's house, and that dervish who cared for nothing left the city and in a day and a half reached Akbarabad,[10] where he contentedly

20

21

در خانهٔ خود واکشید. وقتی که آن جوان گل رخسار و آن سرو تذرورفتار آگاه شد که درویش دل آگاه [...] شد عروس را بخانه آورد و آنجا آب هم نخورد، یعنی همان دم اشک ریزان، افتان و خیزان، سر بصحرا نهاد و قدم در تلاش او کشاد. هر کرا در راه میدید احوال درویش می پرسید. گاهی این طرف گاهی آن طرف می شتافت، پاسبزی که ازو نشان دهد نیافت.

۲۲ ناچار آهی از جگر برکشید و گفت، ای خضر راهِ چون من نابلدی رونما. بی تو هر طرف سرگردانم از طرفی برآ. از خاک برگرفته باشی اگر بدین افتادگی دستگیری نمائی. گنجی یافته باشم اگر در این خرابه به نظر درآئی. جیبی که گل درو می انداختم چاکست؛ سریکه بر بالش ناز داشتم برو خاکست. رحمی که پای رفتنم کوتاهی همی کند؛ لطفی که جز آوارگی کسی همراهی نمی کند. وقت است از لطف بی پایان دریاب؛ خورشیدی، آخر بر ذرهٔ خود بتاب. چه واقع شد که آسودگی از من رو بتافت؛ چه پیش آمد که آوارگی مرا دریافت. (المصنفه)

سخت در کار خویش حیرانم
چه بدل خورد من نمی دانم

settled down in his own house. When that young man—rosy cheeked and cypress tall, possessing a gait as beguiling as a jungle cock's—learned that the dervish had disappeared, he brought his bride home but then did not tarry even for a drink of water. With tears streaming down his face, he immediately set off in search of the dervish. Stumbling and falling, he pressed on, and when he ran into someone on the road he asked if they had seen him. But though he desperately ran in every direction, he did not find anyone who could help him.

Finally he let out a cry from his inflamed heart and said: "Oh Khizr to those who are ignorant like me,[11] show yourself. Appear from somewhere, for without you I run around in vain. You will raise me from dust if you extend your hand to me now, so low I have fallen. But for me it would be like discovering a buried treasure if I caught a sight of you in this wilderness. I used to gather flowers in the skirt of my garment, but now my clothes are all tattered. I used to rest my head in vanity's lap, but now that head is covered with dust. Show me mercy; my feet fail me when I try to move. Be gracious to me, for I have no companion now except vagrancy itself. Now is the time for you to display your unfathomable kindness. You are a sun—shine on this miserable mote of dust. What happened that contentment turned its back on me? And why is it that vagrancy has caught hold of me? (Author's verse:)

I am at my wits' end. What should I do?
I don't know what gnawed through my heart.

22

۲۳ چون گردباد وحشت آماده ام، مگر از طاق دلت افتاده ام. هرچند از کم پائ خود در آزارم، اما هنوز سر توقع میخارم. گر بدشتم آوارهٔ راغم، ور بکهسارم سنگداغم. رخسارم که بر گل تر نواخوانی کردی از تاب آفتاب تفسیده؛ چشمم که بر غزال سیاهی زدی قریب به سفیدی رسیده. تو آفتابی و من سایهٔ افتاده؛ تو سوار دولتی و من پا پیاده. از هر غباری که بلند می شود، منتظر تو می باشم؛ چون بچشم نمی آئ، ناچار از ناله گلو میخراشم. تو تمام اجزائ یعنی کاملی، از حال ناقصان چرا غافلی. نالهٔ می کشید و راهی میرفت، گاهی می ایستاد و گاهی میرفت که ناگاه پیری از پس پشت رو نمود و زبان به لطف و نرمی کشود که ای جوان کرا میجوئی و اینها چیست که می گوئی. علی متقی در اکبرآباد است. برو دست پاچه مشو.

۲۴ چون این مژده بگوش او رسید، دلی که که در سینه قرار نمی گرفت، تسلی گردید. قدم به آرمیدگ در راه نهاد، لب به ادای شکر الهی کشاد. شب در میان داخل شهر مذکور شد. نشان جویان، نام پرسان رسید و بقدمبوس مستعد گشت. اشک شادی بر رخسارهٔ او که رنگ مهتابی داشت دوید؛ رنج ناکامی براحت حصول کامی که در خیالش نبود انجامید.

۲۵ درویش جگرریش نظری بر جمالش کرد که همان نظرِ پاک صاحب کمالش کرد. لطفی فرمود که به تحریر نمی گنجد؛

"You must have cast me out of your heart, for now I wander 23
wild like a whirlwind. But though I am bedeviled by my own
shortcomings, I still pursue every hope. If in a wilderness,
I pine for verdant slopes. And if in mountains, I burn like a
branding stone. My cheeks once put to shame the freshest
rose; now they are darkened from the sun's heat. My eyes
once claimed more beauty than a gazelle's eyes; they are
now almost without sight. You are the brilliant sun, and I a
shadow cast away from you. You are a nobleman riding tall
in the saddle, and I a mere groom running behind. If I see
a cloud of dust rising, I eagerly wait for you to come out of
it; and when you do not appear, I am left to wail and grow
hoarse. What else can I do? You who are perfect in every way,
why must you so neglect those who are imperfect?" Thus he
cried and stumbled along, stopping every few steps, then
marching on. Suddenly an old man appeared from behind
and said to him, ever so gently: "Young man, whom do you
seek? What words are these that you speak? 'Ali-e Muttaqi is
in Akbarabad. Go there. Do not be in such anguish anymore."

When he heard these good tidings, the young man's burn- 24
ing heart found peace. Assured and thankful to Almighty
God, he immediately took to the road. The very next day,
he entered Akbarabad, and seeking out the residence of the
dervish, he quickly arrived in his presence and received grace
by kissing his feet. Tears of joy ran down his face that was
pale as the moon, and grief turned into joy at the success he
had not dreamed of.

The passion-filled dervish cast a glance on him, and with 25
that one glance transformed that handsome man into a
perfect person. He showered upon him kindnesses that

دلدهی کرد که به گفتن راست نمی آید. سرش در کنار کشید و از
لطف بی اندازه پرسید که ای میر امان الله، بسیار در آب و آتش
بودی، یعنی گرم و سرد زمانه آزمودی. غم جدائی اقران نخواهی
خورد. خانمان من خانمان تو، من و غلامان همه از آن تو. خنکی
که طرفه دریای بجوی خویش بستهٔ. شادی که چون سرو دامن
بالازده برجستهٔ. باید که دل جمع کنی و دروازه را بر روی خود
کشی. چندی بخود فرو روی تا خدا را سوی خود کشی.

۲۶   بشنو که وقت دلخواه است، و نکته ها در راه. جامهٔ که عبارت
از جسم باشد عاریتی است. لباس عاریت را پاک باید داشت
و جان را که اشارت با تُست در بند این و آن نباید گذاشت
(لمصنفه)

پاس جان کن، تن ندارد اعتبار
قالب خاکی مزاری بیش نیست

خود را مبین و در خود تامل کن؛ نظر بر خدا دار و توکل کن.
نیازی بهمرسان که نماز دوام بکار نمی آید؛ گداخته شو که دل
بیگداز کاری نمی کشاید. بخود سپردن عیب است. کارها را
بخدا سپار و از خود زبون تری را هم بدست کم برمدار. غرور
بدنمود است؛ زینهار زینهار ازو رو بگردانی. مشق نیازی کن که
بدل چسپیدنی بهم رسانی.

cannot be described, and comforted him in ways that words cannot circumscribe. Holding him fast in an embrace, he said with infinite affection, "*Ai* Mir Amanullah, you have been in terrible anguish and suffered the vagaries of the world. But you shall not grieve for your relatives and friends. My home is your home, and my slaves and I are at your service. Rejoice, for your brook has merged with a mighty river. Be happy, now you stand tall and free like a cypress. You should now be at peace. Closet yourself away from the world and delve within for a while, so that you may draw God to yourself.

"Listen, now is an opportune time, and there are many subtle things that need to be said. This garment that you call your body is something loaned to you. And that which is a loan should be kept unblemished. Your soul is the real you; you should not make it a slave to this and that. (Author's verse:)

26

Respect the soul; the body is worthless.
This mold of clay is no more than a grave.

"Do not take yourself for much; be cautious, rather, with yourself. Fix your eyes on God and depend only on him. Be humble, for even constant praying is of no avail. Soften yourself, for only a melting heart does not fail to succeed. Do not assign yourself much significance. Place all tasks in God's hands. Do not hold in contempt even those who look unworthy to you. Pride is unsightly, inauspicious. Beware, turn away from it. Practice humility instead, for only then will you be able to glue your heart to another.

teachings
of the dervish   31

۲۷ تا توانی علائق را بر گردن خود مبند؛ بعبث خود را زیر این
بار مپسند. دل از نقش غیر بپرداز، تا خانه را رفت و روب نه
کنی قابل مهمان نشود. با موافق و ناموافق بساز، تا آدم اخلاق
پیدا نه کند انسان نشود. رفتگی با همه کس کن که همین مذهب
درویش است. چون غریبان بسر بر که رفتنی در پیش است. عالم
پرسه گاهیست، اینجا رسم دیر ماندن نیست. عالمیان ماتمیان
اند، برای تسلی ایشان دمی بایست. این دشت خوفناک است،
این جا مار و مور بعصا راه میرود. در فکر زاد ره باش که قافله
ناگاه میرود. خواهی که صحیح برآئی ازین بیمارخانه، آب حکیمانه
بخور، طعام پرهیزانه. فقیر آنست که احتیاج به چیزی که داشته
باشد نداشته باشد، و غنی آنکه مملکت عدم بغیر[؟] خود گذاشته
باشد. فقر بما می افتد، غنا بخدا؛ «الله غنی وانتم الفقراء».

۲۸ بدانکه درین چمن یک گل تراست اما به هزار رنگ جلوه گر
است، یعنی یکی است دلدار و جلوه ها بسیار.

"If you can, keep your neck unbound by marital chains. Do   27
not vaingloriously put yourself under that burden. Cleanse
your heart of anyone else's thought, for if a house is not thoroughly swept clean it is not fit to receive a guest. Learn to
live with the pleasant and the unpleasant alike. A man does
not become a human being until he develops moral qualities.
Treat everyone with kindness, for that is a dervish's religion.
Live here like a stranger, for eventually you must leave. This
is no place to tarry; if anything, it is merely a place to condole
with each other. The inhabitants of the world are like mourn-
ers; one moment should suffice to offer them any comfort.
It is a frightening wilderness—here even snakes move with
care. Gather quickly what you may need for the journey, for
the caravan leaves any moment. This is a house of ailment; if
you wish to come out of it in sound health, drink wisely and
eat frugally. A fakir is he who does not feel any need even
for things that should be needed. And that man is considered rich who cares naught for even the kingdom of eternity.
Poverty and need—they befit us; sufficiency belongs to God
alone, for it has been said, 'Allah is Self-Sufficient, it is you
who are needy.'[12]

"Know that only one flower blooms in this garden, but   28
it manifests itself in myriad colors. In other words, he who
steals our hearts is solitary, but the visions he allows of his
beauty are multiple.

33

معشوق در حقیقت اگر بنگری یکیست
هـر کس به جلوهٔ دلِ خود شاد می کند
یکی را به بین و یکی را بدان
یکی را بجو و یکی را بخوان
دوئی کجاست، ز نیرنگ احـولی بگـذر
که یک نگاه میان دو چشم مشترکست

برو، چیزی بخور و بخواب، که از گرد راه رسیدهٔ. پا را بفراغت
دراز کن که محنت بی حد کشیدهٔ. به غلامی اشارت کرد که بالش
نرم زیر سرش بگذارد و خود را در هیچ وقت از خدمت او معاف
ندارد.

حاصل که آن عزیز بفراغت دل می ماند و پدرم برادرِ عزیزش
می خواند. صبح و شام بخدمت درویش آمدی و کسب کمال
کردی. یک لحظه از مراعات خاطر او غافل نمی بود؛ هر روز دری
از مقامات درویشی بر رُخش می کشود. به اندک مدت فقیر کامل
شد. کارش بجای کشید که اگر چشمک زدی عجائبات نمودی،
و اگر آستین افشاندی کرامت ظاهر شدی. اقران او چون خبرش
یافتند مشتاقانه از وطن شتافتند. همسرش برنج باریک مبتلا
گشت و بعداز چندی ازین عالم درگذشت.

٢٩

If you can truly see, there is only one beloved,
And each lover beguiles his heart with whatever he gets
  to see.

See One and know One;
Seek One and think of One.

There is no duality, so transcend the deception of the
  squint you see.
The two eyes may appear opposed, but they share a
  common glance.

"Go, eat something, then rest; you have just arrived after a
toilsome journey. Stretch your legs in contentment now, for
you have suffered aplenty." Then my father told a servant to
prepare a comfortable bed for the young man and not spare
himself in attending to his needs.

To make it short, that honored person—the sayyid—
stayed with us unbothered by any care, while my father
looked upon him as his beloved brother. Mornings and
evenings, the young man would attend upon my father to
seek perfection, and my father, too, diligently tended to his
needs, opening upon him every day the door to some new
state in mystical experience. In just a short time, the sayyid
became a perfect fakir. In fact, he reached such an elevated
state that if he merely looked wonders happened, and if he
barely gestured miracles took place. Hearing the news, his
relatives eagerly came to see him. His wife, meanwhile, came
down with consumption, and shortly passed away.

29

father's disciples

↓
what does this say??

۳۰ القصه آوازهٔ درویشئ آن مرد بلند شد. خلق برو گرد آمدند. عزلت گزید و در ملاقات مردم مصلحت ندید. چون سالی برین بگذشت، پدرم گفته فرستاد که اکنون در فیض بر روی عالمیان باید کشاد. شام گه از حجرهٔ خود برآمد بانداز یکه ملک ترآمد. درویش را سلام داد و در قدم افتاد. گفت ای سید، عجب سکه درست مردی که سکه بزر کردی. هوس آدم را سگ روی یخ می نماید، و نفسِ سرکن سر شخ. تو سنگ قناعت بر شکم بستی و تمنا بر تمنا شکستی.

این کار از تو آید و مردان چنین کنند

۳۱ من دران ایام هفت ساله بودم، با خودم مانوس ساخت و در گریبانم انداخت، یعنی با مادر و پدرم نگذاشت و بفرزندی خویشم برداشت. لمحهٔ از خود جدایم نمی کرد، و بناز و نعمتم می پرورد. چنانچه روز و شب با او می ماندم و قرآن شریف به خدمت او می خواندم.

۳۲ روزی برای سیر جمعه بازار رفته بود. نظرش بر پسر روغن فروشی افتاد. جوان چربی بود، دل از دست داد. پای ثباتی که داشت از پیش رفت، یعنی تاب نیاورد و از خویش رفت. چون روی دل ازو ندید، دست بدل برگردید. هرچند به ضبط خود می پرداخت، اما دل بیتاب باو نمی ساخت. دست بر دوش غلام

In short, the sayyid became renowned as a dervish and   30
people started to gather around him, but he took to isolation
and did not see fit to meet with them. After a year went by in
that fashion, my father sent him a message: "Now you should
open the door of bounty to all mankind." That evening the
sayyid came out of his cell, and his glory put even angels to
shame. He came and saluted my father, then fell at his feet.
My father said, "*Ai* sayyid, you are a sterling person, and what
you have accomplished is solid gold. Greed causes man to run
around like a frostbitten dog, and his impatient lower self
makes him rebellious. But you tied the heavy stone of contentment to your belly and smashed one desire against another.

You have done mightily, and that is how men do."

I was then seven years old. The sayyid showered affection   31
upon me beyond measure and caused me to be more attached
to him than to my mother and father. He treated me as if I
were his own son and never let me be away from him, not
even for a moment, looking after my every comfort. And
so I stayed with him day and night, and learned to read the
revered Qur'an from him.

One Friday the sayyid went out to enjoy the sights of the   32
market. There his eyes fell upon the young and handsome
son of a rich oil seller. In an instant he lost his heart to him.
All his resolves fell by the wayside, and he stood transfixed
by the unbearable sight of his beauty. Then, seeing no sign of
a response in the boy, the sayyid turned around, struggling
to restrain his heart. But no matter how hard he tried, his
distressed heart did not let him be. In the end, placing a hand

داشتی تا قدم بر زمین گذاشتی. بدین سان راه می رفت و با خود
می گفت که ای عزیز، کسی این چنین بد می بازد که تو باختی
و خود را رسوای کوچه و بازار ساختی؟ یا آن عنان داری، یا این
بی اختیاری؟ حرکتی که تو کردی از طفلی نشود؛ راهی که تو رفتی
کوری نرود. دل همچو چیزی نبود که کسی تواضع طفل ته بازار
کند. دل تفتهٔ کسی شدی که در آفتاب گرم از خانه بیرون نیامده.
وارفتهٔ شخصی گردیدی که در پی دل گامی نرفته. این چشم گریان
تر شود، گوئی که منتظر بود همین که دید بدل چسپید. و این
دل طپان تر گردد، همانا که بهانه می جست، همین که دیدهٔ من
واشد طپید. چشم را تا که نگهدارم؛ از دل تا کجا خبر دارم. در
جوانی چشم نه کشودم، اکنون پرافشانی نمودم. اگر خود را جمع
می کنم دل از طپیدن قیامت می انگیزد، وگر بضبط می پردازم
اشک سیلاب سیلاب میریزد. حیرانم که چه سازم و چه تدبیر
نمایم تا این گرهٔ سخت از کار خود کشایم. چاره بجز توجه پیر
نمی بینم. هرچه بادا باد، میروم و می نشینم.

۳۳ بهمان حالت تباهی، در دیده اشک و بر لب آهی، نزدیک بنماز
شام دست بر دوش غلام، در صحبت درویش آمد. حاضران برای
او جا کشادند. اشارت کرد تا در صدر مجلسش جا دادند. گفت که
ای برادر کجا بودی، امروز دیرتر روی نمودی. عرض کرد که برای
سیر جمعه بازار رفته بودم. فرمود، مگر نه شنیده بودی (المصنفه)

on his servant's shoulder for support, he staggered away, scolding himself: "My dear, does anyone act as badly as you just did, disgracing yourself in the middle of a market street? Once you displayed such restraint, and now you have utterly let go of the reins! Even a child would not do what you just did, and not even a blind man would take the path you chose. Your heart is not some cheap treat that you offer any market boy. And yet you set it afire for someone who does not even step outside when the sun is hot, and offered it to someone who cannot be bothered with anyone's heart! Now your eyes shall weep more tears—they were, after all, just waiting to attach themselves to someone. And this heart of yours shall burn ever more fiercely—it had been eager, had it not, for any excuse to burst into flames. How much longer must I guard my sight? And how much further must I watch my heart? When I was young I did not betray my modesty, but now I have acted so recklessly. My heart raises a tumult if I try to hold myself together, and my eyes pour endless tears if I try to restrain myself. I am certainly lost; what should I do? What strategy should I pursue to rid my life of this strife? No, there is no remedy for me except a grace-giving look from my master. So be it, let the worst happen; I must go and sit in his presence."

And so, with tears in his eyes and sighs on his lips, leaning on the shoulder of his slave, the sayyid arrived in the assembly of the dervish—my father—close to the time for the evening prayers. The people in attendance made some space for him, but the dervish indicated to them to bring him forward and had him seated front and center. He then asked him, "Well, brother, where have you been? Today you have

مستمند عشق میداند که سودا میکند

دیـدن طفلان تـه بازار رسـوا می کنـد

برو از تاریکدان خود تا هشت شبانه روز بیرون میا، و سرِ این داستان زینهار مکشا. حق تعالی کریم است. شاید که او را بیارد و ترا عزیز نگهدارد.

۳۴ اتفاق چنین افتاد که هنوز یک هفته نشده بود که شامگه آن ماه دوهفته از منزل خود برآمد و بی تاب بر دکان نشست. پادکانئی استاده بود. پرسید، چه حال داری که امشب برنگ دیگر بنظر می آئی و بیقرارتر می نمائی؟

۳۵ گفت، حالتی که می کشم نمی توانم بر زبان آورد؛ اما ترا آشنا میدانم، اگر با تو گفته شود مضایقه ندارد. امروز روز ششم است که درویشی ازین راه می گذشت. چشمش برعنائی من افتاد، ساعتی بخود فرو رفته باستاد. من که پیش خود برپا بودم ملتفت نشدم. ناچار دم سرد از دل گرم برآورد و رفت. حالیا صورت او از نظرم نمیرود، و خیالش از خاطر من محو نمیشود. اگر بیدارم شوقش نمی گذارد وگر در خوابم چشم بر نمی دارد. چه سازم و دل را بچه پردازم؟ نامش از که پرسم، نشانش از که جویم؟ ره را بکجا برم، غم را بکه گویم؟

40

showed up much too late." The sayyid replied, "I had gone to see the sights of the Friday market." The dervish said, "Perhaps you had not heard that: (Author's verse)

The wretched, favors-seeking lover thinks he has found a
*   bargain,*
But the look he casts on the market lads brings him only
*   ignominy.*

"Go now, and for eight days and nights do not step out of your dark cell. And do not disclose to anyone what has happened. God is benevolent; perchance he would bring him to you and protect your honor."

It so happened that a week had not passed when one evening that "moon at its prime" came out of his house and took his seat at the shop, looking greatly perturbed. A market tout who was standing nearby asked him, "Why, what happened today? Why do you look so greatly disturbed?"

The youth replied, "I dare not speak of what I suffer. But since I regard you as a friend, there may be no harm in telling you. Today is the sixth day since a dervish came by this way. His eyes noticed my beauty, and so, lost to himself, he briefly stopped. But I, in my vanity, paid him no attention. In the end, he drew a deep sigh and went away. Now his face is always before my eyes, and his thought constantly haunts my mind. I long for him when I'm awake, and when I fall asleep my eyes still see him. Tell me, what should I do? How should I console this heart of mine? Whom should I ask for his name? Who can tell me his whereabouts? What road should I take to find him? With whom can I share my grief?"

34

35

41

۳۶ گفت، آن درویشی است نام برآورده، مردی است بخود نسپرده.
خلقی بر آستانش رو نهاده، عالمی دست ارادت باو داده. برادر
خورد علی متقی که مشهور آفاق است و در زیر این سقف منقش
طاق. آستانهٔ او که خاکش بتبرک میبرند بیرون شهر پناه متصل
عیدگاه است. همراه من بیا و از بندِ غم برآ. غرضکه آن مرد کم
بغل جوان را بحضرت پدرم آورد. حقیقت حال شنیده گفت که
آخر عشق بی پروا حیف بی پروائی گرفت. ایما بغلامی کرد که برود
و با برادر عزیز بگوید که بیا، مطلوب تو ترا میجوید.

۳۷ هرگاه این اشارت مع البشارت بآن جگرخستهٔ در بر روی خود
بسته رسید، دست افشان و پای کوبان از کلبهٔ احزان بیرون
دوید. نخستین سر نیاز را بپای بوس پیر برافراخت آن گاه دست
شوق در بغل جوان انداخت، یعنی بکام دل در بر کشید و آن
نخل مراد را بمراد خود دید. پیر هر دو را دست بسر کرد تا بطور
خود بنشینند.

۳۸ چون صحبت درگیر شد و سر حرف وا، درویش گفت که ای
جوان رعنا، من فقیرام و دل بی مدعا دارم. وابستهٔ زلف خودم
نخواهی دانست. خدا داند که سررشتهٔ دل در کجا بند است
و این جان سراپا خواهش برای چه آرزومند. زینهار بر خود نه
چینی و حرف بسر زلف نزنی، مبادا که افسوس کنی. درویشان
اگر چه از دائرهٔ سپهر واژون بیرون اند اما ایشان را بیک پرکار

The tout said, "He is a dervish of great fame, but the fame   36
has not made him vain. A world has laid itself at his threshold. People come in throngs to join his fold. He is the younger
'brother' of 'Ali-e Muttaqi, who is unique and renowned in
the world, and whose blessed abode—people carry away
its dust as a precious relic—is outside the city wall near
the Idgah. Come with me and be released from your bonds
of grief." Then that man of little worth brought the youth
to my revered father. After hearing the youth's story, my
father said, "So the love that pays no attention to anyone
took revenge for not being paid attention to!" Then he told
a servant to go and tell his dear "brother" that the person he
longed for had come looking for him.

When those good tidings reached that tormented man   37
seated in his dark cell behind closed doors, he rushed out
dancing with joy. First he prostrated himself before his
master and kissed his feet; then he turned toward the youth
and, extending his eager arms toward him, embraced him
and looked at him to his heart's content. His master, then,
blessed the two, and gave them permission to leave so that
they could be together at more ease.

When the two sat down together and conversation started,   38
the sayyid said to the young man, "*Ai* handsome youth, I
am a fakir; my heart is devoid of all desires. Do not think
that your tresses have entwined it. God only knows what
my heart has tied itself to, and for whose sake I have become
all desire from head to toe. Beware, do not for a moment be
vain or neglectful, lest you end up ruing the day. Dervishes
are not governed by the rules of the world, and even among
themselves they are not to be treated alike—in other words,

نمیگذارند، یعنی احوال ما مردم مختلف است. برو که رنجی کشیده باشی.

۳۹ گفت که رنجی کشیدم لیکن گنجی یافتم. جاروب کشی این آستان را شرف می دانم. امید که محرومم نه گذاری و چشم لطف از من برنداری. هر صبح می آمد و می نشست؛ کمر خدمت بر میان جان می بست.

۴۰ یکی درویش در حالتی نشسته بود. جوان بسروقت او افتاد. جوان عزیزش خواند و برابر خود به نشاند. نظری در کارش کرد که بکام دل رسید و بهمان لقب شهرهٔ عالم گردید. اکابران شهر عزتش می کردند؛ مریدان خاص رشک برو می بردند. آخر برو حالتی طاری شد که بی دهل رقص میدان معنی شد. آری، چون نظر درویشان اثر میکند، خاک ناچیز را زر میکند.

۴۱ درویش جگرریش، یعنی عم بزرگوار، در هفته یک بار برای دیدن فقیری «احسان الله» نام که بادشاه خود بود، می رفت. چاردیواری سیم گل کرده بکمال پاکیزگی، در بند و دیوارهای بلند، مشهور به تکیهٔ فقیر، آن طرف عیدگاه اکبرآباد داشت. بر دروازهٔ آن دل برشته این دو مصرع بزر نبشته:

the ways of people like us are different. Leave now, lest you suffer later."

The youth replied, "I have suffered, but also found a great treasure. It will be an honor for me to sweep the floor of this sanctuary. I hope you will not deny me that honor, nor turn your benevolent gaze away from me in some other way." Thereafter, the youth, ever resolute to serve him, would come every morning and spend the day in the dervish's company.

One day the dervish, i.e., my "uncle," was seated in a transformed state when the youth happened to come before him. He called the youth Jawan-e 'Aziz and had him sit beside himself,[13] then cast upon him such a glance of grace that the youth at once achieved his heart's goal. Thereon he became known by the title he had received. The notables of the city began to show him deference, and even the select disciples of the dervish greatly envied him. Eventually, such a state came upon that youth that he became a champion in the arena of the spirit. Verily, when the glance of a dervish does its work, it transmutes worthless dirt into purest gold.

The dervish whose heart was sore with pain—namely, my revered "uncle"—used to go once a week to visit a fakir named Ihsanullah, a king in his own right. The latter had a place—whitewashed boundary wall, high house walls, and closed doors—beyond the Idgah of Akbarabad. It was known as the *takiya* of that fakir. And on the door of that man, whose heart was afire, was written this verse in letters of gold:

39

40

41

45

خاطر آسوده خواهی راه آمدشد به بند
چاک در پیراهن دیوار از دست در است

هر که در او را میزد و آواز می داد، خودش می آمد و لب به
جواب می کشاد که احسان الله در خانه نیست. زود برو، اینجا
مایست.

۴۲ یکی عم من قصد دیدن او کرد و مرا همراه برد. چون نزدیک
به دروازه رسید همان جواب شنید، یعنی احسان الله در خانه
نیست. این مرد گفت، اگر احسان الله نیست، امان الله است.
خندید و در را وا کرد. جوانی دیدم، شیراندام، خورشید سوار،
هیبت حق از جبهه اش نمودار. چادر یزدی بر سر، آفتابی در
کمر. چشم سرخش آب چشم از عالمی گرفته، شیر از عشق الهی
بر درش خوابیده. مصافحه به میان آمد. در سایهٔ اراک بتپاک
بنشستند، و احوال هم دیگر گرفتند.

۴۳ گفت که ای میر امان الله، من که در بر روی خود کشیده ام
آدمی باب صحبت نه دیده ام. دل ترا بسیار میخواهد، تا نمی آئی
میکاهد. باری این پسر از کیست؟ گفتا، فرزند علی متقی و گریبان
انداختهٔ عاصی است. فرمود که این بچه هنوز سوزه بال است اما
چنین معلوم می شود که اگر بخوبی پر برآورد بیک پرواز آن طرف
تر آسمان خواهد رفت. باین بابا بگو، بدیدن درویشان همت بر

*If you wish for peace of mind, close the door on comings
  and goings;
For it's a gate's "hand" that splits open the garment of a
  boundary wall.*

When anyone knocked on his door or called out his name, he always himself came to the door and said, "Ihsanullah is not home. Go away. Do not stand here."

One day my "uncle" decided to visit him, and took me   42
along. When we arrived at his door, we heard the same response: "Ihsanullah is not home." My "uncle" rejoined, "So what? If Ihsanullah is not home, Amanullah is here." The fakir laughed and opened the door. I saw an angel-faced man in his prime—broad-chested and narrow-waisted like a tiger—whose looks could fill every heart with the fear of God. He had a Yazdi *chādar* covering his head, and a crimson *lungī* was tied around his waist. His eyes, red from sleepless nights of prayers, could fill any beholder with terror. People stayed away from his door as if a lion, drunk with God's love, lay at his threshold. The two men greeted each other fondly, then settled down to converse in the shade of a *pilu* tree.

The fakir said, "*Ai* Mir Amanullah, if I have shut myself   43
behind closed doors it is because I have not seen anyone worthy of company out there. For you, however, my heart longs, and it frets until you come. But tell me, whose son is this boy?" My "uncle" replied, "He is the son of 'Ali-e Muttaqi, and an adopted son of this sinner." The fakir said, "He is as yet only a child, but it appears to me that if he grows up rightly he shall, in just one flight, reach the other side of the heavens. Instruct him that he should always be

گمارد که ملاقات ایشان برکت بسیاری دارد. پارهٔ نان خشک در آب تر کرده بخورد من داد. طعامی باین لذت نخورده بودم. هنوز ذائقهٔ من بیاد او خمیازه می کشد، و مزهٔ او فراموش نمی شود.

۴۴ گفت که ای یار عزیز، معرفت الهی غزال وحشی این صحرای پرغبار است، و جسم آدمی مرکب، و جان او شهسوار. اگر صید شد، از ضایع شدن مرکب چه میرود، وگر مرکب رو بعدم کرد و آن صید هم رم کرد، حسرتی دست بهم میدهد که عذابی الیم تر ازو نباشد. عذاب قبر عبارت از همین حال است. بیا و بگذر از غرور و هوس، نفس شوم سگیست هرزه مرس. اگر بگفتهٔ او راه رفتی، بریسمان او بچاه رفتی، وگر بخود کشی از خود بگذری، راهی بسر کوچهٔ آدمیت بری. نادان قباحت طول امل را در نمی یابد، عاقل از پی خود ریسمان نمی تابد.

۴۵ آسمان خیمهٔ شب بازی است؛ اشکال عجیب و صور غریب ازین پرده برون می آیند و می روند. این آمدن و رفتن باختیار شکل و صورت نیست، سررشتهٔ کار بدست دیگری هست. دل بدنیا نه نهی که دنیا زال بی حفاظیست. چون پدر از میان میرود هم بستر پسر می شود. کسانیکه اهل سیرت اند و غیرت دارند، مطلقاً روی توجه باین نمی آرند.

۴۶ شیخان ریائی از راه خودنمائی، باین عمر کوتاه که تا چشم بهم میزنی بپایان می رسد، خر خود را چه قدر دراز بسته اند؛ و در

mir being groomed to be a dervish himself

seeking the company of dervishes, for meeting them brings countless blessings." Then he took a piece of dry bread and, moistening it with water, put it in my mouth. I had never eaten anything so flavorful. Even now my palate aches for it, having never forgotten the taste.

Then the fakir began: "My dear friend, true knowledge of the Divine is a wild gazelle in this dust-filled wilderness, and a man's corporeal body is a charger, whose mighty rider is the man's soul. What loss is there if the charger is destroyed but the man catches his prey? However, if his horse dies and the gazelle too runs away beyond his grasp, the man is left crushed with a longing worse than any torment. That is what 'the torture in the grave' means. Come, discard all pride and greed! Man's wretched lower soul is like a stray dog. If you take the road it points to, you will end up in a deep hole. But if you strive and transcend your selfness, you will put yourself on the road to perfect manhood. Fools do not understand the dangers that lurk under their desires; and wise men do not weave nooses for their own entrapment. 44

"The heavens are like a tent wherein puppet shows are performed: strange forms and amazing shapes come out from behind a curtain, then disappear. Their coming and going is not in their control; someone else holds the strings that move them. Do not set your heart on this world. The world is a shameless hag; when her husband dies, she lies down with his son. They who possess character and a sense of honor never for a moment pay it any attention. 45

"Look at these deceitful preceptors—life ends in the flash of a wink, and yet they set themselves up with such pride and pomp. The world is a petty structure of four elements, and 46

چاردیواری عناصر که عبارت از دنیا باشد و از سر او زود باید
برخواست، چون خشت چسان مربع نشته اند. بمعنی بی خبر و
بظاهر هوشیار اند، یعنی از ته کار خبر ندارند. خلوت باصفای
ایشان سراسر کدورت است. ملاقات با چنین مردم چه ضرورت
است؟

۴۷   شایستهٔ صحبت آن بینوایان برگ بیداند که بار سایهٔ درخت هم
بر خود نمی پسندند؛ یا آن فقیران برهنه تن اند که با خدا در یک
پیرهن اند؛ یا آن پهلوانان نطعی پوش اند که در جهاد نفس اماره
می کوشند؛ یا درویشان جگرریش بیگانهٔ یار و خویش، سرهای نیاز
بر خاک، چون آب روان پاک، شیران این آجام، خون دل آشام.
بحرند و نمیجوشند. سیل اند و نمی خروشند. خاک شویان سر
کوچهٔ محبت، نمد مویان بیابان وحشت؛ بندگان باخدا واصل،
دورگردان نزدیک بدل؛ دل داده گان جلوهٔ یار، خاک افتاده گان
سایهٔ دیوار؛ آشنایان بحر حقیقت، مجردان بادیهٔ طریقت؛ آوارگان
بمنزل رسیده، آفتاب از سایهٔ شان دمیده؛ خاک نشینان بر فلک
رفته، عزلت گزینان نام گرفته؛ آشفتگان دشت مهر و وفا، غنچهٔ
خسپان گلزار حیا؛ سنگ سخت بالین سر، علامت شیدائی در بر.
سنگ بر شکم بندند و ننالند، نان خود را بر شیشه نمالند. طعام
لذیذ اگر دست دهد بسوی او نگرایند، نان جوان را بنان خورش
پیر تناول نمایند.

they will leave it soon—but there they sit, smug as a brick in a wall. In appearance they seem wise but, in truth, they are totally ignorant. You foul yourself even when you come in contact with what they hold clean. What need can there be then for you to meet with such men?

"Worthy of company are those indigent *qalandars* who will not oblige themselves even to the shade of a tree; or those naked fakirs whose only garment is God's intimacy; or those acknowledged champions who wrestle down their animal appetites; or those dervishes whose tormented hearts give them no respite. They know not any 'relative,' 'friend,' or 'partner.' Their heads touch dust in humility, but they remain unsullied as running water. Lions they are in this world, but they drink only their own blood. Ocean they are, but deep and placid; torrent they are, but never raging. They lie in Love's lane and sift its dust to find gold, and they crazily rush around in Passion's wilderness seeking what they seek. They are lowly, but united with God; estranged from every-thing, but intimate with their hearts. They gave their hearts to the sight of the beloved's face, and when they found the beloved's house, they lay down in its dusty shade. It's they who have sounded the depth of the ocean of Reality, and it's they who have traveled farthest on the path of Unity. Seem-ingly wandering, they have already gained their destination. And glorious they are, for in their shadow the sun finds its brilliance. They sit in dirt, but the heavens are their abode; they live secluded, but their fame has reached every shore. Gladly they roam the wilderness of fidelity; bashfully they confine themselves to the garden of modesty. They seek no comfort—they use rocks for pillows—and their bodies bear

47

۴۸ طرفه زرد رخسارانند، نام برگشته بیمارانند. مزاج غیوری
دارند، برای دیدن کسی که می میرند سوی او نمی بینند. در
سر غروری دارند. تا تیغ ناز معشوق نه نشیند از پا نمی نشینند.
محبوب حقیقی که متحد با اویند از کمال شوق روز و شبش
میجویند. جنگ آورانند که به هفتاد و دو ملت سربسر کرده اند.
کیمیاگرانند که خاک ناچیز را هزار بار زر کرده اند. متصرف این
کارخانه درویشانند، یعنی هرچه هستند، همین ایشانند. اُنچه
خواهی دست بدعا افراشته میدهند، یعنی حاصل هر دو جهان
دست برداشته میدهند. سخن درویشان بگو، همت ازیشان
بجو، تا باشی ازیشان باش یعنی ازان درویشان باش. راه دریای
لنگردار حقیقت که قفل است، کلید آن زبان ایشان؛ سجاده بر آب
افگندن و بی اندیشه رفتن تصرف درویشان.

۴۹ چون شام خندید گفت، ای یار عزیز، نماز مغرب رسید. اگرچه
دل نمی خواهد که ترا دل دهم اما پیش از غروب آفتاب و طلوع
که وقت خضوع و خشوع است، نمیتوان نشست. برو، سلام من
به علی متقی خواهی رسانید. دست بسر کرد، و در را بربست.

scars from brands of love.[14] Silently they deny their thirst and hunger, and do not hanker after what is another's. Even when someone offers them the most delicious food they do not partake of it. And when perforce they eat, they eat indifferently, mixing the fresh with stale.

"Their cheeks remain pale, but in a peerless way, for what ails them is what they desire. They jealously guard their honor; they may be dying for someone but will never look in his direction. Proudly they offer their necks to the haughty beloved's sword, and do not withdraw from the arena until it rests satisfied. Day and night they zealously seek that true beloved with whom in essence they are one. Warriors they are, but they have made peace with all the seventy-two different sects.[15] Alchemists they are, for they have turned insignificant dust into gold a thousand times. They are the masters of this world, these dervishes—they alone are the ones. No matter what you desire, they raise their hands in prayer and bestow it on you, off-handedly, even if it be the sum total of this world and the next. So, devote yourself to such dervishes, and learn from them to be bold, dignified, and ambitious. Be one of them; so long as you are alive, be one with them. These dervishes—their words alone open the gate that bars the road to the ocean of Reality; and it is for them alone to cast their prayer mats on its waves and fearlessly sail across to the other shore."

When the sun began to set, he said, "Dear friend, the time for the *maghrib* prayers has come. My heart does not wish me to bid you good-bye, but I cannot be with you at two times: sunset and sunrise. Those are the two times when one must pray devoutly and abjectly. So leave now, and give my salaam

48

49

53

عم من از آنجا که آمد، پیش پدرم رفت و سلام فقیر گفت. هر ۵۰
دو دست را بسر برد و فرمود که دیدن احسان الله را احسانِ الله
باید شمرد. میرفته باش و سلام من نیز میگفته باش. روز چهارم
دست مرا گرفته، باز بدرش رفت و دستک زد. آواز داد که در
خانه نیستم. گفت، اگر نیستی باری کیستی که بخانۀ آشنای من
جا گرفتۀ؟ خنده کرد و در را کشاد. سعادت عجبی دست بهم
داد. یعنی سخنان نغز شنیدیم و لطف بسیاری ازو دیدیم.

گفت که ای یار عزیز، عشق از روزی که مرا بر کار بسته است ۵۱
و نقش محبت درست در دلم نشسته، هیچ چیز اینجا بچشم
من نمی آید و دل مطلقاً بدنیا نمی گراید. تجردپیشه ام، بی
اندیشه ام. اگر عالمی برهم خورد جمعیت خاطرم پراگنده نشود.
وگر آسمانی بر زمین بیفتد دلی که دارم که از جا نرود. هرگاه چشم
می بندم نظر بر روی کسی می کشایم که از گلِ صدپردۀ نازک
تر است، یعنی از نگاه گرم رنگ می بازد. چون سر بگریبان فرو
میبرم، تماشائ دلبری می شوم که جلوۀ او از برق هزار مرتبه شوخ
تر است، یعنی دمی با دلم نمی سازد. محشرخرام من اگر خرامد
عالمی ته و بالا گردد. بلندبالای من چون قد برافرازد، قیامت برپا
شود. خاک راه او شو که سران را تاج سر گردی، پایمال او باش که
سرمۀ چشم اهل نظر شوی. دلی بهمرسان که او پسندد، جانی پیدا
کن که باو پیوندد. دست بدستِ به از خودی ده که ازین راه این

54

to 'Ali-e Muttaqi." With that he bade us farewell and bolted the door behind us.

When we reached home, my "uncle" went to my father 50 and gave him the fakir's greetings. My father received them with due deference, and said to me, "Count it a great favor from God that you had a meeting with Ihsanullah. Go to him again sometime, and when you do give him greetings from me too." Four days later, my "uncle" took hold of my hand and again went and knocked on Ihsanullah's door. The response came, "I'm not in." My "uncle" replied, "Who then has taken possession of my friend's home?" The dervish laughed and opened the door. What a wonderful fortune fell into our hands! We again heard profound words and received bounteous favors.

He said, "Dear friend, since the day passion set its task 51 upon me and love was perfectly configured in my heart, nothing here on earth has held any significance for me. My heart does not turn to the world at all; I have no worries or fears, for no ties bind me. If the world were turned upside down, my peace of mind would not be disturbed; and if the heavens were to fall to the ground, my heart—as it is— would not be affected. When I close my eyes, they open upon the face of the One who is lovelier than a hundred-petaled rose—one affectionate glance from him is enough to disclose most amazing sights. And when I cast my head down—bewildered—I catch a glimpse of a Beloved many times more playful than lightning, for he lingers not even for a moment. My Beloved's gait can raise the dead—if he were to take one step, the world would turn upside down. And if the tall-statured Beauty whom I love were ever to display

راهِ دور دست بدست است. زینهار دست بر سر دست منه که
چون دست و پا خشک شوند، راه به بست است.

۵۲ ای یارِ عزیز، مرگ عجب استحاله ایست که در پیش است. از
خصمانهٔ خود غافل مباش، یعنی خود را به چشم دشمن به بین
که دوستی همین است. حال جان هشیار، بعد مفارقت بدن، حال
مستی است معشوق در کنار. چون آنجا تجددِ امثال نیست، پس
از روزگار دراز آن مستی که عبارت از لوث دنیا باشد زایل شود،
دفعتاً ذوق وصل را دریابد. وای بر حال جان ناآگاه که ازین عالم
دور افتد و بآن عالم نسبت نداشته باشد، متاسف بماند. همین
دو حال را عارف دوزخ و بهشت میخواند.

۵۳ ا ی یارِ عزیز، دل اگر دردخور است درخور است. غم اگر
دلخور است، شایسته تر است. دل محزون می جویند نه شایستهٔ
طرب؛ جان دردناک میخواهند نه درمان طلب. روی نیاز بسوی
او آر که بی نیاز است؛ کارها را به او سپار که کارساز است. پا را در
دامن کش و توکل کن؛ سر را بگریبان انداز و تامل کن. اگر جان
به نیاز آید عنقا است؛ دل اگر گداز شود، کیمیاست. (المصنفه)

56

himself fully, the Apocalypse would follow anon. Make yourself the dust in his path, for then even kings will place you upon their heads. Be trodden by his feet, and become the collyrium that visionaries place in their eyes. Make your heart desirable in his sight. Make your soul attach itself to him. Place your hand in the hand of someone who is better than you, for then this long road becomes very short. Do not sit idle with one hand resting upon another, for when your limbs stop striving, no journey forward remains possible.

"Dear friend, death is an amazing sea change that awaits 52 us. Do not fail to be an adversary to yourself. Examine yourself with an enemy's eyes, for that is truly being a friend to oneself. A cognizant soul, after it separates from the body, is in a state of ecstasy—its beloved is in its arms. But in that world there is no perpetual renewal of the likes of this world, and so, as time passes, that ecstasy, which is nothing but an expression of the soul's lingering contamination by this world, fades away. Suddenly the soul discovers the true delight of that union. But woe to that ignorant soul that is cast out of this world and yet has no affinity with that other world—it remains eternally regretful. These are the two states that a gnostic calls heaven and hell.

"Dear friend, if you have a heart that thrives on grief it is a 53 heart worth having; but a grief that consumes your heart is a worthier thing to have. One seeks a grieving heart, and not one that is attuned to pleasures; one desires a pain-ridden soul, and not one that longs for a cure. So turn in humility to the One who needs none, and leave your affairs to the One who looks after everyone. Withdraw from all pursuits and put your trust in God's design. Bow your head in deep

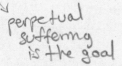
perpetual suffering is the goal

مـدعا نایاب و راه جستجو دور و دراز
پا بدامن همنشین ناچار میباید کشید

۵۴ ای یارِ عزیز، آن معشوق یکتاپیرهن، بهر رنگ که میخواهد،
جامه می پوشد. گاهی گل است وگاهی رنگ؛ جائی لعل است وجائی
سنگ. بعضی از گل دل خوش می سازند؛ برخی با رنگ عشق میبازند.
جمعی لعل را معتبر میدانند؛ جماعتی سنگ را خدا می خوانند.
هشیار، که این مقام منزلةالاقدام است. چشمی باید که بر غیر
او وا نشود؛ دلی شاید که از جای خود نرود. دشمن و دوست همه
از اوست که دلها در تصرف اوست. هدایت و ضلالت هر دو
مظهر اویند؛ مست و هشیار همه او را میجویند. محراب از ابروی
او پیدا آمد؛ میخانه از چشم او هویدا شد. مناجاتیان عبادت
و طاعت گزیدند؛ خراباتیان جام بر سر کشیدند. در محراب به
اقامت خم باید شد و در شیره خانه با حال درهم، یعنی مراعات
هر شأن لازم، و پاس هر مرتبه واجب.

۵۵ ای یار عزیز! هستی واجب محتاج برهان نیست.

reflection, pause and think. If your soul attains to humility it turns into something fabulous; and if your heart becomes tender and poignant it gains transmuting powers. (Author's verse:)

The goal is unreachable, and the search is long and tiring.
Withdraw, my companion; you must perforce retire.

"Dear friend, that uniquely garbed Beloved puts on any 54 costume he desires. Sometimes he is the rose, but another time the rose's hue. In one place he is a ruby, in another place a mere stone. There are some who please their hearts with the rose, and there are others who love merely its color. There are those who hold the ruby in regard, and then there are others who worship the stone. Beware! This is merely a staging place. One should have eyes that do not look at anyone beside him, and a heart that holds still and does not run after everything. Enemies and friends—all are from him, for every heart is under his sway. Guidance and misguidance—both manifest his will; and the sober and the drunk, both seek a way to him. The arch of the mosque is the curve of his eyebrow, and the tavern comes about from his eyes. The prayerful ones sing his praises and bow to him, while the tavern dwellers drink day and night. In front of the arch— one must bow; inside the tavern—one should dance and howl. For it is obligatory upon us to honor and submit to whatever aspect of his own authority and rank he chooses to display.

"Dear friend, that Necessary Being does not require any 55 proof.

59

هرکه بر حق دلیل میگوید
به چراغ آفتاب می جوید

همین که آفتاب بر آمد، روز شد. اگر مالکی در میان نباشد فلک
بیفتد، جبل نه ایستد، خور نتابد، مه نشتابد، آتش نسوزد، هوا
نه سازد، ابر نبارد، برق نتازد، آب نرود، گیاه نشود، گل ندمد،
چمن نخندد، ثمر نباید، شجر نپاید. حق سبحانه تعالی را که کریم
می گویند، نظر بر غلبهٔ این صفت، سررشتهٔ بندگی از دست نباید
داد، که آنجا صاحبی است. وقتی که می نوازد خاک را آدمی می
سازد؛ دمی که به بی نیازی پردازد آدمی را خاک. پیغمبر ما که در
شأن اوست «لولاک لما خلقت الافلاک »، تمام تمام شب نماز
خواندی، و این همه ایستاده ماندی که قدم مبارکش آماس بهم
رساندی. کسانیکه میدیدند، می گفتند یا رسول الله، چرا کار را
بر خود تنگ گرفتهٔ؟ توانی که عالمی را از بند غم وارهانی. متبسم
شدی و فرمودی، چه باید کرد که عالم بندگیست. عزیز من!
نسبت بندگی و صاحبی بسیار نازک است. بندگی پیش آر که از
روی صاحب شرمندگی نه کشی.

سخن اینجا رسانیده بود که جلوداری از صوبه دار شهر رسید،
و نیاز او التماس نموده گفت که نصرت یارخان برای قدمبوس
می رسد. فرمود که خوش باشد. هرچند دهن ملاقات فقیران

۵۶

60

He who offers proofs for God's existence
Lights a lamp to seek the sun!

"For when the sun comes out, it *is* day. If there were no Overlord, nothing would happen—the heavens would fall; the mountains would flatten out; the sun would not blaze; the moon would not mark time;[16] the fire would not burn; the air would not nurture; the cloud would not give rain; the lightning would not flash; the water would not flow; the grass would not grow; the rose would not blossom; the garden would not bloom; the fruit would not appear; the trees would not stand firm. It is for that reason that Almighty God, worthy of all praise, is called "the Munificent." One should never cease to be obedient to him, for he is a master who, when generous, makes dust into man; and who also turns man into dust, whenever he chooses to disdain. Our Prophet—in whose praise God has said, "But for thee I would not have created the heavens"[17]—used to pray all night. And in his prayers he would stand so long that his feet would swell. Those who noticed would say to him, "Prophet of God, why put so heavy a task upon yourself when you have the power to release the world itself from bonds of sorrow?" He would smile and reply, "I am merely a slave. What else can I do?" My dear, the relationship between a slave and his master is most subtle; so always practice obedience, lest you disgrace yourself before your Master."

The discourse had reached here when a servant of the *subedar* of the city arrived and, after presenting the *subedar*'s abject greetings, said, "Nusrat Yar Khan is on his way to kiss your feet."[18] The dervish replied, "Let it be. He is not really

56

61

ندارد اما مرا از روی او شرم می آید که بارها برگشته رفته است.
اگر این بار هم برود، خدا داند که باز ملاقات شود یا نشود. چون
بدروازه رسید از فیل فرود آمده دوید، و بسعادت پابوسی سر بر
آسمان رسانیده پنج اشرفی نذر گذارنید. گفت که خوش آمدی و
صفا آوردی.

۵۷ عرض کرد که زهی طالع من که بخدمت شریف رسیدم و روی
مبارک را بکام دل دیدم. چون روی دل از فقیر دید، رو انداخت
که گاهی به نگاهی این رو سیه را باید نواخت. گفت که دل قوی
دار که روی تازه داری، یعنی خدای عزوجل ترا اینجا بر روی کار
آورده است، اغلب که آنجا هم روسفید برآئی. شکرانهٔ این نعمت،
روانداختگان را بنواز، یعنی رو از سنگ و آهن مدار و روی ایشان
بر خاک مینداز. از خدا رودار و بر خود مچین. در کارِ غربا روی
کسی مبین. زینهار که از بی کسان رو نتابی، مبادا که در عرصات
رو نیابی. حالا برو که یار عزیز شیشه جان و نازک مزاج است، و
من در پاسداری این مرد لاعلاج. صوبه دار چون غریبان خاکسار
پارهٔ رو بر زمین مالیده آستانهٔ فقیر را بکمال اعتقاد بوسید و رفت.

۵۸ در همان حال پسر خوانندهٔ ساده روئی، مرغوله موئی، عودی
رنگی، سیر آهنگی، طنبور بر دوش، حلقهٔ زر در گوش، از آن راه
گذشت. نظر فقیر بر آن افتاد، اختیار دل بدستش داد. بعم من
گفت که این را بخوان و بنشان. چون آن پسر آمد و نشست،

fit to meet with fakirs, but I feel embarrassed sending him away—he has already gone back disappointed several times. God knows if we would meet again if he is turned away today as well." When the *subedar* arrived, he descended from his elephant at the door, ran forward, and raised his head sky high by placing it on the dervish's feet. He then presented an offering of five gold coins. The dervish responded, "Your coming is pleasing, and your gift is pure."

The *subedar* then submitted, "All praise to my good fortune that I was able to reach your presence and fully gratify myself with the sight of your noble visage."[19] Seeing that the dervish was kindly inclined toward him, he added, "Please cast a glance of kindness every so often toward this black-faced sinner." The dervish replied, "Be brave, for you are held worthy in the sight of many. God, the most exalted and glorified, has made you a man of rank in this world; most likely he will make your face shine in the other world too. Express gratitude for this blessing by being generous to those who turn their faces to you in expectation. Show them respect; do not betray their trust by saying no to them. Strive to become worthy in God's sight; do not be vain. Serve the poor and do not hold back because of anyone. Do not turn your face away from the helpless, lest you lose face on the Day of Judgment. But now you must leave, for my dear friend here is precious to me. He is by nature as delicate as crystal, and I must be vigilant with respect to his feelings." The *subedar* humbly touched his forehead to the ground, kissed the threshold of the dervish's abode, and left.

Just then a singing boy—smooth faced and curly haired, aloe skinned and fine voiced, with a lute on his shoulder and

57

58

خودبخود این شعر آمده را در دوگاه که پردهٔ ایست مشهور و بیگاه میخوانند، برخواند.

بیا که عمر عزیزم بجستجوی تو رفت
ز دل نـرفتی و جانم ز آرزوی تـو رفت

فقیر را تواجد دست بهم داد، و حظ بسیاری برداشت. گفت که ای عزیز، امشب پیش فقیر بمان و چیزها را که میدانی بطور خود بخوان. التماس نمود که سعادت و بر جان منت.

چون شام قریب بود، ما را رخصت کرد و در را بربسته بیاد الهی به نشست. شنیده شد که فقیر قصد نماز خفتن نموده اشرفیها را زیر بالین گذاشت. خوانندهٔ سیه دل دید و بعد از ساعتی به بازار رفت. کاسهٔ شیری درو زهر داخل کرده آورد و بمبالغهٔ پیش بخورد فقیر داد. بمجرد خوردن شیر حالش دگر گشت. دست و پا زدن آغاز نمود، یعنی زهر کارگر افتاد. آن بی چشم و روی نادرست اشرفیها را گرفت و گریخت. نصف شب آه آه دلخراش فقیر خواب از چشم همسایگان برداشت. مضطرب دویدند، محتضرش دیدند. کسان تلاش آن عیار طرار بسیار کردند. چنان در پردهٔ گلیم شب پنهان شد که به نظر کسی نیامد. چون شب بسر دست آمد، چشم فقیر بطاق افتاد و جان شیرین را

64

gold rings in his earlobes—happened to pass by. The fakir saw him and immediately lost his heart. He said to my "uncle," "Get him to come and sing." The boy came, sat down, and spontaneously sang this verse in *dogāh*, the popular mode also known as *begāh:*

Come—my precious life was spent looking for you;
I died of that desire, but my heart still longs for you.

The dervish, deriving tremendous pleasure from the verse, entered into a state of ecstasy. He said, "My dear, stay here tonight and sing to me in your special manner whatever you know." The boy replied, "I'd give my life for that honor."

Since it was getting close to evening, the fakir bade us good-bye and, bolting the door, busied himself in his remembrance of God. Later we heard that when the fakir was getting ready for the late-night prayers, he put those gold coins under his pillow. That blackguard of a singer saw him do it, and a while later went to the market and brought back a bowl of milk that had some poison in it. He then placed it before the fakir and made a great show of begging him to drink it as a favor. No sooner had the fakir drunk the milk than the poison did its work, and the fakir began to thrash about in pain. Then that shameless wretch grabbed the gold coins and disappeared. At midnight, the heart-rending cries of the fakir stole sleep from his neighbors' eyes. They came running, greatly perturbed, and found him on the verge of death. Some of the people searched high and low for that crafty rogue, but he had so concealed himself in the cover of night that no one found him. As the night came to an

59

بتلخی تمامی داد. اعیان شهر افسوس کنان، پشت دست گزان بر جنازهٔ او حاضر شدند، و موافق وصیتش در تکیهٔ فقیر بخاک سپردند. هنوز آن مکان زیارت گاه عزیزان ست. (لمصنفه)

فلک زین گونه خون بسیار کرد است
عـــزیـــزان را بسی آزار کـــرد اســـت

۶۰ آسمان خم تنک عشوه هائی لاجوردی دارد، و نازهائی هرمزی. هر روز با خاک افتادگان می ستیزد، هر شب فتنهٔ تازه می انگیزد. کسی را بزهر هلاهل هلاک می سازد، و کسی را به تیغ ستم بخاک می اندازد. مستان شوق را باید که از گردش این ایمن نشوند. تا سخت نخورند از جای خود نروند.

۶۱ عم مرا ذوق صحبت درویشان و شوق دیدن این جگرریشان بیشتر بود. روزی از شخصی شنید که درویشی بایزید نام، متصل سرائی گیلانی که بنایش سیلاب به آب رسانیده بود، در یکی از حجره های او که چون دل عاشقان هزار ره دارد افتاده میباشد، دیدنی است. چون ازو نشانِ درویش یافت دلش را آرزو گرفت، و همه چیز از فکر افتاد. مرا از سر وا کرده، بسرعت تمام رفت. جوانی دید بلندبالا، با کمال استغنا. ملکی وارد این عالم، نی نی عزیزتر از جان آدم. بالش از سنگ، بستر از خاک، هر ساعت

66

end, the fakir's eyes became transfixed, and he gave up his sweet life after a bitter struggle. The notables of the city, grief-stricken and despairing, gathered for his burial, and following the fakir's instructions buried him where he had died. That place is still a shrine in the sight of worthy men.

The heavens have committed many such bloody deeds;
they have always hurt worthy people a great deal.

The crooked heavens are stingy, and their ways, though   60
coy and colorful, are treacherous and full of guile. Every day they cause some great grief to the downtrodden, and every night they incite against them some new iniquity. Some they kill with bitter poisons; others they cut down with the sword of tyranny. Those who are intoxicated with the wine of desire should never think they are safe from the heavens' wiles. Instead, they should remain steadfast and not stir, lest they be made to swallow a bitter draught.   *did the fakir err?*

My "uncle" greatly relished the company of dervishes and   61
was always eager to visit with these love-tortured people. One day someone told him that a dervish, Bayazid by name, had arrived in town and was staying in the dilapidated ruins of the Gilani Inn—in a cell that had as many holes as a lover's heart—and that he was definitely someone to be seen. When he heard of the dervish, my "uncle" forgot everything else, and leaving me at home, he immediately set off in great haste. He found a young man of goodly height, whose mien displayed scorn for the riches of the world—verily, an angel come down to earth and a being more precious than life's breath. With the dirt as his bed and a rock as his pillow,

مهیای هلاک. شکسته دل و کشاده رو، برشته جان و فتیله مو.
دلداده، خاک افتاده؛ خود را بخدا سپرده، راهی بکام دل برده.
اگر خوش چشمی از پیش او رفتی بالای چشمت ابرو نگفتی. با
کسی برنخوردی، به بی کسی بسر بردی. چشم را اکثر اوقات بسته
میداشت و دل را بی یادحق نمی گذاشت. نان را برغبت ندیدی،
آب را از گلو بریدی. باریک بین و مشکل پسند، در لباس قلندران
برگ بند. پرسید که چه نام داری و از کجائی؟ دردمند و عاشق
پیشه می نمائی! گفتا، این جائیم، و میر امان الله نام دارم. گفت،
بنشین که با تو دمی چند خوش برآرم.

۶۲   میگفت که چون زبان بازی بمیان آمد سر کرد که ای عزیز، راه
ها بریدم، رنجها کشیدم. از خود رمیدم، در کوچها دویدم. چون
ابر ایستادم، چون برق افتادم. عمری سرگردان شدم، مدتی دل
پریشان شدم. چندی با چشم تر گشتم، آوارهٔ دشت و در گشتم.
شبها نخفتم، روزها نگفتم. دست در دامن امیران زدم، سر بر
دروازهٔ فقیران زدم. تا آن شوخ چشم را بر من گذری افتاد و بحال
دگرگون گشتهٔ من نظری کرد:

he was always prepared for the moment of death. Broken-hearted he was, but always smiling. His soul was on fire, and his mind tormented. He had given his heart away and humbly cast himself in dirt, and by thus resigning himself to God's will had found the way to be content. If some doe-eyed person were to cross his path, the dervish would never even throw him a glance. He sought favors from no one, and lived independent of everyone. Most of the time he kept his eyes closed, and did not for a moment let his heart forget God. Never did he look at any food with appetite, and he always begrudged a sip of water to his lips. Possessor of a discerning eye and a subtle mind, he was dressed in the leathern garb of certain *qalandars*.[20] He asked, "Where do you come from? What is your name? You seem like a person given to love and pain." My "uncle" replied, "I hail from here and my name is Amanullah." The dervish said, "Sit, and let me enjoy a few pleasant moments with you."

My "uncle" used to say that when conversation began, the dervish told him, "Dear one, I have walked many a path and suffered many a torture. I fled from myself and went pursuing others. I rose high like the clouds and then, like lightning, fell down. I was confounded; my heart was distressed for years; and as I roamed through jungles and towns I kept shedding tears. For days on end I did not speak, and for countless nights I did not sleep. I tugged at the garments of nobles to seek favors, and knocked my head against the doors of fakirs to seek their help. I did it all. Only then did that Coquettish One turn to me and cast a glance at my distressed state. 62

دیر بر سر آن غزال دورگـرد آمـد مرا

از طپیدن های دل پهلو بدرد آمد مرا

اگر میخواهی که در زمرهٔ سختی کشان او باشی، باید که دل از
آهن و جگر از سنگ تراشی.

ای عزیز، اگر آن محبوب سراپا ناز پیش چشم است، بهشت ۶۳
جاوید، واگر از نظر رفت، همان دوزخ عاشق ناامید. بدانکه سر
کلافه پیدا نمی شود، یعنی بر ما هیچ هویدا نیست. نمیدانم که
زاهدان ریاضت پیشه چه در سر دارند و بی خودان شوق آن مست
سرانداز از که خبر. جمعی را خلش خواهشی، جماعتی را کاوش
کاهشی. کسانیکه حق شناسند مبرا از امید و یأسند. عزیزانیکه
ناخدایند، دلدادگان رضایند. جان عاشقان را که بتلخی کار
است، خون ایشان شیرین بسیار است. رنج را بر خود گوارا کن
تا شایان راحت شوی. کار را بسیار با خود تنگ بگیر تا بفراغت
روی. دل برداشتن ازین عالم خوب است. اگر معرفت حق میسر
نشود، اینهم خوبست. عمارت دنیا در گردیدنی است، بنای این
بر وهم گذاشته اند. طاق آسمان نیلی افتادنی است، در هوایش
معلق داشته اند. اگر بمقصود رسیدنی خواهی، در دلی راه کن؛
هرچه از دست کوته خدمتت بر آید، لله کن. اگر آشنای دریائی ته
دار حقیقت نمی توانی شد، باری بر کران باش، یعنی اگر دفعتاً بر

70

That far-ranging gazelle took so long to come near me
that a pain settled in my breast as my heart throbbed.

"So steel your heart and be firmly resolute if you wish to
be among those who bear the hardships he enjoins.

"Dear friend, it is like being in paradise for you if that   63
Beloved, that embodiment of coquetry, is before your eyes,
but it is hell for the hopeless lover if he is hidden from his
sight. You should understand that this secret is like a tangled
skein whose end is nowhere to be seen. We know nothing;
we have been told nothing. These ascetics undergoing amazing hardships—I do not know what they seek. And these
people drunk on the love of that vain Beloved, I do not know
what impels them. One group is in anguish, for it desires
something; the other wastes away, for it pursues something.
Those who can recognize Truth are guiltless of both hope
and despair. Those who are with God give themselves over
to his will. Lovers drink the bitterest dregs, but find in them
the sweetest pleasure. Strive to accept grief, that you may
become worthy of receiving joy. Make life hard for yourself,
that you may pass it in comfort. It is well to detach your heart
from this world; and if it does not bring you the knowledge of
God, that is fine too. This edifice—the world—has no perma-
nence; it is based on mere conjecture. And this lofty blue
arch of the sky will crash down one day, for it only hangs in
thin air. If you wish to achieve what you desire, seek the way
into someone's heart. And do only for God's sake whatever
your puny hands can serve to do. If you cannot fathom the
depthless ocean of Reality, that's fine—stand at least on its
shore. That is to say, since you never have the power to give

مردن خود قادر نیستی، آمادهٔ دادن جان باش. خود را از قید دیر
و مسجد وا رهان، یعنی با خدا باش و در همه جا بمان.

عارفان دو گروه اند. مردم یک جماعت نقش دیواراند، گوئی
که زبان ندارند، یعنی حیران تازه کاری آن صنعت گر پرکاراند.
دیده اند انچه دیده اند؛ فهمیده اند، انچه فهمیده اند. مردمان
جماعت دیگر را، چون بادام، زبان مغزدار است، یعنی هر یکی
زبان دان چشم سخن گوی دلدار است. هرگاه شرح طرز دیدن
او می کند، هزار رنگ لب می کشاید. کیفیت مژگان بهم زدنش
بصد زبان ادا می نماید. چنانچه کمالات آن مست ناز از حدِ شمار
افزون، کلمات این بی اختیار هم از حیّز بیان بیرون.

اول صحبت بود زود برخاست؛ رنج فقیر زیاده برین نخواست.
پیش پدرم آمد و احوال او همگی بیان نمود. او گفت،

هر گلی را رنگ و بوی دیگر است

درویشان اهل بخیه کجا بهم می رسند. اکثرش می دیده باش.

یکی بعد از نماز پیشین، قصد دیدن او کرد و مرا همراه برد.
درویش به عنایت تمامم برخوانده، رو با روی خود به عزت
بنشاند. چون خوردسال بودم، رو به عم من کرد و کلاه از سرم
برداشت، یعنی متفحص احوال شد. التماس نمود که فرزند علی
متقی است. گفت، چه پرسیدنست. پدر این بابا مردیست کلان
کار، دانای اسرار، خورشید آسمان درویشی، مشهور جهان، جان

۶۴

۶۵

۶۶

72

up your life, at least remain always prepared to do so. Free
yourself from bondage to mosques and monasteries. Be with
God, and go everywhere.

"Gnostics are of two kinds. The men of one group are like   64
a picture painted on a wall—silent, as if they do not even
possess a tongue. They are lost in amazement at the ever-
new creativity of that marvelous Creator—they have seen
what they saw, and have grasped what they grasped. Those
in the other group are like an almond—they possess the
sweet kernel of a tongue. All of them know the language the
Beloved's eloquent eyes speak. They tell in myriad colorful
ways how to look at him, and put into thousands of words
what the Beloved does in a wink. Just as the marvels of he
who is intoxicated with his own beauty are countless, so are
the exclamations of the second group of men beyond any
description."

Since it was their first meeting, my "uncle" left early, not   65
wishing to trouble the dervish further. Coming to my father,
he told him everything. My father said, "*Every flower has
its unique color and fragrance.* A dervish of such a congenial
nature is not easily found. You should visit him often."

Another time, after the early afternoon prayers, my   66
"uncle" decided to visit the dervish and took me along. The
dervish welcomed me most graciously and had me sit facing
him. Since I was still young in age, he turned to my "uncle"
and asked about me. My "uncle" replied, "He is the son of
'Ali-e Muttaqi." The dervish said, "Say no more. His father
is a man of great deeds and a knower of profound secrets.
He is the resplendent sun among dervishes, renowned in
the world, the very soul of dervish-hood—an ocean from

درویشی. دریای است کزو گوهر تر برون می آید. ما فقیران کنار
خشک داریم، از ما چه می کشاید. ای پسر، بعد از نیاز من خواهی
گفت که کوتاهی از شوق بی پایان نیست. شکسته پائی کوچه نمی
دهد وز بخت کم مدد نیز گذر نیست، می خواهد که ازین خرابه
سر بیرون نه نهد. تو قلندر مضبوط الاحوال، من به نسبت تو
کوچک ابدال. در حق چون منِ بی سروپای بشرط مساعدت وقت
دعای.

۶۷   طرح سخن بطور دیگر انداخت، عم بزرگوار را مخاطب ساخت
که ای عزیز، همه گوش شو و سخن فقیران بشنو. عبادت ما
برای ماست. آنجا خدائی ست، کرا پرواست. طاعت ما این همه
نیست که بر خود بچینیم و برو تکیه کرده بنشینیم. اگر بپذیرند
احسان بهشت کنند، ما بنده ایم و بر بحساب نگیرند جز این نمی
توان گفت که شرمنده ایم. اینکه نفس ترا چیزی قرار دادۀ شوی
محض است. چون خوب بکنه خود رسی، محرومی محض. آن
سروناز مائل رنگین رفتن خود است و جلوۀ او و بهزار رنگ سرگرم
آمد و شد. چه گمان بردۀ، چه قرار دادۀ، چه خیال کردۀ، بچه دل
نهادۀ؟ گاهی گل در آب می افگند ، گاهی گل بر سر خاک میزند.
زینهار که دل شکنی کسی نه کنی و سنگ ستم بر این شیشه نزنی.
دل را که عرش می گویند ازین راه است که منزل خاص آن ماه
است.

which emerge only the finest pearls. I am a mere pauper—
what can I give to anyone? Son, give my humble greetings to
your father, then tell him what I say to you now: 'My lapse
in not attending upon you is not due to any lack of fervor
on my part. An innate weakness does not allow me, and my
unfriendly fate does not help either—it dictates that I should
not stir out of these ruins. You are a *qalandar* of established
rank and power; compared to you, I am a mere novice. Please
pray for this helpless person when you find some propitious
time.'"

Then he changed the subject, and addressing my "uncle" 67
said, "Dear friend, be all ears now and listen to what this
fakir says. Our devotions and prayers are for our own sake.
He is God, what does he care? Our obedience lies in our
not becoming vain and not taking his kindness for granted.
It is only his absolute generosity if he accepts our service
and rewards. We are slaves; he remains our master even if
he chooses not to take us to task. We can only say that we
are sorry in his sight. That your lower soul has made some
promise to you is nothing but a misfortune, for you will
only be disappointed when you realize who you are. That
Master of coquetry is engrossed in his own colorful ways,
and his manifestations, taking on manifold forms, appear
and then disappear. What have you conjectured? What have
you conjured? What do you think it all is? What have you
set your heart upon? One moment he instigates a fight, the
next he raises someone high. Never break anyone's heart;
never cruelly cast a stone on a piece of glass. People call the
human heart the highest of heavens. Why? Because it's the
exclusive site where that Moon grants us his sight.

نـيازارم ز خـــود هـرگز دلی را

که می ترسم درو جای تو باشد

۶۸ ای عزیز، آن محبوب محبت دوست است، یعنی با عاشقان
سری دارد، و با آن بی پروائی بحال ایشان نظری. چون مراقب
میگردند، در دل جلوه گر است؛ چون چشم می بندند، در پیش
نظر. از هر دری که می خواهند می آید؛ بهر رنگی که می جویند رو
مینماید. انقباض و انبساط وابسته بحال ایشان است. اگر خوش
می شوند گرفتگی ازین چمن میرود، وگر محزون می گردند غنچه وا
نمی شود. اما طور ایشان از راه و روش بیرون. معشوق در آغوش،
و دلها همه خون. گاهی متفکر، گاهی متحیر. قرار نمیگرند؛ تسلی
نمی شوند. خدا داند که از خدا چه می خواهند. خواهشی ندارند
و می کاهند.

۶۹ نشنیدهٔ که در عهد موسیٰ علیه السلام خشک سال شد. مردم
در معرض تلف افتادند. گفتند که یا موسیٰ، در جناب احدیت
عرض کن که باران نمی بارد. خلق عالم تاب تعب ندارد. مفت
هلاک میشوند و بر باد فنا میروند. موسیٰ علیه السلام بر طور
رفت. عرض داد. خطاب آمد که کلک خسپ پریشان گوی دارم
که در فلان گلخن افتاده می باشد. با گپ زدن او خوش داشتم.
از چندی رو بآسمان نمی کند، و بطور خود حرف نمیزند. نزول

I never willingly hurt any heart,
For I fear it might be your abode.

"My dear, that Beloved cherishes love. That is to say, he 68
cares for lovers and, despite his disdainful airs, looks after
them. He appears in the lovers' hearts when they fall into
contemplation; and when they shut their eyes, he comes
into vision. He comes to them through whichever door they
want him to, and shows himself to them in whatever form
they pursue. Despair and joy are tied to what the lovers feel.
When they are happy this garden is freed of gloom, and if
they are grieving not a single bud in it can bloom. But the
ways of the lovers are indeed strange—their beloved is beside
them, and yet their hearts pine and bleed. One moment they
are pensive; another, they are wonder-struck. They are
always restless and never satisfied. Only God knows what
they want from God, for they hold no desire and yet they
pine and languish.

"Have you not heard that once there was a severe drought 69
during Moses's time? When people began to die in large
numbers, they came to him and said, "Moses, please tell
God that there has been no rain, and that his creatures
cannot bear this severe hardship. All are dying, and for no
reason." Moses went up Mount Sinai and made his petition.
The response came: "There is a destitute man of confused
speech who lies in the discarded ashes of a certain bath—his
crazy words used to give me much pleasure. But for some
days now he has not raised his head skyward and spoken in
that manner. The coming down of the rains depends on his
letting loose his tongue." On hearing that response, Moses

باران موقوف بر واشدن اوست. چون ازان جناب این جواب
شنید، بسوی همان گلخن شتافت. باری آن بلاکش شوق را
دریافت. مردی دید بالای تودهٔ خاکستر، گلیم سیاهی در بر. از
سرتاپا همه ذوق، مستغرق دریای شوق. یکه بیت دیوان تجرید،
فرد اول جریدهٔ تفرید.

بمجرد دوچار شدن زبان بکشاد که یا موسیٰ گذرت بر مزابل از
چه افتاد؟ بچه دل نهادهٔ که اینجا افتادهٔ؟ گفتا که امساک باران
است. کاری از دست دعای کس نمی کشاید. زندگانی دشوار می
نماید. روی نیاز بجناب پاک حق برده بودم، چنین ظاهر شد تو
که سکوت اختیار کردهٔ، انقباض است. تا بعادت قدیم سخن
سر نه کنی ابر را باد نیارد و باران رحمت نبارد. خدا را، دمی رو
بآسمان به نشین. چیزی بگو و این بلا را برچین. گفت، ای موسیٰ
تو آن فریبنده را نشناختهٔ، و بطور من دل را در راه او نباختهٔ.
عبارت آن طرار کنایه ها میزند؛ اشارتش دل بصد جا می افگند.
استغفرالله. من بگفتهٔ او کی راه میروم. اما اگر پاس رسول او نکنم
کافر میشوم، که گفته اند، «با خدا دیوانه باش و با نبی هشیار
باش.» غرضکه آن مقید عشق مطلق و آن حیرتِ کمالاتِ حق رو
بفلک کرد و بساط سخن را بطورخود به گسترد که ای سراپا فریب
و ای دشمن شکیب، پیش ازین ابر و باد و باران مسخر تو بودند.
اکنون حکم کش من اند که اگر من خواهم گفت باد خواهد

hurried to that bath, and after a search found that "bearer of Love's burden"—a man wrapped in a dark blanket, lying on a heap of ashes, a man who was the total embodiment of exquisite discrimination but drowning in an abundance of longing; call him "the key verse in the book of abstinence" or name him "the chief of those who cut off worldly ties for the love of God."

"When their eyes met, the man asked Moses, "What brings you to this dunghill? What have you set your heart upon, Moses, that you come here?" Moses replied, "No rain has fallen this year, and no one's prayers seem to have any effect. All life is at risk. When I made my humble petition to God, it was revealed to me that it is your falling silent that has caused the drought. Unless you address him again in your own manner, the winds will not bring clouds and the rains will not come down. In God's name I beseech you, raise your head heavenward for a moment and remove this curse by saying a few words." The man replied, "Oh Moses, you do not know that Trickster. You have not given away your heart to his cause the way I have. That Cunning One's words are too allusive. Even his smallest gesture can totally confuse anyone. God forbid! I cannot let him lead me down that path. But, on the other hand, I become an infidel if I disobey his prophet. For they have said, '*Be crazy with God, but be careful with his prophet.*' Then that prisoner of Absolute Love, that wonder-struck observer of the perfections of the Truth, turned his face heavenward and began to speak in his own special manner: "Oh Embodiment of deceit! Oh Enemy of the heart's peace! Till now the clouds, the wind, the rain, all were under your command—suddenly they have become my

70

وزید، ابر خواهد آمد، بارش خواهد شد؟ بلی، حق بر طرف تست،
ترا دخلی نیست. متصرف این کارخانه منم. بیا! این فریبندگی
را بگذار و بر حال خلایق رحم آر. دو سه بار ازین قسم سخنان
پریشان گفته بود که ناگاه بادی وزید و ابر سیاهی سفید شد.
سیلاب سیلاب بارید.

٧١ ای عزیز، کدام معشوق این قدر پاس عاشق می کند؟ حیف
است اگر تعلق بدو نگیری و در طلب آن سرمایۀ جان نمیری.
دل اگر برای او خون شود بهتر؛ جان اگر در راه او رود خوش تر.
محو او برنگی شو که برنگ او برآئی؛ بطریقی گم گرد که باز رو نه
نمائی. رباعی:

نی دل بخیال زلــف و رو بایــد داد
نی جان به هـوای رنگ و بو بایـد داد
اینجا دل را چه قدر و جانرا چه محل
خــود را همـه او کرده، باو بایـد داد

٧٢ درین حال وقت نماز عصر رسید. برخاستیم و باو نماز گذاردیم.
بعد فراغ رو بمشرق نشست و گفت، ای میر امان الله، امروز چیزی
خورده ام که نخورده بودم، و دست به چنین طعامی نه کرده
بودم. عم من قدری گستاخ شده بود، گفت که ای درویش مبالغه
را حدی و تکلف را نهایتی است. قامتت از بار فاقها خم است، و

80

slaves, have they? Now I must order the wind to move, the clouds to gather, and the rain to fall? But of course—you are always right! You have no say in these matters. I am in sole control here. Come on! Stop these tricks of yours, and take pity on your creatures." He had spoken in that crazy fashion just a few times when suddenly a wind started, bringing piles of dark clouds, and rains came down in torrents.

"My dear, what other beloved cares so much for a lover? 71 Pity on you if you do not tie yourself to him, or do not give up your life in seeking that treasure! What could be better for your heart than to be crushed for his sake? And what is happier for your life than to be lost in his pursuit? Be absorbed in him in such a manner that you efface yourself and take on his manners. Become lost, so lost that you are never found again.

> *No, it's not enough to lose your heart to his face and*
> *   tresses,*
> *Nor is it enough to devote your life to pursuing his many*
> *   shapes.*
> *In this matter of Love, your heart and life are worthless;*
> *Instead, make yourself totally him, and put yourself in*
> *   his hands."*

Meanwhile the time for the late-afternoon prayers had 72 arrived. We got up and prayed together with him. Afterward, he sat down facing east and said, "*Ai* Mir Amanullah, today I had something so delicious, the like of which I had never eaten before." My "uncle," who had by now become somewhat bold with him, said, "*Ai* dervish, there are limits

سنگ قناعت بر شکم. برای یک دمِ آب استخوان می شکنی، نان گربه را به تیر می زنی. هر روز برای مرگ آمادهٔ، با صد خرابی درین خرابه افتادهٔ. کجا طعام لذیذ و کجا تو؟ از دهن خود زیاده مگو.

٧٣ گفت، والله که من زیاده سر و سبک پا نیستم. جائیکه احتمال دروغ باشد نه ایستم. بشنو که از صبح آتش جوع زبانه می کشید و نفس شوم چون سگ پاسوخته می گردید، یعنی می خواست که بشهر بروم و پیش کس و ناکس سائل شوم. باری سنگ در زیر سر گذاشتم، و غیرت خود را بزور نگهداشتم. یکایک موشی نیم نان خشک در دهن گرفته برآمد و درین حجرهٔ شکسته تر از دل عاشق درآمد. من که بمعنی شیر شرزه بودم و بظاهر از فاقه کشیها گربهٔ لاوه، چون مرا دید، آن نیم نان را انداخته گریخت. نصف دل خوش برخواستم و برداشتم. آبی میسر نه بود که پاکش کنم. منتظر خضری نشستم. بعد از ساعتی آواز سقای بگوشم خورد. کوزهٔ دسته شکستهٔ خود را برده آب آوردم، و آن نیم نان خشک را شسته تر کردم و خوردم. خدا شاهد است که لذت نعیم بهشت می داد. عزیزِ من، در سخن درویشان تصنع و تکلف نمی باشد. ایشان شاگرد چرخ دولابی نیند که اگر صد کوزه بسازد یکی دسته ندارد. در صحبت این طایفه شیشه بند کردن سنگ بدل زدن است. زبان را نگه باید داشت که شکرآب ایشان شربت شهادت بی ادب می شود.

to hyperbole and bounds to extravagance! Here you are—bent from a lack of food, with the rock of contentment tied to your belly; breaking your bones to find even a little water; indigent enough to steal even a cat's supper; lying destitute in these ruins and facing death—how could you have had some fancy food! Enough; do not make big claims."

The dervish said, "By God, I am not insincere or given to boasting. I do not tarry a moment where there is any possibility of lying. Listen, since this morning the fire of hunger was ablaze in me, and my wretched lower soul was restless like a dog with scorched paws. It wanted me to go into the city and stretch my hand like a beggar before all and sundry. Somehow, with great struggle, I persisted in my ascetic practice and managed to protect my honor. Suddenly a mouse, holding half of a piece of dry bread in its mouth, came scurrying into this cell—this place that has more holes than a lover's heart. On seeing me—a growling lion inside, but on the outside thin like a tipcat pussy[21]—it dropped that piece of bread and ran away. Perforce, I went and picked it up. But now I did not have any water to purify it, so again I sat down and waited for my 'Khizr.' After some time passed, I heard the cry of a water carrier. I went out with my cracked cup and got some water from him. I then cleaned that piece of bread and ate it. As God is my witness, that dry bread gave me the same pleasure as the finest delicacy from paradise. My dear, dervishes do not make specious or artful remarks. They are not votaries of falsehood. To indulge in mockery in their company is like casting stones at someone's heart. One should watch one's tongue. The dervishes' annoyance can be fatal to the insolent."

۷۴ عم بزرگوار از خطاب او خجالت کشید، و عذر هرزه چانکی خواست. چون متنبه یافت بر سر عنایت آمد و گفت که ای عزیز، من ترا از جان عزیزتر دارم. این قدر تنبیه ضرور بود که چانهٔ بیجا زدن از ادب درویشی دور است. همدران هنگام روز تمام شد و شام افتاد. رخصت خواستیم. گفت، خدا برو. از آنجا که آمدیم، بخدمت شریف پدر رفته سلام و پیام فقیر رسانیدیم. گفت که عنایت ایشان. اگر باز با عم خود بروی، البته نیاز من هم برسانی.

۷۵ صحبت سیم بخدمت او رسیدیم. دیدیم که بیحضوراست، و بیک پهلو افتاده آه آه می کند. چون عم مرا دید دم سرد کشید و پیش خواند، و این بیت حکیم شفائی بر زبان راند:

پرستاری ندارم بر سر بالین بیماری
مگر آهم ازین پهلو بآن پهلو بگرداند

۷۶ پرسید، چه حالت است که این قدر ملالت است؟ گفت، ای عزیز، سینه ام بحدی می سوزد که گوئی در درون من کسی آتش می افروزد. نالهٔ که می کشم، زبانهٔ آن آتش است. آهی که می کنم، لائحهٔ همان شعلهٔ سرکش.

Thus addressed, my "uncle" was shamed to tears, and   74
begged to be forgiven for his improper words. The dervish,
seeing him repentant, became kind again, and said, "Dear
friend, I hold you dearer than life itself. But the reprimand
was necessary. It does not befit a dervish to make foolish
and irresponsible remarks." By then the day was coming to
an end, and so we asked his leave. He said to us, "Go with
God." As soon as we got home, we went to my father and
gave him the dervish's greetings and his message. My father
said to me, "That was most kind of him. When you next
visit him with your 'uncle,' be sure to give him my respectful
greetings."

When we went to the dervish the third time, we found him   75
indisposed and lying on his side. He was groaning. Upon
noticing my "uncle," he sighed and called him to draw near.
Then he recited this verse by Hakim Shifa'i.[22]

I lie on my sickbed; there is no caretaker by my side;
I turn over to the other side by raising an anguished cry.

"What has happened?" my "uncle" asked. "Why are you   76
so despondent?" The dervish replied, "My dear, my breast
burns as if someone has lit a fire in it. The cries that issue
from me are flares from that fire, and the sighs I draw are
flames of the same.

من نمیدانم که دل می سوزد از غم یا جگر

آتش افتاد است در جای و دودی می کند

اگر مرگ بفریاد من رسد خوش بهشتی است وگرنه دوزخی است
که نتیجهٔ عمل زشتی است. اکنون بار بستن جان فتوح است، که
آمد و رفت دم سوهان روح است. شب بیخوابم و روز بیتابم؛ چه
سازم، بچه پردازم که تا بمیرم قرار بگیرم.

روزی بشب کنم بصد اندوه سینه سوز

شـب را سـحر کنم بامیــد کــدام روز

بادی که می وزد دامن بر آتش من می زند. آبی که می خورم
کار روغن میکند. دوای مناسب مناسبتی ندارد، تدبیر موافق
موافقتی نمی کند. اگر بباغم ببری از سوز درون ناخوشم، ور
بعمانم بیندازی من همان در آتشم. کاش سینهٔ من بشگافند و
دل و جگر را زود برآرند. یا مرا ازینجا ببرند و زنده بزیر خاک
بسپارند.

القصه، احوال آن دل سوختهٔ جگرکباب تا بزوال آفتاب بهمین
یک وتیره بود. گاهی دست بدیوار داده می ایستاد، گاهی می
نشست و می افتاد. گاهی چشم می کشاد و نومیدانه میدید، گاهی
چون ماهی بی آب می طپید. ناگاه از زبان من شنید که وقت نماز

٧٧

Is it the heart that smolders, or is it the liver? I don't know.
But a fire has kindled somewhere in me, and the smoke
  rises.

"It would be a boon from heaven if death came to my rescue; otherwise, I am already in hell for my bad deeds. It would be a godsend if life were to pack up right now and leave this body, for even the coming and going of breath is a torture to me. I cannot sleep a wink during the night, and I thrash in anguish all day long. What should I do? How may I contrive to die and thus find rest?

I brought today to its end with the help of many
  consuming pains;
What hope of a tomorrow should I use to carry this night
  to its end?

"If a breeze comes my way, it fans this fire; and if I take a sip of water, it is as if I have poured oil on it. Well-tested medicines do not work on me, and other appropriate measures also fail in my case. If you were to take me to a garden, I would still remain in anguish; and if you were to cast me into an ocean, the fire inside me would continue to burn. I wish people would cut open my breast and pull out my heart and my liver, or otherwise take me away from here and bury me alive."

To make the story short, that is how that tormented man 77
was until the sun passed the meridian. Sometimes he would sit up; sometimes he would stand and lean against a wall— only to collapse to the ground again; sometimes he would open his eyes and look at us in despair; sometimes he would

ظهر رسید. بخضوع و خشوع سجودی برد. «سبحان ربی الاعلی»
گفت، و بمرد.

آتش عشقش بسی را سوختست
لیک زین سان کم کسی را سوختست

عم بزرگوار با چند غلام به تجهیز و تکفین او بپرداخت، و در
همان حجرهٔ شکسته تر از دل عاشق مدفون ساخت. از شنیدن
این خبر جناب پدرم پشت دست گزید و گفت که آدمی روشی
این چنین دیر پیدا می شود، صد حیف که زود رفت.

شبی در خواب عم من آن دلسوختهٔ از جهان رفته می آید، و
می گوید: «دیدی که عشق چه آتشی در من زد و چنانم سوخت.
چارهٔ کار من جز مرگ نبود. چون بی تابی جان مرا دیدند در بحر
مواج رحمتم انداختند و با گوهر مقصود هم کنارم ساختند. یعنی
تسلی گردیدم و آرام گرفتم. و بکام جان ازان نگارِ بهشت رو کام
گرفتم.» از دیدن این واقعه وحشت در مزاج شریف او پیدا آمد.
مدتی با کس انس نگرفت. اکثر اوقات میگفت که بایزید عجب
سوخته جانی بود. داغ جدائی او که بر جان منست تا زنده ام
سیاهی نخواهد افگند.

بر سبیل حکایت این خواب را بخدمت پدرم نقل کرد. گفت،
چه عجب که حق تعالی کریم مطلق است. نشنیدهٔ که عارف نامی

۷۸

۷۹

88

thrash around like a fish out of water. Then he heard me say, "It is now the time for the *zuhr* prayers." All of a sudden, he prostrated himself on the ground most abjectly, and devotedly exclaimed, "Praised be the Almighty Lord!" The next moment he was gone.

The fire of Love has burned many a one,
But few are consumed in this manner.

My "uncle," with the help of some servants, made arrangements for the dervish's shroud and grave, and had him buried in that room that was more ruined than a lover's heart. When my father heard the news, he expressed much grief and remarked, "A true man like him comes by only rarely. Too bad that he died so soon."

One night that soul on fire, who had cut all ties with our world, appeared to my "uncle" in a dream and said, "Did you see the fire Love lit in me? And how it burned me down? There was no way out for me but death. When he saw the anguish of my soul, he cast me into the ocean of his mercy so that I might obtain the pearl I sought. In other words, I was comforted and relieved—my soul rejoiced in his vision." As a result of that dream, my "uncle" became very disturbed, and for some time shied away from all human company. Often he would remark, "Bayazid was a soul on fire, unique, such that a separation from him has scarred my own soul. I shall bear that scar till the day I die." 78

One day my "uncle" mentioned that dream to my father. My father responded, "Why are you surprised? God Almighty is absolute kindness. Have you not heard? The 79

بایزید بسطامی همسایهٔ دیوار بدیوار ترسای بود و از چهل سال
باو آشنائی داشت. او هر سحر تختهٔ می زد، و این می گفت که
ای ترسا، ازین تخته زدن در فردوس بر روی تو باز نخواهد شد.
اگر نجات میخواهی، بیا اسلام قبول کن. یکی بخاطرش رسید که
بایزید آدمی سهلی نیست. چهل سال است که دعوت اسلام می
کند، خالی از چیزی نخواهد بود. سرزده در مجلس او رفته میگوید،
ای شیخ، تو که هر صبح می گوئی مسلمان شو، ضامن نجات من
می توانی شد؟ شیخ را حالت سکر بود. کاغذی از کاغذگر طلبید و
ضامنی نجات او نوشته داد. رفت و مسلمان شد. اتفاقاً در همان
هفته فجائةً بمرد. ورثه آن نوشتهٔ شیخ را بگریبان کفن چسپانده
بخاکش سپردند. چون شیخ بخود آمد، بخود فرو رفت. مریدی
باعث حیرت پرسید. گفت، درحالت مستی متعهد امری شده
ام که از عهدهٔ آن بیرون نمی توانم آمد. گفتا، دران حال ترسای
دوست روی، از دست شیخ ضامنی نجات خود نویسانیده، برده
بود. می گویند که مسلمان شد و مرد. شیخ غش کرد چون این
سخنش بگوش آمد. آب بسیاری بر رویش زدند تا بهوش آمد.
سر کرد که من در نجات خود ترددی داشتم، این جگر از کجا
بهم رساندم که متکفل نجات دیگری شدم. افتان و خیزان بگور
آن نومسلمان شده رفت و متوجه باطن شد. در معامله اش دید
که همان کاغذ بدست دارد و میگوید که ای بایزید، نوشتهٔ تو

famous Sufi Bayazid-e Bistami had a Christian as his next-door neighbor, whom he had known for forty years. Every morning the Christian would beat on his simandron,[23] and every morning Bayazid would say to him, 'Ai Christian, your sounding that piece of wood will not open the doors of paradise for you. Come on; accept Islam, if you desire salvation.' One day that Christian said to himself, 'Bayazid is not an ordinary man. And for forty years he has been inviting me to accept Islam. There must be something to it.' Impulsively, he immediately went to Bayazid—who was seated in his assembly—and said, 'Ai Shaikh, every morning you ask me to become a Muslim. Can you guarantee my salvation?' It so happened that Bayazid was then in a transformed state of ecstasy. He sent for some paper from the papermaker, and writing down a guarantee to that effect gave the paper to the Christian. The latter left, and converted to Islam. By sheer chance, that very week, he suddenly fell ill and passed away. The man's heirs sewed Bayazid's guarantee note to his shroud and had him buried. Meanwhile, when Bayazid finally came to himself, he fell into utter despair. A disciple asked him why he was so worried. He replied, 'When I was not in my senses I took upon myself some task that I will never be able to fulfill.' The disciple said, 'Yes, a friendly looking Christian had come during that time; he got you to write him a note guaranteeing his salvation. We hear that he then became a Muslim, but soon passed away.' Upon hearing those words, Bayazid fell down in a faint. His disciples splashed some water on his face and revived him. He then cried out, 'Here I am, absolutely unsure of my own salvation—how did I become so reckless that I took on someone

هیچ بکار من نیامد. پیش از نمودن این پرچه که دست پیچ نجات خود کرده بودم، بطرزی کریم سوی خودم خواند که چشم فرشتگان مقرب حیران کار من ماند. موجب دل پریشانی خود مشو؛ قلم بند کردهٔ تو این است، بگیر و برو. هرگاه کرم او بدان را این چنین در می یابد، آن فقیر خود از خوبان روزگار بود، اگر بدریای رحمتش غوطها نخوردی این ماجرا بسیار آب بردی.

۸۰ ای برادر عزیز، چون دانستی که آن گل همیشه بهار بهزار رنگ بر می آید و این چمن رسانیدهٔ اوست و این رنگها ریختهٔ او، اگر بینا شوی بتامل شو، وگر قدم کشائی فهمیده رو. در همه ذرات کائنات پرتو همان آفتاب است. اگر شناسای طرز او شدهٔ، دلت کامیاب است. کسی را که دیده و دل بینا است می داند که حباب و موج از دریاست. حق بر طرف عاقلیست اگر غافل نماند. بر ساحل افتاده از دریا چه داند. بیا که برخیزیم و از میان رویم، شاید که بکام جان همه او شویم. موسم جوانی رفت؛ لطف زندگانی رفت. عمر بشست سالگی کشید، پیرانه سالی در رسید. قامت خم شد، طاقت کم شد؛ دماغ ضعیف، جسم نحیف؛ روانی از طبیعت رفت و تیزی از هوش، بینائی از چشم و شنوائی از گوش؛ ذوق بیذوق، دندان بیزور؛ پا ناتوان، سر بی شور؛ موی سفید، دل نامید. زنگ و زنجیر از کمر واکن. ایام آرایش فقیری رفت، زنجیرِ سر در پا کن. هنگام زینت قلندری گذشت.

else's burden?' In desperation, he somehow found his way to that man's grave, and there meditated upon what was within it. He saw that Christian, who held out to him a piece of paper as he said, '*Ai* Bayazid, your note was of no use to me. Before I could even present it—this note that I had taken to be the token of my salvation—he drew me so close to himself that even the most intimate of his angels were left amazed. So do not fret so much. Here is the note you wrote; take it and go home.' When God in his kindness bestows so much even on those who were not good, it would have indeed been strange if that fakir—who was among the best of his time— had not drowned in the ocean of his mercy and kindness.

"Dear brother, you know that that ever-blooming flower   80 takes on a thousand hues, that this garden was nurtured by him, and that these colors here were splashed by him. Therefore, if you truly wish to be among the seeing, look attentively; and if you wish to move forward, do so with deliberation. In every particle of the universe there is the reflection of that one and the same Sun. If you are able to discern his signs, your heart has met with success. He who has eyes and a heart that can see knows that the waves and the foam do not exist except for the sea. Truth is by the side of the wise if he does not persist in remaining ignorant, for then his case is like that of he who casts himself on the beach and learns nothing of the ocean. Come, let us arouse ourselves from our sleep and withdraw from all this; perhaps then we may obtain what our souls seek and become all him. The time of youth has passed. Life's pleasures have vanished. I am now close to sixty, and old age has come upon me. My back is bent; my strength has declined. My mind has grown weak and my

۸۱ در معاش پاس مشهور کن و در معاد مراعات معقول، یعنی ظاهر را مطابق نقل بیارا، و باطن را موافق عقل نما. اگر یار در حرم جلوه گر است، مسلمان شدن هنر است؛ مقصود دل اوست از هر دریکه برآید. وگر جلوۀ او در دیر لاریب است، پس کافر شدن چه عیب است؛ منظور چشم اوست از هر جا که رو نماید.

بـــدیر و کعبـه میگــردیـم، گاه ایـنجا و گاه آنجا
که مطلب جستجوی اوست، خواه اینجا و خواه آنجا

۸۲ باید که عزلت گزینی و چندی تنها نشینی. سرمۀ خفا در چشم کش و بر هیچ چیز التفات مکن. نظر بر خدا دار و هرگز با کسی ملاقات مکن. بسیار با مردم سردرهوا برخوردی، وقت آنست که مژگان بهم زدی و مردی. سر پیچ زدن تا کجا؟ غفلت را بگذار؛ اگر دقیقه فهمی سر ازین مضمون برآر:

body is decrepit. I have lost all spontaneity, and I cannot think fast anymore. My eyes cannot see; my ears cannot hear. My appetites are gone; my teeth are not strong. My legs wobble; my brain is listless; my hair has turned white; and my heart is hopeless. Untie the chains of a fakir from your waist, for the days of decorating ourselves as fakirs are over; remove the chain of a *qalandar* from your forehead and place it on your legs, for the time to preen ourselves as *qalandar*s has passed.

"In the matters of here and now, pay attention to what is 81 known to one and all; and in that which concerns the world we must return to, listen to your intelligence's call. In other words, your outer self should be in accord with *naql*, but your inner self should be in tune with *'aql*.[24] If the Beloved has made himself manifest in the Kaaba then it is virtuous to be a Muslim—for no matter what door he comes out of, he is the heart's goal. But if forsooth he is manifest in a temple, then how can one be faulted for becoming an infidel? For he is the cynosure of our eyes, no matter where he reveals himself.

> *We go to the temple and visit the Kaaba—we are here and*
> *we are there.*
> *We only aim to seek him out—be it here or be it there.*

"You must seek seclusion and be by yourself for a while. 82 Put the collyrium of concealment in your eyes and turn your back on everything. Fix your sight on God and do not meet with anyone. For a long time you pleased yourself in the company of men distraught in love; now it is time that you closed your eyes and died.[25] How much longer must

دیده ام در علم صحبت های رنگین صد کتاب

کــــرده ام یک مصرعــهٔ تنهانشــــینی انتخاب

۸۳ نمیدانم که چه می سگالی که سر زخم خود نمی مالی. پیش
ازین سرگران هوا و هوس ممان. سر را از نشهٔ یاد حق سبک
گردان. نظر بر ریش سفید شانه کاری منمائی، یعنی بفریب و
تملق با کسی یاری ننمائی. قصد خرق عادت نکنی. گاو در خرمن
زورمندی چون خدا بستن خود را بخریت شهرهٔ شهر کردنست. ور
بی اراده کرامتی ظاهر شود، چون شجر شاخ بر دیوار نکنی که ثمرهٔ
آن شاخ از پشیمانی برآورد. شاه اندازی را فقیران عیب میدانند،
یعنی متکبر و مغتمز را آدمی نمی خوانند.

۸۴ وقتی که رخصت شد، با خود قرار داد که آینده جای نروم و
روزی دو بار حاضر شوم.

۸۵ یکی پدرم گفت که ای برادر عزیز، دماغ آخر میرود، یعنی هر
روز ضعیف میشود. اگر صرف حفظ قرآن شریف شود چه طور
است؟ التماس کرد که خوب بخاطر گذشت. چنانچه در مدت
یک و نیم سال مصحف مجید را یاد گرفتند.

۸۶ روزی باهم نشسته بودند و دور میکردند که درویش، «اسد
الله» نام، پیراهن نیلی در بر و کلاه نمد بر سر، وارد شد. چون
دوچار پدرم گشت، گفت که ای سیرابه پژِ کبود جامه، چرا سفر

96

you slumber? Discard this negligence, and draw your lesson from this verse if you claim to be intelligent.

I read a hundred books on the science of joyful company,
But took to my heart just one line: Sit alone by yourself.

"I do not understand what is in your mind that you give no thought to finding a cure. Henceforth, do not go crazy after base desires. Drink the cup of God's remembrance and lighten your head of all burdens. Consider the whiteness of your own beard and do not indulge in flattering and deceiving others. Do not even think of performing a miracle. To claim the powers that belong to Almighty God alone is to have oneself proclaimed an ass all over town. And if perchance a miracle comes about without your intending it, do not let it turn your head. Do not be proud of it, for only a fall will follow. Fakirs consider boasting a terrible fault, and he who is boastful and vain—they do not even consider him a man."   83

My "uncle" took his leave and vowed to himself that henceforth he would not stir out of the house, and would visit with my father twice a day.   84

One day my father said to my "uncle," "Dear brother, the mind is being used up anyway, i.e., it grows weaker every day. How about it if it were used for memorizing the Noble Qur'an?" "That is a fine idea," my "uncle" replied. And so, in eighteen months, they memorized the Glorious Book.   85

One day, as the two were sitting together going over what they had memorized, a dervish by the name of Asadullah arrived, dressed in a blue robe and a felt cap. Upon seeing him, my father asked, "*Ai* stew maker of Kabud Jama,[26] what   86

دور و دراز اختیار کردی و شداید راه خوابیده بر خود هموار
ساختی؟ آن عزیز دوید و در قدم افتاد. سرش در کنار گرفت و
قریب خود جا داد.

عم من حیران این اختلاط شده پرسید که این بزرگ کیست؟ ۸۷
گفتا آشنای قدیم منست. حیران تر شد و التماس نمود که برای
رابطهٔ این چنین ملاقات بسیار شرط است. این مرد را گاهی ندیده
ام. گفت که من و این مرید یک پیریم. در دو سال یکبار بخدمت
ایشان حاضر میشد. یکی سوال کردم چه شود که آثار مرگ بر من
ظاهر شود، تا بکار گور پردازم و دل را بچیز دیگر مشغول نسازم.
ارشاد شد که هرگاه این سیرابه پژ کبود جامه را بینی، یقین به دانی
که تا سال دیگر زنده نمانی. دانسته باش فرصت عمر من بسیار
کم است. عموی بزرگوار از استماع این کلمات سخت متالم شد
و گفت، انشاءالله من از این واقعه را نخواهم دید، یعنی آن روز در
جهان نخواهم بود و این غم نخواهم کشید.

دمی که با آن تازه وارد سر حرف وا شد، نقل کرد که از چندی ۸۸
دوکان من نمی گردید، یعنی سیرابهٔ مرا کسی نمی خرید. شب می
پختم روز می انداختم. دم و دودی که داشتم صرف خسارت
شد. ناچار دل بدریا افگنده لب خشک و چشم تر بر خاک افتاده
بودم. ناگاه خوابم در ربود. دیدم که پیر بر سر استاده است و می
گوید که ای اسدالله، هرچند صعوبت سفر بسیار است و راه دور

made you undertake this long journey? Why did you put yourself under so much hardship?" The man rushed forward and threw himself at my father's feet, but my father gathered him in his arms and had him sit by his side.

My "uncle," amazed at this intimacy, asked, "Who is this saintly person?" My father responded, "He is an old friend." My "uncle" was now even more amazed, and said, "But such intimacy between people comes about only through numerous and frequent meetings—I have never seen this person before!" My father replied, "He and I are disciples of the same master. He used to come to see the master once in two years. One day I asked my master, 'Is it possible that when my death draws nigh I could see some sign of it? So that I may get busy preparing for the grave, and disengage my heart from everything else.' My master replied, 'When next you see this stew maker of Kabud Jama, know that you would not live to see another year.' Now you must understand that the days left to me are very few." My revered "uncle" was devastated when he heard those brutal words, and said, "God willing, I shall not see that day. I shall already be dead and not have to endure that grief."

When conversation with the new arrival began, the man said, "Lately my shop was not doing so well, for people were not coming to buy my stew. Each night I would make the stew for the morning, and at each day's end I had to throw it away. What little money I had saved got used up covering the loss. One day I was lying on the floor in despair—my lips chapped, my eyes tearing, ready to kill myself—when suddenly sleep grabbed me, and I had a dream. I saw that our master stood at my head and was saying to me, "*Ai* Asadullah, it will be an

87

88

اما یکبار برخوردن تو با علی متقی ضرور. در میان من و او اشاره
ایست. همین که تو خواهی رسید او خواهد فهمید. باید که زود
بروی، و از کساد بازاری پریشان دل نشوی که چون از آنجا برگردی
دکانت آنچنان گردد که سیرابه تو تبرک گردد. برخاستم و دوکان
را بشاگرد گذاشتم، و نیم نان خشک بطریق زاد راه برداشتم.
باندک زمانی از جهانی بجهانی آمدم، یعنی از کبودجامه با اکبرآباد
رسیدم، و ترا بمراد دل مشتاق دیدم. اکنون رفتن من باختیار
تست. هرگاه خواهی گفت، انداز آنطرف خواهم کرد.

۸۹   پدرم متبسم شد و گفت که ای اسدالله، اینهمه بآهو سوارشدن
از برای چه؟ سیرابه ضایع نمی شود که این همه دست پاچه می
شوی. از گرد راه رسیدهٔ، رنج بی پایان کشیدهٔ. اگر مشتاق ما فقیران
نۀ، چندی برای رفع ماندگی خود بمان. شتاب چیست؟ رخصت
هم اتفاق میشود. بغلامی اشارت رفت که فرش خوابش در حجرۀ
عم من درست کند و آب بدست او ریزد. حاصل که ساعتی از خود
جدا نمی گذاشت، و بدلجوئی و مزاج گوئی می داشت.

۹۰   یکی آن مهمان عزیز سوال کرد که در مسئلۀ رویت تردددی دارم.
خداخوانان دو جماعت اند. جماعتی بران است که روزی آن
غیرت ماه را چون بدر کامل تماشا خواهیم کرد. عقیدۀ جماعت
دیگر اینکه ادراک آن آفتاب از بصر بشر امکان ندارد. فرمود که ما
فقیران را هیچ تردد نیست. چون مقرر شد که او عین عالم است،

arduous and long journey, but it is imperative that you visit 'Ali-e Muttaqi. Between him and me a sign is agreed; he will recognize it when you arrive. Leave immediately, and do not worry about your failing business. Your shop will do so well on your return that your pot of stew would never satisfy the demand." I immediately got up, handed over the shop to my apprentice, and meagerly equipped, set out on the journey. In no time I left one world and arrived in another—i.e., I traveled from Kabud Jama to Akbarabad, and found you as my heart desired. Now my departure is in your hands; I shall go back whenever you command."

My father smiled and said, "*Ai* Asadullah, what's the big   89
rush? Is your stew likely to go bad that you fret so and are in such terrible haste? You have just arrived after having had a hard time of it. Stay a while. Get rid of your fatigue even if you may not be keen for the company of us fakirs. What's the big hurry? You can leave in due course." Then he instructed a servant to prepare a bed for the guest in the cell of my "uncle" and to look after all his needs. To put it briefly, my father did not let him out of his sight for a moment and did everything to keep him pleased.

One day that beloved guest said, "I am bothered about   90
something related to the question of our having a 'vision of God.' God's votaries come in two groups. One group believes that they shall one day see that Beautiful One as clearly as they now see a full moon; the other, however, declares that human eyes can never comprehend the vision of that Sun." My father responded, "For us fakirs there is no fear in that regard. Since it has been established that he is the Essential Reality of this world, he appears to our eyes whichever way

بهر جا که نظر می افگنیم او به نظر می آید. در هرکه می نگریم او
رو می نماید. آن معنی بهر صورت جلوه گر است، و دیدار او بشرط
نظر میسر. القصه بعد یک هفته رخصت شد و گل بانگ بر قدم زد.

۹۱   صبح عید عموی من تبدیل رخت کرده بمصلیٰ رفت. از آنجا که
آمد دردی در سینه اش ظاهر شد بشدتی که رنگ رویش شکست،
و قرار از دل رخت بست. والدِ مرا طلبید و گفت، دردی دارم که
بکمال بی دردیست. یافته ام که این درد عاقبت ندارد. و خفکی
بمرتبه ایست که نفس تنگی می کند. غالباً جان ناتوان طاقت ندارد.
عبای را از تن من بکشید که خوش نمی آید. کلاهم دور بیندازید
که بر سر گرانی می نماید. جانم ناتوان است، بیمار من گران است.

۹۲   چون شام شد، آن درد عام شد. شور آه آهش بلند گشت. همگی
یکدل دردمند گشت. دمی که بضبط پرداختی خود را غنچه ساختی.
گهی که از درد نالان شدی، چون گل پریشان شدی. وقتی دلش
بسیار گرفتی آه آتشناک کشیدی. دود جگر که کباب گذشته بود
به آسمان رسیدی. اگر سخن راندی این رباعی خواندی. لمصنفه:

وقت است که رو بمرگ یکباره کنیم
آن درد نـداریم که ما چـاره کنیم
بیماری صعب عشــق دارد دل ما
گر جامه گـذاریم، کفن پاره کـنیم

102

we turn. He shows us his face in whatever we look at. That Essence is revealed in every form that we see here. A vision of him is available to anyone who knows how to see." To make the story short, our guest stayed a week, then took his leave and set off on his journey home in great haste.

On the morning of the Id, my "uncle" changed clothes and went to pray in congregation. When he returned, a pain started in his chest. It was so intense that his face turned pale and his heart lost all peace. Sending for my father, he said to him, "I am seized by a severe pain that I am sure will not have a good end. And I feel so strangulated that I can hardly breathe. Evidently, my life will not endure. Please remove my undershirt, for it discomforts my body, and throw away my cap, for it sits heavy on my head. My strength ebbs. My sickness grows worse."

When evening arrived, that pain spread throughout his body. His cries grew so loud you might say he became an embodiment of pain. When he held his breath to suppress the pain, he appeared clenched like a rosebud; and when he let go his cry of pain it left him like a torn rose. When the pain would grow worse each breath he would draw would be like a flame, and each sigh he would then release would be the smoke from his consumed heart reaching for the sky. And if he said anything, it was only this quatrain (Author's verse:)

It's time I faced my death with resolution,
For the pain I suffer is not for me to cure.
An intractable Passion plagues my heart—
I would tear my shroud even when dead.

91

92

103

۹۳ چون پاسی از شب گذشت، کار از بی طاقتی برو تنگ شد. با
پیر گفت که آخر دلِ سختی دیدهٔ من کبابِ سنگ شد. تو خود
آگاه راز این میخانهٔ. اگر تهِ شیشه از عمر من باقی مانده باشد،
بکسی دیگر بده که درد نوشی باین درد کشیدن جگری می
خواهد. من ازین جان شیرین تلخیِ مرگ را صدمرتبه گواراتر
می بینم. توجهی کن که آسان بمیرم؛ بخشائی که آرام بگیرم.
آخرِ شب کلاه شب پوش را بمن بخشید و چشم از غلبهٔ ناتوانی
بپوشید. دمی که شب شکست، یعنی سفیدهٔ صبح دمید، جان
المناک او بر لب رسید. موذن مسجد «أللّٰه اکبر» گفت، آن
بیمارِ شب زنده دار بخفت، یعنی دست بر دل نهاد و جان
بجان آفرین داد.

۹۴ پیر او دستار بر زمین زد و گریبان درید، و ازین واقعهٔ جانکاه
الفها بر سینه برید. مریدانش خاک بر سر و داغ بر جگر، با صد
پریشانی چنانکه میدانی، برسمیات مردهٔ او پرداختند و جنازهٔ آن
دردمند را درست ساختند.

عشق دردی بی دوائی بوده است
بهرِ جان و دل بلائی بـوده است

هرگاه برای نماز استادند، اکثری بر خاک افتادند. پدرم گفت
که ای ناواقف پاسِ آشنائی، دیر معلوم شد که بیوفائی. آنچنان

۱۰۴

When some of the night had passed, his weakness 93
grew worse. He then spoke to my father, his master: "My
tortured heart feels like a roasted piece of meat. You well
know the secrets of this tavern. If there still remain some
dregs of my life, please give them to someone else, for it
takes a much stronger person to drink such bitter dregs.
I would rather take the poison of death a hundred times
than this last gulp of life's nectar. Hold me firm in your
thought, that I may die easily; be merciful, that I may find
rest." Near the end of the night, he gave me the cap he wore
at night and, overwhelmed by weakness, closed his eyes.
And when night ended and dawn's whiteness gleamed, his
pain-wracked life came to an end. From a mosque arose
the call to prayers—"*Allāhu Akbar*"—and here that sick
man ended his nightlong vigil and fell asleep. That is to
say, he placed his hand over his heart and submitted his
life to its Creator.

My father flung his turban to the ground, tore open his 94
shirt, and scarred his breast in anguish at this soul-consum-
ing event. His disciples—dirt in their hair, scars on their
heart, and utterly distressed—did all that was necessary for
a proper burial.

Love is a pain that has no cure—
It's a curse on our hearts and souls.

When the gathering lined up for the funeral prayers,
many of them collapsed in grief. My father cried out, "*Ai*
stranger to the duties of friendship, I learned too late that
you were fickle. You sped away with such heat that my heart

گرم رفتی که سینهٔ مرا تفتی. یاران این چنین نمیروند؛ غمخواران بیمروت نمی شوند.

چه شد آن وفا و عهدی که تو وعدها نمودی
بتو من چه گفته بودم، تو بمن چه گفته بودی

۹۵ بزرگان دوش بزیر تابوت گذاشتند، یعنی بعزت تمامش برداشتند. آه پیر برسم علم مردگان پیش پیش روان، معتقدانش سیلاب سیلاب سرشک افشان. مردهٔ او را بیرون شهر بردند و بگوشهٔ باغی بخاک سپردند. گلها افشاندند؛ فاتحه خواندند. ملالت بیحد کشیدند؛ چارهٔ جز صبر ندیدند.

۹۶ روز سیوم که عزیزان شهر برای فاتحه آمدند، پدرم گفت، کسیکه این چنین عزیزش مرده باشد اگر او را عزیزمرده گویند می افتد. از امروز مرا «عزیزمرده» می گفته باشند. چنانچه در شهر بهمین لقب شهرت گرفت. روزی صدبار گریستی، بحال مردگان زیستی. منکه بغل پروردهٔ او بودم، حوائج خود را باو می گفتم، با او می خوردم، با او می خفتم، روزها یاد میکردم، شبها فریاد میکردم.

still smolders. Friends do not run away in that manner, and comforters do not turn so heartless.

> *What happened to the fealty you had promised, that oath*
> *of consistency?*
> *Remember what I had said to you? And what you had*
> *then said to me?"*

The elders placed his coffin on their shoulders and with solemn reverence carried it outside. The cry of his master went before it like the banner that goes ahead of a coffin, while behind the coffin trailed his many devotees, their eyes overflowing with tears. Thus it was when they went outside the city walls and had him buried inside a garden. Then they placed flowers on his grave and recited the prayers for his salvation. Finally they returned to the city burdened with grief, knowing that they had no option but to resign themselves to God's will. [95]

On the day of his *siyum*,[27] when the notables of the city gathered for formal prayers, my father said, "If someone loses to death a person so *'azīz* to him, it behooves that he should be called 'Aziz Murda."[28] Therefore, from this day onward, please call me only by that name." And so it happened that he became famous in the city as 'Aziz Murda. He burst into tears a hundred times every day, and lived as if he were already dead. While I, who had been brought up so lovingly by the deceased—telling my needs to him alone; having all my meals with him; sleeping next to him on his bed—perforce remembered him all day long and cried for him every night. [96]

107

new name

درویش عزیزمرده بدلجوئی می پرداخت، و بهیچ وجه آزرده دلم
نمی ساخت. گاه می گفت که ای پسر من ترا بسیار میخواهم،
اما ازین غم میکاهم که من نیز بر سر راهم. گاه می گفت که ماه
من، نه طفل هاله، الحمدلله که ده ساله. چه به کاهش افتاده،
آخر درویش زاده. دل را قوی دار، خود را بخدا سپار. شاد بزی و
خوش بمان. مرا طرح کش خود بدان. جان من، مگر طفل شیری
که هر زمان دلگیری؟ اندیشهٔ خود چرا داری؟ وارث چون خدا
داری. رفتگان باز نمی آیند؛ گذشتگان رو نمی نمایند. ای پسر
دنیا در گذر است، و هر کرا می بینی در جناح سفر. نه پنداری
که جای بودنت جهان است، این قرار داده مجلس روان ست.
حاضران رفته اند؛ نشستگان گذشته اند. غنچه پیشانی مشو،
چون گل شگفته رو می باش. بهار این چمن رفتنی است، بعبث
دل مخراش. مقامرخانهٔ آفاق را چنان ساخته اند که درو چون تو
بسیاری دل باخته اند. تا واقف راه و رسم این جا نشوی، زینهار
که این راه نروی. در حریفان سخت باز و طرار، مثلیست: قمار
و راهِ قمار. هر روز ازین قسم سخن کردی و بناز تمام پروردی.

روزی به تلخ کامی تمام حلوای مرگ قسمت می کرد که جوانی
سرواندام، احمد بیگ نام، شکری رنگ، دانهٔ چند شکرانگور بر
دست گذاشته، نذر گزرانید و گفت، تازه از ولایت آمده ام و
ارادهٔ حج دارم. چون وارد شهر شدم آوازهٔ درویشئ تو شنیدم،

kind of emotionally repressed father-son relationship

My father, the dervish 'Aziz Murda, made every effort   97
to console me and never did anything that could make me
feel bad. Sometimes he would say to me, "My son, I love
you greatly, but I am also much anguished by the thought
that I too must soon depart." Then at other times he would
say, "Moon of mine, you are not a baby anymore. Allah be
praised, you are ten years old. Why are you in despair? After
all, you are the son of a dervish. Keep your heart strong and
put yourself in God's hands. Live happily; keep smiling. You
should know that I'm always ready to fulfill your every desire.
Ai soul of mine, are you an infant that you cry all the time?
Why must you worry when you have a guardian and protector in God? The people who go away do not come back; they
passed away and will never again show their faces. *Ai* son,
this world is transitory; everyone you see here is bound to
depart. Do not consider this world to be a permanent place
for you; nay, it is just a momentary assembly. They who were
present here have moved on, and they who were seated here
are gone. Do not clench your brow like a bud; smile, and open
up like a flower. Spring in this garden is transitory. There is
no need to anguish over it. He made this gambling house of
a world in such a way that there are scores of you who have
gambled their hearts away. Do not set foot on this path until
you have learned how to walk. Among astute gamblers there
is a well-known proverb: 'There is gambling, and then there
is a right way to gamble.'" That is how he talked to me every
day and nurtured me with utmost care.

One day my father, with the bitter taste of grief still on   98
his tongue, was distributing sweets to commemorate his
beloved friend when a young man arrived. Cypress bodied,

مشتاق شده بخدمت سامی رسیدم.

گفت مگر نشنیدهٔ:

چرا بپای خود ای کعبه رو نمی افتی
همان توئی که بفرسنگ می نمایندت

اولا خود را دریاب، انگاه برای کعبه بشتاب. کعبه عبارت
از دلهای خستهٔ درویشان است، و مقصود دست و بغل ما این
جگرریشان. اگر دل ایشان بدست آید، کعبهٔ مراد بی سعی رو
نماید. ازین جاست که کسی گفته رفته است.

ز کعبه آیم و رشک آیدم به خوننابی
که از زیارت دلهای خسته می آید

دل درویشان جای خوشست. این ویرانه را هوای خوشست.
دل را منزل آن ماه می گویند؛ مقصود از همین در می جویند.
سالکی به طواف کعبه رفته بود. کسی را در آنخانه ندید. با دلِ
پرآرزو ناکام برگردید. در همان حال گفت:

sugar colored—his name was Ahmad Beg. He presented some Shakar grapes to my father and said, "I have newly come from abroad, with the intention of going on to perform the Haj. On arrival here, I heard the fame of your saintliness and became eager to attend upon you."

My father replied, "Perhaps you have not heard: 99

Ai traveler to the Kaaba, why not throw yourself at your
    own feet?
For it's you whom he shows to you in the mile markers on
    this road.

"You should first find yourself, and only then hurry to the Kaaba. The Kaaba stands for the shattered hearts of the dervishes, and these anguished persons are what we most cherish. If one gains their hearts then one can obtain the Kaaba of one's desire without any effort. That is why someone has said:

I return happy having seen the Kaaba, but I envy the man
Who paid homage to shattered hearts with tears of blood.

"The heart of a dervish is a lovely place—this wilderness has a pleasant air. People say the human heart is the abode of that Beauty, and they seek in it what they ultimately desire. Once a seeker on the path of Truth went to circumambulate the Kaaba and found that the House of God was empty. Disappointed, he turned around, his heart's desire still unfulfilled, and in that state remarked:

کعبــه را دیـدم، دل من درد تنهـائی گــداخت

مجلس آرائی که ما را خواند خود مهمان کیست؟

آنچه تو می گوئی محرم حرم نیز همین گوید. کسی را که تو می
جوئی، کعبه هم او را می جوید.

هـر کرا دیـدم چـو من گم گشـتۀ تحقیق بـود

کعـــبه را هـم بی تـکلف در بیـابان یافتـم

گرد دلها بگرد که طواف حرم اینست؛ بلاگردان خود شو که
مطلب عمده همین است. وجود غیر موجود نیست و کسی بی
او مشهود نی.

گفـتم بحـرم محـرم این خانه کـدامسـت

آهســـــته بمن گفت که بیگانه کدامست

مرا بر جوانی تو رحم می آید که رنجها خواهی کشید و بمطلب
نخواهی رسید. سخن درویشان بگوش جان بشنو. چندی فروکش
کن وازینجا مرو.

جوان چون روی دل از درویش دید، سر را از فرمان نه پیچید، ۱۰۰
یعنی رحل اقامت انداخت و بریاضت شاقه پرداخت. ذهن
سلیمی داشت؛ کسب کرد و در مدت هفت ماه بمرتبۀ کمال

I went to the Kaaba, and its desolation consumed my
heart.
Whose house did he go to grace after inviting me to his
house?

"You say your aim is to see the Kaaba, but that is what they too say who are intimates of the Kaaba. In fact, the Kaaba also seeks the One whom you seek.

Everyone I came upon was lost in a search the way I was;
to be frank, I found the Kaaba itself lost in a wilderness.

"Circumambulate human hearts, for that is the true circumambulation of God's abode. Be a votary of yourself, for there is no finer goal. Nothing exists besides him; nothing is manifest without him.

I asked the House, "Who is the Intimate of the House?"
It softly asked back, "But who is a stranger here?"

"I feel pity for your young age, for you will suffer a great deal but never reach the goal you seek. Listen carefully to what the dervishes say. Do not leave; stay for a few days."
When the young man saw the dervish so inclined toward him, he submitted to his command, and settling down he vigorously engaged himself on the Sufi path. Since he possessed a fine mind, he learned fast—within seven months he reached perfection. The world had rarely seen and people had scarcely heard of an old master of such quality and a young man of such beauty—an old master in such a height-

100

رسید. پیری باین خوبی، جوانی باین محبوبی؛ پیری باین حالت،
جوانی باین کیفیت؛ پیری باین کمال، جوانی باین حال؛ پیری باین
عنایت، جوانی باین ارادت؛ پیری باین نظر، جوانی باین اثر دیدهٔ
روزگار کم دیده و گوش جهانیان کم شنیده. روز و شب چون
شکر و شیر، یعنی صحبت بسیار درگیر. پیر را دمی نمی گذاشت،
بجوان عزیز شهرت داشت. اتفاقاً زر توفیقی از جای بدست پیر
آمد. جوان را گفت که برین متصرف شو و بسفر حجاز برو. بعد از
نماز صبح زیرپیچ دستار و سجادهٔ محرابی عنایت کرد و رخصتش
نمود.

روزی درویش عزیزمرده برای عیادت همشیره زادهٔ برادر عزیز
که محمد باعث نام داشت، عالم، فاضل، متصوف کامل بود،
بعالم گنج که محله ایست مشهور از اکبرآباد، در آفتاب گرم
رفت. چون شام بروز سیاهی زدن آغاز کرد، از آن جا باندازخانه
روان شد. عشائین را در مسجد خود آمده ادا نمود. هرگاه بر فرش
خواب رفت و من حاضر شدم، گفت، ای پسر، حرارت آفتاب
در مزاج من تاثیری کرده است. صداعی دارم. از آثار معلوم
میشود که تپ خواهم کرد. غذای شب نخورد و خوابید. صبح
که برخواست، تپی بشدت داشت. طبیب «ابوالفتح» نام معالج
قدیم او بود، آمد و تبرید کرد. تسکین نیافت. مبالغه در مبردات
فوق الحد نمود، سودمند نیفتاد. تپ درویش بندی شد، یعنی هر

۱۰۱

ened state and a young man so touched with grace—an old master so perfect and a young man so select—an old master so benevolent and a young man so devout in intent—an old master so effective and a young man so receptive. They stayed together day and night, as inseparable as sugar in milk. Not for a moment did the young man leave his master, and he soon came to be known as Jawan-e 'Aziz.[29] One day the master received some money—God's bounty—from somewhere. He said to the young man, "Here, take this money and set out on your journey to Hejaz." The following day, after the dawn prayers, he gave him a skullcap and a prayer rug and bade him farewell on his journey.

One midday, my father, the dervish 'Aziz Murda, went to Alamganj, a well-known neighborhood in Akbarabad, to visit with Muhammad Ba'ith, who was ill. The latter was the nephew of the late Mir Amanullah, and himself a learned man and a perfect Sufi. When evening began to darken the sky, the dervish turned homeward and, arriving at his mosque, performed there the two combined evening prayers. When he finally lay down on his bed and I presented myself before him, he said, "*Ai* son, the heat of the day has affected me. I have a severe headache, and it seems that I'm going to have a fever." He did not eat the evening meal and went to sleep. When he woke up the next morning, he was running a very high temperature. Abul Fath, his regular physician, came and gave him a cooling potion to drink, but it brought him no relief. He then gave him stronger coolants—some excessively so—but all to no avail. His fever set in, that is, it gripped him every evening and lasted the night through. They tried many other ways to break the fever's grip, but

101

115

روز شام می آمد و تمام شب می ماند. برای تپ بستن تدبیرهای بی شمار میکردند، اما از هیچ یکی این عقدهٔ سخت کشاده نشد. پس از ماهی مشخص گردید که این تپ متشبث بقلب است و استخوانی شده است، یعنی این درویش نحیف که مشت استخوانی بیش نیست مبتلای رنج باریک است.

١٠٢   بمن گفت که ای پسر، جان من از صرف نیاز است و جسمم وقف گداز. رغبتی با غذایم نیست. اگر می خورم گرانی می کند. دوائیکه صبح طبیب می دهد تا صبح دیگر کفایت است. می خواهم که تا بمیرم ترک غذا بگیرم. پنج شش دسته های نرگس از بازار بطلب که بشرط حیات گاه گاه بو کرده آید. بموجب ارشاد طلب داشتم و پیش او برابر گذاشتم. هرگاه چشم می کشاد، دسته بدست گرفته بو می کرد و می گفت، الحمدلله که سیر شدم.

١٠٣   چون بترک غذا پرداخت ما بیکسان را از خود نامید ساخت. طاقت از دست و پا رفت. کار ناتوانی بالا رفت. سخن بسیار کم راندی، نماز باشارت خواندی. بیست و یکم رجب طبیب، بعادت قدیم، کاسهٔ تبرید آورد. درویش ابرو ترش کرد و نخورد، وآن کاسهٔ دوا را بر زمین زده گفت که ای مرده شو برده، تاثیر دوا از روز اول ظاهر بود. من پاس تو میکردم که میخوردم. افسوس که نه فهمیدی. برو، دست از من بدار. ناقباحت فهمی مرضی است که علاج ندارد.

none succeeded. After a month it was diagnosed that the fever had taken hold of his heart and had even penetrated into the bones. In other words, that enfeebled dervish who was no more than a handful of bones was dying of consumption.

He then said to me, "*Ai* son, my soul is all submission and my body is burning away. I feel no desire for food. If I eat anything, it sits heavy with me. The medicine that the physician gives me in the morning suffices me till the next day. I now wish to have no food till the day I die. Send for a few bunches of dried narcissus flowers from the market so that, life permitting, I might inhale their fragrance every so often." I followed his order, and, getting the flowers, kept them by his side all the time. Whenever he would open his eyes he would hold a bunch in his hand and smell the flowers; then he would say, "Allah be praised! Now I feel satiated."

102

When he stopped eating, we miserable ones lost all hope for his recovery. His legs and arms were drained of the little strength they had, and an utter weakness overwhelmed him. He spoke very little and used only gestures when he prayed. On the twenty-first of Rajab, the physician as usual brought him a bowl of the cooling potion. But the dervish became angry and did not drink it. Instead, he hurled it to the ground and said, "You wretch! From the first day it was clear just how effective your medicine was. I have been taking it only out of consideration for you, but you do not seem to learn a thing. Now go away, and leave me alone. Foolishness is itself an illness that has no cure."

103

۱۰۴ انگاه حافظ محمد حسن برادر کلان مرا، که برادراندر بود،
طلب نمود و فرمود که من فقیرم و هیچ ندارم، مگر سه صد
جلد کتاب. روبروی من بیارید و حصهٔ برادرانه کرده بگیرید. او
التماس کرد که من طالب علمم. کرم این کار مرا بیشتر است، و
این برادران ربطی بکتاب ندارند. کناره های اوراق چیده خواهد
شد. یکی کاغذ باد خواهد ساخت، یکی در آب خواهد انداخت.
اگر پیش من امانت گذارند خویست، وگرنه مختار اند. پدر از
مزاج ناساز او خبر بود. شانه گیر شد و گفت، چه شد که ترک
لباس کردهٔ لیکن کج پلاسی تو هنوز نرفته است. می خواهی که
طفلان بیچاره را بازی دهی، و پس از مرگ دل بخرابی ایشان نهی.
دانسته باش که حق تعالی غیور است و غیور را دوست میدارد.
غالب که میر محمد تقی دست نگر تو نشود. اگر بنوع دیگر
پیش خواهی آمد کاسه بر سرت خواهد شکست، و نقش عزت تو
پیش این بابا نخواهد نشست. خواهی دید اگر بمراد خواهی رسید؛
برای یک جلد کتاب پوست تو خواهد کشید. کم کاسه شایستهٔ
بی اعتباری است. بخل و حسد دلیل ذلت و خواری است. خوب
است، کتابها را ببر و نگاه دار.

۱۰۵ پس انگاه روی سخن بمن کرد. گفت که ای پسر، قرضدار سه
صد رویپهٔ بذالان بازارم. امید که تا ادا نکنی مردهٔ مرا برنداری
که من سکهٔ درست مردی بوده ام، و در همه عمر دغابازی نه

He then sent for Hafiz Muhammad Hasan, who was my 104
half-brother and older than I, and said to him, "I am a fakir.
Except for three hundred books I have no other possessions.[30] Bring them here and divide them up with your brothers." He replied, "I am a student, and I am diligent in what I
do. These brothers of mine have no interest in books. They
will only tear their pages out. One would use them to make
kites, the other would turn them into paper boats. It would
be better if you left the books in my trust—otherwise, you are
the master." My father was well aware of his wicked nature,
so he admonished him and said, "It makes no difference if
you have dressed yourself in humility, for your meanness
has not left you. You only wish to cheat these boys, and cause
them more trouble after I am gone. But you should know
that Almighty God jealously guards his honor and also loves
the people who similarly guard theirs. I strongly believe that
Mir Muhammad Taqi will never have to stretch his hand in
front of you. If you treat him wrongly, he will expose you in
public. Your name will matter little before this child's fame.
If you gain your aim, you will see that he will punish you
severely. No one trusts a stingy person, and meanness and
jealousy lead only to disgrace. All right, take the books and
look after them carefully."

Then my father turned to me and said, "Son, I owe 300 105
rupees to the shopkeepers in the market. I hope you will not
bury me until you have paid off that debt, for I have been a
man of integrity, and never in my life did I cheat anyone."
I meekly responded, "There is nothing worth anything in
the house except for the books, and you have already given
them to my elder brother. How am I going to pay off the

نموده ام. عرض کردم که غیر از جلدهای کتاب دم و پوستی بنظر
نمی آید. آنها را ببرادر کلان سپردید. ادای قرض چسان توانم کرد.
چشم پرآب نمود و گفت، خدا کریم است، دل تنگ نباید شد.
کاغذ زر در راه است. قریب می رسد. می خواستم که تا رسیدن
زر زنده بمانم اما فرصت عمر کم است، ماندن نمی توانم. در
حق من دعا کرد و حوالت با خدا کرد. ساعتی نفس شمرد آخر
حساب سپرد.

۱۰۶ درویش چون چشم پوشید، جهان در چشم من سیاه گردید.
حادثۀ عظیمی رو داد، آسمان بر من بیفتاد. دریا دریا گریستم،
لنگر از کف دادم؛ سر را بر سنگ زدم، بر خاک افتادم. کل و
مکل بسیار شد؛ قیامت پدیدار شد. برادر کلان من ترک مردم
داری گرفت و بی چشم و روی اختیار نمود. دید که پدر آستین
کهنه داشت و به بیکسی جامه گذاشت، قرضخواهان دامن
گیرمن خواهند شد. پهلو تهی کرد و گفت، کسانیکه همگیر ناز و
نعم بودند آنها دانند و کار آنها. من در حیات پدر دخیل کاری
نگشتم، از وقف اولادی هم گذشتم. سجاده نشینان او سلامت
باشند. سر را می کنند، وجهه را میخراشند. انچه مصلحت وقت
خواهد بود، خواهند نمود.

۱۰۷ منکه تازه بیکس شده بودم، چون سخنان بی ته او را شنودم،
غم و غصه بسیاری خوردم. التجا باو نبردم. کمر را محکم بستم،

debt?" Tears came into his eyes as he said, "God is munificent. Do not despair. A bill of payment is on its way; it
should reach here very soon. I had wished to stay alive until
it arrived, but no more life is allowed to me. I must depart."
He prayed for my welfare and entrusted me to God; then he
took the few breaths he still had to account for and died.[31]

When the dervish closed his eyes,* the world darkened   106
before my eyes. It was a terrible calamity, as if the sky had
fallen upon me. My tears gushed out in torrents. I lost all
control—I rolled in dirt and hit my head against the walls.
There was so much noise and such turmoil that you might
have thought the day of reckoning had arrived. My elder
brother gave up all pretensions of civility and started to
behave shamelessly. Seeing that our father had been indi-
gent and died in poverty and that his creditors were going to   *father dying*
press their demands, he separated himself from us, saying,
"They who received favors and affection from the deceased
should now take care of their responsibility. I had no say in
any matter while my father was alive. Now I renounce even
my claims as a son. May they live long who are now his spiritual heirs. They are tearing their hair and scratching their
faces—they will do whatever is needed."

When I, who had just been made abjectly helpless, heard   107
his foolish remarks, I felt tremendous anger and pain.
However, I did not plead with him. Instead, I girded my waist
in readiness and waited, setting my eyes only on God. The
market people came with another 200 rupees and pleaded
with me to accept the money, but I did not. I was bound to

* C. 1734.

نظر بر خدا نشستم. بذالان بازار دوصد روپیه دیگر آوردند، و
سماجت از حد بردند. پاس وصیت درویش بود، قبول نکردم.
همه را بزبان داشتم، یعنی ملول نکردم. در همین حال آدم سید
مکمل خان که مرید عم بزرگوار من بود با هندوی پانصد روپیه تازه
سکه رسید، و دردشریک من گردید. سه صد روپیه بقرضخواهان
داده، فارغخطی گرفتم و بصد روپیه درویش را برداشته بردم و
در پهلوی پیر او بخاک در آوردم.

۱۰۸   بی مروتی های آسمان را دیدم. ستمهای روزگار کشیدم. نی
نی گناه فلک و جرم زمانه چیست، من ستاره نداشتم که سایهٔ
چنین آفتابی از سر من رفت. هر چه کرد طالع من کرد. غیر از
دست خود بر سر نیافتم، یعنی کسی را سایه گستر نیافتم. خانمان
بر سرِ غیرت نهادم؛ زینهار بر در کس نه ایستادم. لبم بحرف
طلب آشنا نگردید؛ چشم من به هیچ چیز ندوید. سایهٔ دست
کسی نه گرفتم و سردستی بمن کسی نگرفت، یعنی خدای کریم
مرا شرمندهٔ احسان کسی نکرد، و دست نگر برادر که سر بسرِ
من داشت نساخت. نقل ماتم درویش قسمت ساختم، کار را
به لطف خداوند انداختم. دم خود را ببرادر خورد سپرده بتلاش
روزگار در اطراف شهر استخوان شکستم. لیکن طرفی نه بستم،
یعنی چارهٔ کار در وطن نیافتم، ناچار بغربت شتافتم. رنج راه
برخودِ هموار کردم، شدائد سفر اختیار کردم.

honor the dervish's last wish. However, since I did not wish
to hurt their feelings, I mollified them with gentle words.
Just then a man sent by Sayyid Mikmal Khan, a disciple of
my revered "uncle," arrived with a bill of payment worth
500 rupees, newly minted, and shared my grief. I gave 300
rupees to the creditors and obtained a full receipt of clear-
ance. Then I spent another 100 rupees and had the dervish
properly buried next to his spiritual master.

I suffered the inhumanities of the heavens and the
cruelties of the times. No, no! It was neither a fault of the
heavens nor a crime of the times. What happened was my
misfortune alone. It was in my stars that I should lose the
comforting warmth of that sun. I discovered that now I
was my own guardian, there was none else to look after
me. I put my trust in my sense of honor and never went
to stand at someone's door. No word of asking came on
my lips; no glance of mine went chasing after things. I did
not seek anyone's help, and no one came to hold my hand.
In short, the munificent God did not let me be burdened
under anyone's favors; nor did he make me depend on my
mean and hostile older brother. I distributed the "sweets
of mourning" to commemorate my father, then placed my
affairs in the bountiful hands of God. Putting my younger
brother, Muhammad Razi, in charge at home in my place,
I strained my legs roaming the environs of the city to find
some way to gain a living, but found none. Not obtaining
any relief in my own city, I was compelled to leave home
and resign myself to the hardships of a journey.

108

١٠٩ بشاهجهان آباد دهلی رسیدم؛ بسیار گردیدم، شفیقی ندیدم.
خواجه محمد باسط که برادرزادهٔ صمصام الدوله امیرالامرا بود
عنایتی بحال من کرد و پیش نواب برد. چون مرا دید، پرسید که
این پسر از کیست؟ گفت، از میرمحمدعلی است. فرمود از آمدن
این پیداست که ایشان از جهان رفته باشند. پس از افسوس
بسیار سخن زد که آن مرد بر من حقها داشت. یک روپیه روز از
سرکار من باین پسر میداده باشند.

١١٠ التماس نمودم، اگر نواب لطف میفرماید دستخط کرده بدهد
که جای سخن متصدیان نماند. التماسی که نوشته بودم از کیسه
برآوردم. ناگاه از زبان خواجهٔ مذکور برآمد که وقت قلمدان
نیست. چون این سخن شنیدم، بقاه قاه خندیدم. نواب در روی
من در دید و سبب خنده پرسید. عرض نمودم که این عبارت را
نفهمیدم. اگر ایشان می گفتند، قلمدان بردار حاضر نیست، این
حرف گنجایش داشت. یا آنکه وقت دستخط نواب نیست بابتی
بود. وقت قلمدان نیست انشای تازه است. قلمدان چوبی بیش
نمی باشد. وقت و غیروقت نمیداند. بهر نفریکه اشارت رود
برداشته بیارد.

١١١ نواب بخنده درآمد و گفت که معقول میگوید. غرض تکلیف
مرا بر خاک نیفگنده، قلمدان طلبید و آن التماس بشرف دستخط
رسید. روز دربار بادشاه بود. کمر بسته باستاد، بعنایت تمامم

124

went to Delhi @ 12 after his father's death

When I arrived at Shahjahanabad, i.e., Delhi,* I strove a   109
great deal but could not at first find anyone with compassion.
Then Khwaja Muhammad Basit, the nephew of Amir-ul-
Umara Samsam-ud-Daula, showed kindness to me and took
me to the nawab, the Amir-ul-Umara. On noticing me, the
nawab asked him, "Whose son is he?" The khwaja replied,
"Mir Muhammad 'Ali's." The nawab then said, "The boy's
coming here means that that worthy man is no longer in this
world." After expressing much grief, he added, "That man
had rightful claims on me. And so this child should be given
one rupee per day from our treasury."

I humbly requested the nawab to favor me with a signed   110
order so that the account keepers should not raise any objection. And I took out of my pocket the petition I had prepared
and brought with me. Suddenly the aforementioned khwaja
exclaimed, "This is not the time of the 'pen case.'" On hearing those words, I burst out laughing. The nawab stared at
me and asked the reason for my laughter. I humbly replied,
"I do not understand the words he spoke. Had he said, 'The
pen case bearer is not present,' it would have made some
sense to me, as it would have too if he had instead said, 'This
is not the time for the nawab to sign orders.' But 'This is not
the time of the pen case' is something new and strange. The
pen case is no more than a piece of wood. It does not know
one particular time from another. Any servant you glance at
will immediately bring it to you."

The nawab burst into laughter and said, "What he says   111
makes sense." Then, asking for his pen case, he honored my

---

* C. 1735; Mir was then barely twelve.

میان داد. تا عهدیکه نادرشاه بر محمدشاه که حالا بفردوس
آرامگاه ملقب است مسلط شد و نواب مذکور بسبب پیش جنگی
کشته افتاد، آن روزینه می یافتم. نان و نمک میخوردم و بسر
میبردم.

١١٢   بعد این انقلاب، باز روزگار سنگین دل کار را بر من تنگ گرفت.
کسانیکه پیش درویش خاک پای مرا کحل بصر می ساختند، یکبار
از نظرم انداختند. ناچار بار دیگر بدهلی رسیدم، و منتهای بی
منتهای خالوی برادر کلان که سراج الدین علی خان آرزو باشد
کشیدم. یعنی چندی پیش او ماندم و کتابی چند از یاران شهر
خواندم. چون قابل این شدم که مخاطب صحیح کسی می توانم
شد، نوشتهٔ اخوان پناه رسید که میرمحمدتقی فتنهٔ روزگار است.
زینهار به تربیت او نباید پرداخت، و در پردهٔ دوستی کارش باید
ساخت. آن عزیز دنیادار واقعی بود. نظر بر خصومت همشیره
زادهٔ خود بد من اندیشید. اگر دوچار می شدم، چار چار می زد،
وگر اعراض می کردم نواخوانی میکرد. هر روز چشمش بدنبال من
می بود؛ اکثر سلوک مدعیانه می نمود. چه بیان کنم که ازو چه
دیدم؛ چگویم که چه حالت کشیدم. هرچند پنبه دهانی اختیار
میکردم، او از حلاجی دست نمی داشت. با صد هزار احتیاج یک
روپیه ازو نمی خواستم. اما سلاخی نمی گذاشت. خصمی او اگر
به تفصیل بیان کرده آید دفتری جداگانه می باید.

humble petition with his signature of approval. Since it was a day for the emperor's audience, the nawab arose to go there, and with much affection gave me permission to depart. From that day onward till the time when Nadir Shah overwhelmed Muhammad Shah—who is presently called "Resting in Paradise"—and the nawab was killed in the battle,* I received the daily allowance and sustained myself on it frugally.

After that reversal of fortune, cruel times once again gripped me. The people for whom, during the dervish's life, the dust from my feet was the collyrium for their eyes, the same people now turned away from me. Having no other recourse, I betook myself to Delhi once again, where I suffered the boundless indignity of being obliged to Sirajuddin 'Ali Khan Arzu, the maternal uncle of my older brother[32]—that is to say, I stayed with him for a while, and also studied with him a few insignificant books. When I had learned enough to hold a proper conversation with someone, a letter arrived from my "revered" half brother. It said, "Mir Muhammad Taqi is a snake in the grass. Do not make any effort toward his upbringing—in fact, in the guise of friendship, have him killed." That worthy person, Arzu, was worldly to the core. Seeing that his own sister's son was against me, he too became my enemy. If I came before him once, he abused me twice over, and when I avoided him, he made cutting remarks about me to others. Daily he schemed against me, and frequently caused me actual harm. How can I describe what he did to me! In what words can I put what I suffered! I sealed my lips, but he persisted in abusing me.

112

Family conspiring against Mir Taqi

---

* February 13, 1739.

2 *Mir Taqi suffered abuse*

۱۱۳ خاطر گرفتهٔ من گرفته تر شد، سودا کردم. دل تنگم تنگ تر
گردید، وحشتی پیدا کردم. در حجرهٔ که می بودم درش می بستم،
و باین کثرت غم تنها می نشستم. چون ماه بر می آمد، قیامت بر
سر می آمد. هرچند از آن هنگام که دایه ام دم رو شستن «ماه
ماه» می گفت و من بسوی آسمان می دیدم نظری بماه میداشتم،
لیکن نه باین مرتبه که کارم بدیوانگی کشد و وحشت بجای رسد
که در حجرهٔ من باندیشه باز کنند و از صحبتم احتراز نمایند.
در شب ماه پیکری، خوش صورت، با کمال خوبی از جرم قمر
انداز طرف من می کرد، و موجب بی خودی می شد. بهر طرف که
چشم می افتاد، بران رشک پری می افتاد. بهر جا که نگاه میکردم
تماشای آن غیرت حور میکردم. در و بام و صحن خانهٔ من ورق
تصویر شده بود، یعنی آن حیرت افزای از شش جهت رو می نمود.
گاهی چون ماه چهارده مقابل، گاهی سیرگاه او منزل دل. اگر نظر بر
گل مهتاب می افتاد، آتشی در جان بی تاب می افتاد. هر شب باو
صحبت، هر صبح بی او وحشت. دمیکه سفیدهٔ صبح می دمید،
از دل گرم آه سرد می کشید، یعنی آه می کرد و انداز ماه می کرد.
تمام روز جنون میکردم؛ دل در یاد او خون میکردم. کف بر لب
چون دیوانه و مست، پاره های سنگ در دست. من افتان و
خیزان؛ مردم از من گریزان. تا چار ماه آن گل شب افروز رنگ تازه
می ریخت، و از فتنه خرامیها قیامت می انگیخت. ناگاه موسم

128

Though oppressed with hundreds of needs, I didn't ask him for even a rupee—and yet he called me all sorts of names. If I were to describe his enmity in detail it would require a separate book.

My tortured mind grew more tortured; my already oppressed heart became more oppressed. A dreadful solitariness took hold of me, and I became mad. I closed the door of my tiny room, and though overwhelmed with grief sat inside alone. Every night when the moon rose in the sky, it brought upon me a calamity. When I was a little child my nanny, as she washed my face, would say to me, "Moon! Moon!" to keep me from fidgeting, and I would look up at the sky. Ever since that time I had been fascinated by the moon. But not to the extent of going mad! Now, however, I became so crazy that people were scared to open my door or come near me. Every night, a moon-faced lovely form came toward me from the moon and caused me to lose my senses. Wherever I looked my glance fell upon that person more beautiful than a fairy, and no matter what direction I turned, I saw only that fair houri. The walls, the terraces, the courtyards of the house appeared like paintings, for that same bewitching form appeared to my sight wherever I looked. Sometimes she showed me her face openly like the full moon of the fourteenth;[33] at other times she hid herself within my heart's confines. If ever my glance fell on the moon in the sky, I felt as if someone had poured more fire on my consumed soul. Each night blessed me with her company, and each morning made me crazy with her absence. No sooner a dawn gleamed on the horizon than she heaved a deep sigh and disappeared into the moon. I tortured my heart with her thought and raged

113

Mir Taqi's obsession w/ the moon

129

↳ descent into madness

گل رسید. داغ سودا سیاه تر گردید. یعنی چون پریدار شدم و
مطلق از کار شدم. صورت آن شکل وهمی در نظر، خیال زلف
مشکینش در سر. شایستهٔ کناره گیری شدم، زندانی و زنجیری
شدم.

۱۱۴   همسر فخرالدین خان که مرید درویش بود و قرابت قریبه
داشت، زر بسیاری خرج نمود. پریخوانان افسون دمیدند؛
طبیبان خون کشیدند. تدبیر اطبا سودمند افتاد. پائیز آمد و
بهار ریخت. سلسلهٔ جنون از هم گسیخت. نقشی که وهم بسته
بود از صفحهٔ خاطر محو شد. درسی که از جنون خوانده بودم،
فراموش گشت. لب با سکوت مالوف شد؛ پریشان گوئی موقوف
شد. ترطیب دماغ کردند، خواب افزود. طاقت رفته باز رو نمود.
یعنی بحال آمدم و بدخوابی رفت. از پیش نظر آن چهرهٔ مهتابی
رفت. پس از چندی رو بصحت کامل آوردم، و شروع بخواندن
ترسل کردم.

۱۱۵   روزی بر سر بازار، جز کتابی در دست نشسته بودم. جوانی
میرجعفر نام ازان راه گذشت. نظرش بر من افتاد و تشریف
داد. بعد از ساعتی گفت که ای عزیز، دریافته میشود که ذوق
خواندن داری. من هم کشتهٔ کتاب ام، اما مخاطبی نمی یابم.
اگر شوق کاملی داشته باشی چندی می رسیده باشم. گفتم، دستی
ندارم که خدمتی از من بیاید. اگر لله این رنج برخود گوارا کنی،

insane all day long—frothing at the mouth like a madman and carrying stones in my hands. And as I stumbled around in that state, people ran away from me. For four months, that night-illuminating beauty showed herself to me, ever anew every night, causing each time a new tumult. Then spring arrived, and my madness took a darker hue. I became totally overwhelmed, devoid of any power to act. That imaginary shape remained before my eyes, and a passion for her dark musky tresses occupied my mind. I deserved to be isolated, and so it happened—I was placed in confinement and put in chains.

The wife of Fakhruddin Khan had been a disciple of my father, and was also closely related. She spent a great deal of money on my treatment. Spell casters were brought to try their spells; physicians came and drew blood. The latter's efforts bore fruit. Then spring left and autumn arrived, and the chain of my madness also snapped. The shape that had so taken hold of my mind now completely vanished. The lessons that madness had taught me were totally erased from my mind. My ravings stopped, and my lips became reacquainted with silence. The doctors removed the dryness of my brain, and I began to sleep more. The strength my body had lost returned. My insomnia disappeared, as did the moon face that had earlier constantly haunted my eyes. In other words, I became normal again, and started studying the "Letters."[34]

One day I was seated by the roadside in the market, with some pages of a book in my hand, when a young man named Mir Ja'far happened to come by. Noticing me, he sat down near me, and after a few moments said, "My dear, I can see

114

115

Mir Taqi's recovery! + treatment

عین بنده نوازی است. گفتا، اینقدر هست که ته پا تا نباشد پا بیرون نمی گذارم. گفتم، خدای کریم آسان خواهد کرد، اگرچه اگرچه من هم چیزی ندارم. پاورقهای آن نسخهٔ درهم را مطابق سرصفحهای آینده کرده داد و رفت. ازان روز اکثر ملاقات آن ملک سیرت و آدم صورت اتفاق می افتاد، و بلطف نهایتم زبان میداد. یعنی دماغ خود می سوخت و مرا چیزی می آموخت. تا مقدور من نیز بالش نرم زیر سر او میگذاشتم، یعنی صرف او بود انچه میسر میداشتم. ناگاه خطی از وطن او که عظیم آباد بود رسید، و آنمرد رخت خود، کام و ناکام، بآن صوب کشید.

۱۱۶ بعد از چندی با سعادت علی نام سیدی که از امروهه بود برخوردم. آن عزیز مرا تکلیف موزون کردن ریخته، که شعریست بطور شعر فارسی بزبان اردوی معلی بادشاهان هندوستان و دران وقت رواج داشت، کرد. خودکشی کردم و مشق خود بمرتبهٔ رساندم که موزونان شهر را مستند شدم. شعر من در تمام شهر دوید، و بگوش خورد و بزرگ رسید.

۱۱۷ یکروز خالوی کذائی بر طعامم طلبید. تلخی ازو شنیدم، بیمزه شدم. دست در طعام ناکرده برخاستم. چون پای چراغی نداشتم، شام از خانهٔ او برآمده راه مسجد جامع پیش گرفتم. اتفاقاً راه غلط شد. بر حوض قاضی که آبگیر خوردی نزدیک بحویلی وزیرالممالک اعتمادالدوله واقع است رسیدم، و آب کشیدم. آنجا علیم الله

132

that you have an aptitude for studies. I too am a martyr to books, but I cannot find anyone to talk to about them. If you are really keen I can once in a while spend some time with you." I replied, "I have no means to return the favor. But it would be a boon to this humble person if you would take the trouble in God's name alone." He said, "The only thing is that I do not leave my house unless there is something for a snack." I replied, "The munificent God will solve that problem, though I too possess nothing." He then arranged the pages of my book in their proper order and left. After that day I often met with that angelic man. He spoke with great affection, and taxed his own mind to teach me something. On my part, I too made every effort to make his life easy, and put at his disposal whatever I received. Then one day a letter came to him from Azimabad, and willy-nilly he hurried back home.

Sometime later I met a sayyid from Amroha named Sa'adat 'Ali.[35] That noble person urged me to compose poetry in *rekhta,* which is a kind of verse in the Persian manner but written in the language of the "Imperial Camp" of the kings of Hindustan, and which was becoming popular at the time. I worked at it very hard, and soon carried my compositions to such heights that the poets of the city considered me an authority. My verses spread throughout the city, reaching the young and old alike.

One day that uncle of mine summoned me to eat with him. But when he spoke to me nastily, I was disgusted and got up without touching the food. Since I expected nothing from him, I left his house in the evening and took the road to the Jami' Masjid. However, somehow I lost my way and ended up at Hauz Qazi, which is a small reservoir of water near the

116

117

133

نام شخصی پیش آمد و گفت که شما میرمحمد تقی میر نباشید؟ گفتم، از چه شناختی؟ گفتا، طور سودائیانهٔ شما مشهور است. رعایت خان که پسر عظیم الله خان یزنهٔ اعتمادالدوله قمرالدین خان باشد، از روزیکه زادهٔ طبع نکته انگیز باو رسیده است، اشتیاق ملاقات بیش از بیش دارد. اگر بدست من او را دیده شود سبب مجرائی من گردد. رفتم و دیدم. آدمیانه برخورد، و با خود رفیقم کرد. تمتعی ازو بستم و از قید تنگدستی رستم.

۱۱۸ هنگامی که شاه درانی بلاهور آمد و شاهنوازخان پسر ذکریاخان که صوبه دار آنجا بود گریخت، وزیر و صفدرجنگ وایشر سنگه پسر راجه جی سنگه که زمیندار کلانی بود، بادشاه زاده احمد شاه را با خود گرفته بجنگ او برآمدند. آن طرف سرهند بوزیر گوله رسید، و زمیندار مذکور بس خم زد. صفدرجنگ و معین الملک، که پسر وزیر شهید باشد، احمد شاه را سوار کرده جنگ بافغانان زدند. من درین سفر با خان مسطور بودم و خدمتها می نمودم.

۱۱۹ هرگاه شکست فاحشی بر لشکر افغانان افتاد و گریخت، معین الملک ناظم لاهور شد. خان مذکور، چون عضو از جا رفته، ترک رفاقت او گرفته با صفدرجنگ روانهٔ شهر شد. قریب پانی پت که شهریست مشهور چهل کروهی شاه جهان آباد، خبر رسید که محمد شاه بآن جهان خرامید. عالمی لکد روزگار خورد. صفدرجنگ لکد برابر زده چتر و تخت پیش احمدشاه آورد. نوبت

134

mansion of Vazir-ul-Mamalik I'timad-ud-Daula. As I was getting a drink of water, a man named 'Alimullah approached me and asked, "Are you not Mir Muhammad Taqi Mir?" "How did you guess?" I asked. He replied, "Your crazy ways are well known. Since the day he heard some of your subtle verses, Ri'ayat Khan—a son of A'zimullah Khan, the husband of I'timad-ud-Daula Qamaruddin Khan's sister—has been most eager to meet you. If you would meet him through me, it would also provide me a way to pay him my respects." I went with the man and met Ri'ayat Khan. He received me civilly and made me his companion. I gained some succor from him and was thus freed from the clutch of indigence.

When Ahmad Shah 'Abdali Durrani attacked Lahore and Shah Navaz Khan (son of Zakariya Khan), who was the *subedar,* fled from Lahore, the vazir, I'timad-ud-Daula Qamaruddin Khan, and Safdar Jang and Ishar Singh (son of Raja Jai Singh, a prominent *zamīndār*) took Prince Ahmad Shah, the son of the Emperor Muhammad Shah with them and went out to do battle.* They had reached beyond Sirhind when the vazir was hit by a cannonball and the aforementioned *zamīndār* decamped. Then Safdar Jang and Mu'in-ul-Mulk (the son of the martyred vazir) placed Prince Ahmad Shah on an elephant and attacked the Afghans.† I was with the aforementioned Ri'ayat Khan on that journey and performed many services.

The Afghans were roundly defeated, and Mu'in-ul-Mulk was made the governor of Lahore. Then Ri'ayat Khan,

118

119

* January 1748.
† March 1748.

135

سلطنت باو رسید. با کروفر تمام داخل شهر شد. اینجا جاویدخان که خواجه سرای بادشاه مرحوم بود بخطاب نواب بهادر مخاطب گشت، و اختیار سلطنت بدست او افتاد.

هـر روز اخـتیار جـهان پیش دیگر یسـت
دولت مگر گداست که هر روز بر دریست

وقتیکه نظام الملک آصف جاه در دکن فوت گشت، منصب وزارت به صفدرجنگ رسید، و سادات خان ذوالفقارجنگ به بخشیگری سرفراز گردید. امارت وزیر حال بجای رسید که یال و گوپال او را شاه هم نداشت. بخشی حال راجه بخت سنگه را که زمیندار کلان کار نام گرفتۀ بود، و برادر کلانش ابهه سنگه ریاست جوده پور داشت، نیابت صوبۀ اجمیر داده بر روی او دوانید. راجۀ مذکور خان را سردار فوج نموده با خود برد. در ظاهر سامهر که قصبه ایست معروف، بیست کروه این طرف اجمیر، هر دو لشکر طرف شدند، و جنگ توپ خانه بمیان بیمان آمد. مردمان طرف ثانی پاس نمک نکرده چون غیرت بحرامان یک روز هم تن ندادند، تا بجان دادن چه رسد. ناچار رئیس آن طرف ملهار را که در سرداران دکن نام برآورده مردی بود، در میان داده سر بسر کرد و رفت. من پس از صلح برای حصول سعادت زیارت درگاه فلک اشتباه خواجۀ بزرگ رفتم، و سیر آن نواحی کرده برگشتم.

۱۲۰

disdained like a useless limb, parted company with him and proceeded to return to the capital with Safdar Jang. When we were near Panipat, which is a well-known city about 40 *kurohs* (80 km) from Shahjahanabad, the news arrived that Muhammad Shah had passed away.* Everyone was devastated. Safdar Jang, however, put on grand airs and brought the royal throne and umbrella to Prince Ahmad Shah, who now became the emperor and entered the city with much pomp and show. Now Jawid Khan, who had been the master of the seraglio of the late king, received the title of Nawab Bahadur, and all authority of the state passed into his hands.

Every day the world finds a new master—
Power must be a beggar, going from door to door.

When Nizam-ul-Mulk Asaf Jah died in the Deccan, Safdar 120
Jang was made the vazir in his place and Sadat Khan Zulfiqar Jang was honored with the position of the *mīr bakhshī* or the imperial paymaster. The new vazir's pomp and power grew so great that even the emperor could not rival him. The new *mīr bakhshī* assigned the governorship of the *sūba* of Ajmer to a senior and prominent *zamīndār,* Raja Bakht Singh, whose older brother, Abhay Singh, was the ruler of Jodhpur, and had him challenge the authority of his older brother. Bakht Singh made Ri'ayat Khan the chief of his army and set out. Outside Sambhar, a well-known town about 20 *kurohs* this side of Ajmer, the two armies came face to face, and a battle of artilleries began. The men in the army of the other party,

---

* April 16, 1748.

137

۱۲۱ اینجا در امری زبانبازی بمیان آمد. راجه بخت سنگه ابرو
ترش کرد. صحبتِ خان و او قروتی شد. ستارقلی خان کشمیری که
صورت بازی بیش نبود، برو صد ده دهن خواند. کار بنزاع کشید.
خان صرفهٔ خود ندیده مرا فرستاد و عذر ده زبانی خواست. رفتم و
از جانب او مصحف خوردم که آینده چنین نخواهد شد. اما دلش
آبی نخورد و صرفه نداد. زر تنخواه مردمان رساله همگی فرستاد،
و خیرباد کرد. باری بخیر گذشت. خان از آن جا واسوخته بشهر
آمد، و چندی در خانه نشست.

۱۲۲ شب ماه بر مهتابی پسرخواندهٔ روبروی خان نشسته بود و می
خواند. چون مرا دید، گفت که میرصاحب دو سه شعر ریختهٔ خود
باین بیاموزید که این طفل دربسته بکار درست کرده بخواند.
گفتم که من نقش این کار ندارم. گفت، شما را بسر من. چون
پای تبعیت در میان بود، ناچار حکم او کشیدم و چار پنج شعر
ریخته باو آموختم. اما بسیار بر طبع نازک من گران آمد. آخر
بعد از دو سه روز خانه نشین گشتم. هرچند لطف فرمود نرفتم،
و ترک آن روزگار گرفتم. مروت ذاتی آن مرد نگذاشت که فقیر را
ناکام گذارد. برادرم میر محمد رضی را نظر برفاقت من از اسپ از
خانهٔ خود داد و نوکر کرد. چون پس از مدت مدید رفته ملاقات
نمودم، عذر بسیاری نمود. گفتم، گذشته را صلوٰة.

i.e., Abhay Singh of Jodhpur, were not true to his salt—they made no effort on his behalf. Left with little choice, Abhay Singh got Malhar Rao Holkar—a prominent name among the Maratha chieftains—to mediate and, after a truce was obtained, left the field. Once peace was established, I went to pay homage at the heavenly shrine of the great Khwaja Mu'inuddin Chishti at Ajmer, and after enjoying the sights of that area returned to the camp of Ri'ayat Khan.*

Here there was an altercation between Ri'ayat Khan and   121
Raja Bakht Singh. Raja Bakht Singh lost his temper, and the relationship between the two deteriorated. It further worsened when Sattar Quli Khan Kashmiri, a mere jester, made all sorts of remarks. The khan, who saw no gain in all this, sent me to the raja to seek his forgiveness for the loose talk. I went and on his behalf swore on the Qur'an that such a thing would never occur again. The raja, however, remained bitter and chose not to give him another chance. He sent the khan the money for the salary of his soldiers and bade him goodbye. At least it ended well enough. The khan turned around and returned to the capital, and for some time stayed home.

One moonlit night, a young singer was performing before   122
the khan on the terrace. When the khan saw me, he said, "Mir Sahib, please teach this boy a few *rekhta* verses of yours so that he might properly set them in the *basta* mode and sing for me." I replied, "I cannot possibly do that." He said, "Please, for my sake." Since I was dependent upon him, I had to obey; I taught the boy a few couplets. But it sat heavy on my delicate nature, and after a few days, I stopped visit-

* C. August 1748.

۱۲۳ هرگاه چندی بر این گذشت، تلاش روزگار بخانهٔ نواب بهادر کردم و نوکر شدم. اسدیار خان بخشی فوج او احوال مرا نقل کرده اسپ و تکلیف نوکری معاف کنانید. پاس من از حد بیشتر میکرد و پهلو میداد. خدایش خیر دهاد.

۱۲۴ ایامی که قائم خان پسر محمد خان بنگش بجنگ رهیله ها کشته شد و صفدرجنگ برای ضبط کردن خانهٔ او رفت، من بتقریبی باسحاق خان نجم الدوله سیر جهت آن طرف رفتم. چون با احمد خان برادر خورد قائم خان جنگ عظیم رو داد، فوج وزیر شکست خورد و اسحاق خان کشته افتاد. بآن لشکر شکسته باز بشهر رسیدم، و تصدیع بی حد کشیدم. وزیر بار دیگر لشکر کشید و افغانان را مغلوب ساخته به تسلط تمام در حضور آمد.

۱۲۵ در حینی که ذوالفقارجنگ میربخشی بسبب خصومت نواب بهادر از پایهٔ خود افتاد، نوبت امیرالامرائی به غازی الدین خان فیروز جنگ پسر آصف جاه رسید، و او برای نظم و نسق صوبهٔ دکن رفت و در راه هیضه کرده درگذشت. خلعت بخشیگری عمادالملک پسرش پوشید. بنده ترک ملاقات عزیزان گرفته، بخواندن مطول مشغول شدم.

140

ing him. The khan sent kind messages, but I did not go and renounced my position in his household. That noble man did not like to leave this fakir in need, and so, out of regard for me, he gave my brother, Mir Muhammad Razi, a horse from his own stable and employed him in his service. When, after quite some time, I went to see him, the khan apologized profusely. I responded, "What is past is done with."

After things went on that way for a while, I sought employ- 123
ment in the household of Nawab Bahadur Jawid Khan and was successful. The *bakhshī* of his army, Asad Yar Khan, informed the nawab of my condition and got him to excuse me from the requirements of keeping a horse and being in attendance constantly. He, Asad Yar Khan, used to respect me a great deal, and also helped me a lot. May God be kind to him.

When Qa'im Khan (son of Muhammad Khan Bangash) 124
was killed in the war with the Rohillas,* Safdar Jang went forth to take possession of his home and property. I too went along in the company of Ishaq Khan Najm-ud-Daula to enjoy the sights. There was a major battle with Ahmad Khan, the younger brother of Qa'im Khan. The vazir's army was routed, and Ishaq Khan was killed.† I returned to Delhi with the battered army and had a very hard time of it. The vazir then put together a second army, and after fully subduing the Afghans returned to the court.

When Zulfiqar Jang, the *mīr bakhshī*, due to the animosity 125
of Nawab Bahadur, lost his position, the rank of Amir-ul-

---

* November 12, 1749.
† September 13, 1750.

۱۲۶ موسمی که صفدرجنگ نواب بهادر را به دغا کشت، روزگار عالمی برهم خورد. من نیز بیکار شدم. مهانراین دیوان وزیر، بدست داروغهٔ دیوان خانهٔ خود میرنجم الدین علی، سلام تخلص، که پسر میرشرف الدین علی پیام بود، چیزی فرستاد و باشتیاق بسیار مرا طلبید. دست در دامن پهلودار او زدم، و چند ماه بفراغت گذرانیدم.

۱۲۷ هنوز خون خواجه سرای مظلوم نخوابیده بود که روزگار سرپای زده فتنهٔ عجیبی را از خواب بیدار ساخت، و طرح هنگامهٔ عظیمی انداخت. یعنی وزیر را توهمی پیدا شد. سر از فرمان بادشاه پیچید. هرچند بدر صلح زدند، اما سر از غرور ثروت فرود نیاورد. ناچار بادشاه از پی او رسن تابید. آخر از شهر برآمده، آمادهٔ جنگ خداوند نعمت شد. اینجا عمادالملک نبیرهٔ آصف جاه که منصب بخشیگری داشت و انتظام الدوله خالوی او پسر اعتمادالدوله شهید، و دیگر سرداران فوج بادشاهی به حفاظت شهر پرداختند. شهر کهنه تمام بغارت رفت. تا شش ماه جنگ در میان بود. اگرچه بالقوه خصمانهٔ او نداشتند لیکن کسان فوج شاه آنچنان پا فشردند که کار را پیش بردند. پای ثبات وزیرِ سرکش از پیش بدر رفت. ناچار پیغام صلح فرستاد. بادشاه هزیمت او را غنیمت دانسته دستوری صوبه اش داد. وزیر انتظام الدوله شد.

Umara was bestowed upon Asaf Jah's son, Ghaziuddin Khan Firoz Jang. He left for the Deccan to put things in order but succumbed to cholera on the way.* Now the robes of the rank of *mīr bakhshī* were put on by his son, 'Imad-ul-Mulk.[36] During that time I stopped meeting with nobles and devoted myself to studying the *Mutawwal*.[37]

When Safdar Jang had Nawab Bahadur killed through   126 deceit and a world of people suffered,† I too lost my position. Then Maha Narain, the *dīwān* of the vazir Safdar Jang, sent me something through his own *dīwān*, Mir Najmuddin 'Ali—his *takhallus* was Salam, and he was the son of Mir Sharafuddin 'Ali "Payam"—and expressed great desire to see me. I put my trust in his bountiful lap, and spent some months in comfort.

The bloody affair of the murder of the poor eunuch, i.e.,   127 Jawid Khan Nawab Bahadur, was still fresh in memory when the wretched hands of Time set into process a new disaster: the vazir developed certain suspicions and turned rebellious. People tried to create peace between him and the Emperor Ahmad Shah, but his head, filled with the pride of his wealth, was not willing to bow. The emperor then made plans to punish him. The vazir marched out of the city and got ready to do battle with his own master. While here in the city, 'Imad-ul-Mulk, the grandson of Asaf Jah and the king's *bakhshī*, and his uncle, Intizam-ud-Daula, who was the son of the late I'timad-ud-Daula, and other officers of the royal army made preparations for the city's defense. The Old

---

* October 1752.
† August 27, 1752.

۱۲۸ درین ایام، من از نامساعدت ایام همسائگی خالو گذاشته، نظر برین که مرا بچشم کم خواهد دید، در حویلی امیرخان مرحوم که امیر کلان عهد محمد شاهی بود و صوبه داری اله آباد و رگ خواب سلطنت در دست داشت، و انجام تخلص اوست، بخوش سلیقگی و طلاقت لسان زبانزد مردم است، و موجب مهم علی محمد روهیله شده بادشاه را برآورده او را بگیر آورده بود و انجام کار از دست یکی از نوکران خود بر دروازهٔ دیوان خاص کشته شد، سکونت اختیار کردم، و بلطائف الحیل بسر بردم.

۱۲۹ عمادالملک در اندک مدتِ زور بهم رسانیده، سرداران دکن را از خود ساخته، بجرم رفاقت صفدرجنگ بر سورج مل که زمیندار زورآوری بود، لشکر کشید. و از سربتوئی قلعهٔ او محاصره کرده، کار را تنگ گرفت. پسر ملهار در همان جنگ کشته افتاد. زمیندار مذکور نوشت و خواندی با وزیر داشت. این معنی سبب نفاق طرفین شد.

144

[handwritten: civil war, a coup → downfall of society]

City outside the walled city of Shahjahanabad was entirely ravaged as the fighting continued for six months. Though the royal army was essentially no match for the vazir's forces, it fought with such great determination that it succeeded. The rebellious vazir lost all confidence and was forced to seek peace.* The emperor, considering it a good enough victory, gave him his previous governorship of Avadh. Intizam-ud-Daula was made the new vazir.

[handwritten: take up residence w/ another nobility]

During that time, in view of the trying circumstances, I chose not to remain a neighbor to my uncle lest he should treat me with contempt, and found quarters in the mansion of the late Amir Khan. He had been a senior noble during the reign of Muhammad Shah, holding the governorship of Allahabad and wielding great authority in state affairs. His *takhallus* was Anjam, and his elegance and eloquence were proverbial. He had initiated the campaign against 'Ali Muhammad Rohilla, made the emperor come out of the city with him, and eventually crushed his Rohilla enemy. He, Amir Khan, was eventually killed at the gate of the Diwan-e Khas by one of his own retainers. I lived in the compound of his mansion, and somehow or other managed to survive.

[handwritten: 128]

In little time, 'Imad-ul-Mulk gained a great deal of strength and won over to his side the Maratha chieftains; he then set out to punish Suraj Mal, a mighty *zamīndār*, for having previously sided with Safdar Jang. With careful thought, he laid siege to Suraj Mal's fort, and made life hard for him. The son of Malhar Rao Holkar was killed in

[margin: 129]

---

* March–November 1753.

۱۳۰ بادشاه برآمد، و بست کروه آنطرف آب جمن قریب سکندرآباد خیمه کرد. روزی شام خبر رسید که سرداران دکن و عمادالملک با سورج مل طرح آشتی انداخته، بارادهٔ غارت دائرهٔ لشکر بادشاه حاضر یراق جنگ گردیده، دویده اند. قریب است که برسند. بادشاه، بمصلحت صمصام الدوله میرآتش و حرام کوزهٔ چند که بکارپردازان بخشی گری ساخته بودند، ناموس را هم گذاشته مضطرب و سراسیمه گریخت. آنجا نزدیک بصبح فوج دکن رسید، و لشکر را همگی بغارت برده متعاقب آمدند و آنروی آب خیمه ها زدند.

۱۳۱ نسق شد که از مردمان بادشاهی کسی در قلعه نماند. اگرچه آن حرام توشه ها پیشتر ازین برخاسته رفته بودند. بعد از بندوبست عمادالملک آمد و قلمدان وزارت گرفت. وزیر مغزِ خرخورده از غردلی بکنجی خزید، و بادشاه خرد گم کرده متوجهٔ باغ گردید. پس از ساعتی یاران غدار بغدر دستگیر نمودند و میل در چشمش کشیده نبیرهٔ بهادرشاه را بر تخت نشاندند و عالمگیر ثانیش خواندند. مردمان بی ته در عرصه درآمدند. هرچه شد بیجا شد. صمصام الدوله که از عقل بهرهٔ نداشت امیرالامرا شد. من درین سفرِ وحشت اثر با احمد شاه بودم. آمده، عزلت اختیار نمودم.

seige of Delhi
by the Marathas

that battle. The aforementioned *zamīndār* had continued
to correspond with the vazir, and that became the cause for
enmity between the two parties.

The emperor came out of the city, crossed the river
Jamuna, and after marching some 20 *kurohs* encamped near
Sikandarabad. One evening the news came that the Maratha
chieftains and 'Imad-ul-Mulk had made peace with Suraj
Mal, and after fully preparing for war were now rushing to
attack the emperor's camp—that in fact they were quite
close. The emperor, advised by Samsam-ud-Daula,[38] the
commander of the artillery, and a few other traitors who had
conspired with the officers of the Bakhshi, 'Imad-ul-Mulk,
cast to the wind all considerations of honor and fled back
to the city in utter panic. The Maratha forces arrived at the
royal camp near dawn and plundered it totally; then they
set out in pursuit, and arriving across the river, opposite
the city, set up camp.

It was announced that all officers of the royal household
should leave the citadel, but the treacherous lot had in fact
already slipped away. After things settled down, 'Imad-ul-
Mulk came and took over the office of the vazir. The previous
vazir, an idiot and a coward, slunk off to some corner of his
own, while the emperor, having lost his senses, proceeded
to his garden. But the traitors shortly took him prisoner
and blinded his eyes.* Then they put on the throne a grandson of Bahadur Shah and called him 'Alamgir II. Unworthy
people took on positions of authority. Whatever happened
was wrong. Samsam-ud-Daula, who had no intelligence at

130

131

* June 2, 1754.

lots of royal
infighting

147

۱۳۲ درین حال خبر رسید که صفدرجنگ بساط حیات درپیچید، و ریاست صوبه بشجاع الدوله پسر او قرار یافت. خالوی من بادیه پیمای طمع شد، یعنی در لشکر شجاع الدوله باین توقع رفت که برادران اسحاق خان شهید آن جا هستند. نظر بر حقوق سابق رعایتی خواهند کرد. جز باد بدستش نیامد. لکد زمانه خورد، و هم آنجا مرد. مردهٔ او را آوردند و در حویلیش بخاک سپردند.

۱۳۳ بعد از دو سه ماه راجه جگل کشور که در وقت محمد شاه وکیل بنگاله بود و بثروت تمام میگزرانید، مرا از خانه برداشته برد و تکلیف اصلاح شعر خود کرد. قابلیت اصلاح ندیدم. بر اکثر تصنیفات او خط کشیدم.

۱۳۴ در این هنگام راجه ناگرمل که در سلطنت فردوس آرام گاه بدیوانی خالصه و تن ممتاز بود، به نیابت وزارت و خطاب مهاراجگی و عمدةالملکی سرفراز شد. چون مظلومان شهر را در خانهٔ خود جا میداد و بداد ایشان می رسید، کار آن سرکرده بدشمنی کشید. اگر به دربار میرفت، خودش با حزم تمام و کمال طمطراق، و فوج او همه حاضر یراق. فریب یاران بدپرداز نمی خورد. ببالاچاقی بسر می برد. درین ولا صمصام الدوله که عبارت از میر بخشی حال باشد، بمرض سل درگذشت. پسرش که بی حقیقت محض است بجای او مقرر شد.

all, became the Amir-ul-Umara. During that terrible journey I had been with Ahmad Shah, but I took to seclusion after I returned home.

At this time the news arrived that Safdar Jang had folded up the dice board of his life* and that his state had been passed on to his son, Shuja-ud-Daula. Consequently, my uncle, i.e., Arzu, went chasing in the desert of greed; that is to say, he journeyed to Shuja-ud-Daula's camp in Avadh, expecting that the brothers of the late Ishaq Khan who were already there would be favorable to him in view of his previous claims on them. But he received nothing but a fistful of air and, kicked around by Time, died.† His corpse was brought back to Delhi and buried in his house.

After two or three months, Raja Jugal Kishore, who had been the agent of the governor of Bengal during the reign of Muhammad Shah and led a prosperous life, came and took me to his house and requested me to look over his verses and make corrections. I did not find them worthy of correction and scratched a line across most of them.

Meanwhile, Raja Nagar Mal, who had been Muhammad Shah's *dīwān* of *khālisa* and *tan*,³⁹ was elevated to the position of deputy vazir and given the titles of maharaja and 'Umdat-ul-Mulk. Because he gave shelter in his own house to the oppressed of the city and did justice to them, many in power became his enemies. And so when he attended on the emperor he was himself a magnificent and awe-inspiring sight, and his soldiers accompanied him fully at the ready.⁴⁰

becane the editor of another Mughal noble [handwritten marginalia]

132

133

134

* October 5, 1754.
† January 27, 1756.

۱۳۵ در این اثنا شاه درانی که هزیمت خورده از سرهند رفته بود و در سر خیال هندوستان داشت، با لشکری گران به لاهور آمد. وضیع و شریف آنجا چه ستمها که نکشیدند و چه جفاها که ندیدند. یعنی معین الملک پیشتر مغلوب او شده بعد از چندی از اسپ افتاد و رو بوادی عدم نهاد. چون مانعی نبود، از انجا قصد شهر نمود.

۱۳۶ از آمدآمد او بنگ از کلهٔ یاران پرید. از بادشاه و وزیر هیچ نه شد. آخر برسم پذیرهٔ او رفته قید شدند. راجه ناگرمل با بعضی رؤسا مثل سعدالدین خان خانِ سامان و غیره برای حفظ خود بقلعه جات سورج مل رفت. قریب یک ماه بر شهر سختی مصادره ماند. انگاه شاه بعالمگیر سلطنت بخشیده وزیر را با خود گرفت و انداز اکبرآباد کرد. فوج او دست غارت کشاد. متهرا که هژده کروه این طرف شهری بود با کمال رونق و آبادی قتل شد. چون هوا متعفن گردید، شاه از خوف طاعون معاملت سورج مل را ملتوی گذاشته دفعةً کوچید، و دختر محمد شاه را بحبالهٔ نکاح درآورده بالابالا رفت. عمادالملک در نواح اکبرآباد ماند. نجیب الدوله که در جنگ صفدرجنگ نوکر وزیر شده بود، ترقّی نمایان کرده میر بخشی گردید و مختار سلطنت شد.

He did not let himself be deceived by those who wished ill of him, and lived towering above others. At that time, Samsam-ud-Daula, the *mīr bakhshī,* died of consumption, and his son, an utterly worthless fellow, was appointed in his place.

Meanwhile, the Durrani king, Ahmad Shah 'Abdali, who had returned home after the defeat at Sirhind but still had thoughts of Hindustan in his head, arrived with a huge army at Lahore.* There is no tyranny or oppression that the worthies of that city did not suffer. Mu'in-ul-Mulk, already vanquished, fell from a horse after a while and died. Since there was no one to bar his way, the Durrani king started for Delhi.   135

As he came closer, our "friends" here came to their senses in a hurry. But neither the emperor nor the vazir was able to do anything. Finally they rode out to receive him and were taken prisoners. Raja Nagar Mal, together with other nobles such as Sa'duddin Khan, the master of the household, and others, went away for protection to the forts of Suraj Mal. For nearly a month, the city suffered extreme hardship. Then the Durrani king returned the imperial authority to 'Alam-gir II and, taking the vazir, 'Imad-ul-Mulk, into custody, set out for Akbarabad. His army stretched forth its hand of destruction, and Mathura, which was a prosperous and populous city, 18 *kurohs* this way, was put to the sword. When the air turned evil with the stench of dead bodies, the Durrani king, fearful of plague, decided not to settle the issue with Suraj Mal at that time. He quickly broke camp, and after taking for a wife a daughter of Muhammad Shah, hurried   136

---

* December 20, 1756.

151

۱۳۷ اینجا راجه ناگرمل با سرداران دکن برخورده، وزیر و احمد خان
و آنها را بر نجیب الدوله برد. او شهربند گشت. جنگ توپ خانه
بمیان آمد. بعضی از سرداران که برای خویش بودند باندک غلبه
انداز خرابی شهر میکردند. راجهٔ مذکور که مدعایش جز نیک
نامی وزیر هیچ نبود، برای ممانعت بر کار سوارشده آنها را باز
میداشت، و می گفت که بر شهر زدن شما بر قالب زدنست. فوج
دکن ناموس عالمی بر باد خواهد داد. شما برّه بند این کار نه اید.
نه شود که شهر بغارت رود و بدنامی عاید شود. اصلح آنست که
روهیله ها را بصلح برآریم، و شهر راسلامت نگهداریم. پایان کار
با نجیب الدوله سر بسر کرد، و از شهر برآورد. او به سهارن پور
که در فوجداری خود داشت، رفت. وزیر و اعزهٔ دیگر داخل شهر
شده، فوج دکن را رخصت نمودند. داروغگی توپ خانه به پسر
راجه تقرر یافت، و میربخشی گری به احمد خان شد.

joining the winning side

away without coming back to Delhi.* 'Imad-ul-Mulk stayed on in the vicinity of Akbarabad, while in Delhi, Najib-ud-Daula, who had joined the service of the vazir during the war with Safdar Jang, made notable progress and became the chief paymaster and the designated master of the realm.

Meanwhile, Raja Nagar Mal joined hands with the Mara-   137
thas and subsequently brought them to Delhi, together with the vazir, 'Imad-ul-Mulk, and Ahmad Khan Bangash, to challenge Najib-ud-Daula. The latter closed the gates of the city, and an artillery battle started. Some of the generals, who had only their own interest in mind, wished to indulge in plunder anytime they gained a little victory. The raja, wanting nothing but a good name for the vazir, held firm to his purpose and in every instance stopped them. He told them, "It would be absolutely foolish for you to do such a thing. The Maratha soldiers would then plunder everything and everyone. You have no experience in that regard. So do not do it, lest the city be destroyed and you earn a bad name. What is best for us is to get the Rohillas out peacefully and keep the city safe." Eventually he induced Najib-ud-Daula to make a compromise and come out of the city. Najib-ud-Daula marched off to Saharanpur, which was part of his assigned territory. The vazir and other nobles bade farewell to the Maratha army and entered the city.† Rai Bahadur Singh, the eldest son of the raja, was appointed the *dārogha* of the artillery, while Ahmad Khan Bangash was made the *mīr bakhshī*.

---

* April 1757.
† September 1757.

۱۳۸ یکی پیش راجه جگل کشور شکایت روزگار کردم. آن عزیز از خجلت سرخ و زرد شده گفت که من شال کهنه دارم. اگر دستی می داشتم، چشم نمی پوشیدم. روزی سوارشده بخانهٔ راجه ناگرمل رفت و تقریب من کرده طلب داشت. رفتم و بدست او ملاقات نمودم. لطف بسیاری کرد و گفت، ضیافت شیراز حاضر است، یعنی حصهٔ شما هم خواهد رسید. باری تسلی شدم و برخواستم. روز دیگر که صحبت شعر اتفاق شد، گفت که هر بیتِ میر مانا بعقد گهر است. طرز این جوان مرا بسیار خوش می آید.

۱۳۹ بهمین وتیره چندی رفتم اما چیزی بدست نیامد. چون کارد باستخوان رسیده بود، یکی بعد از نماز صبح بر در ایشان رفتم. جی سنگه نام میردهٔ چوبداران پیش آمد و گفت که این کدام وقت دربار است؟ گفتم که حالت اضطرار است. گفتا، شما را مردمان درویش میگویند. مگر گوش زد نشده است که «لا تتحرک ذرة إلا باذن الله». اینجا از علو مرتبت پروای کسی نیست. صابر و شاکر باید بود. همه چیز در گرو وقت است. این راه اندکی دور است. دیدن پسر کلان ایشان ضرور است. تر آمدم و برآمدم.

۱۴۰ شبی بگفتهٔ او بر در رای بهادر سنگه رفتم. دربانی ممانعت کرد و گفت دیدن ایشان این وقت امکان ندارد. ناچار برگشته آمدم. شب دیگر بعد از نماز عشا باز رفتم. دیدم که در بی

One day I complained of the hard times to Raja Jugal   138
Kishore. That noble person turned pink with shame, and
said, "'My own shawl is full of holes.' Otherwise, I would not
deny it to you if I possessed anything." Then one day he rode
out to the house of Raja Nagar Mal and, after mentioning
me to the raja, had me sent for. I went and was introduced
to the raja by him. The raja greeted me warmly and said, "It
is a poor man's banquet, but you will get your share of it." I
was relieved and took my leave. Another day, when there was
some occasion to recite poetry, the raja remarked, "Every
couplet of Mir's is like a string of pearls. I find this young
man's style most pleasing."

In similar fashion I visited him several times but failed to   139
get anything. Since my condition was already dire, I became
desperate and early one morning, after the prayers, I went
to the raja's house. Jai Singh, his head mace bearer, met me
at the door, and said, "Is this any time for an audience?"
I replied, "But I am desperate for subsistence." He said,
"People call you a dervish. But you do not seem to have
heard that 'Not a particle may move but when commanded
by God.' No exceptions are made here. You should be more
reconciled and patient. Everything has its fixed time. You
have just a little more to go. But first you must go and see
the raja's eldest son." Abashed, I returned home.

Subsequently one night, I went to the house of Rai Bahadur   140
Singh, the raja's son. His doorkeeper stopped me and said,
"It is not possible to see him at this time." I had no choice but
to turn back. Another night, after the 'ishā prayers, I went
again and found that the doorkeeper was absent. I asked
someone: "Where did the doorkeeper go?" He replied, "He

درنبانست. پرسیدم که درنبان کجا رفت؟ گفتند، امروز درد سرش
بحدی گرفته بود که نمی توانست نشست. دانستم که ارادهٔ حق
تعالیٰ متعلق است. بدیوان خانه درآمده دریافتم، و صحبت شعر
داشتم. خواجه غالب که جوان زورمندی بود و با من تعارفی
داشت، احوال مرا مفصل گفته چیزی مقرر کنانید. تا یک سال
می یافتم. شبی بخدمت راجه حاضر شدم. ایشان زر یک سالهٔ
مرا تنخواه نموده گفتند، اکثر مرا می دیده باشید. ازان روز بعد
نماز عشا بطریق ملازمان در خانه باغ ایشان می رفتم و تا دو پهر
شب می ماندم. گل این خدمت آن بود که بشگفتگی خاطر اوقات
میگذرانیدم.

۱۴۱   اکنون خامهٔ زبان دراز طرح سخن بطور دیگر می اندازد.

۱۴۲   سرداران دکن ملک را از خود میدانستند، و خیال جنگ شاه
در سر میداشتند. تیمورشاه پسر شاه درانی و جهان خان سردار
فوج را با مردم قلیل شنیده و از دنبالهٔ آن پروا نکرده یلغز به
لاهور رفتند. فوج کم شاهی تاب جنگ نیاورده گریخت. اینها تا
برودخانهٔ اتک متصرف شده، صاحبا نام سرداری را برای ضبط
آن طرف گذاشته، روانهٔ وطن که عبارت از دکن است گشتند.

۱۴۳   چون نوشتن این سانحات بر سبیل اجمال منظور داشتم، اکثر
مقدمات مثل چشم سخت کردن عمادالملک بر شجاع الدوله و
مصلح بودن راجه؛ و هنگامهٔ بی ادائی بدخشیان و زبون گشتن آنها

156

had such a bad headache that he could not be here tonight."
Taking it to be a sign that God was inclined toward me, I
entered and proceeded to the audience hall, where I met the
master of the house. A session of poetry recitation followed.
Khwaja Ghalib, who was a robust young man and acquainted
with me, told Rai Bahadur Singh all about me, and had me
assigned a regular salary. I received it for one year. Another
night I attended on Raja Nagar Mal. He too fixed a salary
for me, and also gave me a year's arrears. He told me, "You
should come and see me often." After that, like his regular
retainers, I used to attend upon him in his house-garden after
the *'ishā* prayers and stay till midnight. In return, I was able
to live a pleasant life.

Now the impetuous pen starts discoursing in a different   141
manner.

The Maratha chieftains, believing the entire country was   142
theirs, had thought of engaging in battle the Shah 'Abdali
Durrani for some time. And so when they heard that Timur
Shah, the son of the Durrani king, and Jahan Khan, the
commander of the garrison, had only a small number of
soldiers with them, they attacked Lahore on their own,
ignoring any thought of the terrible consequences that
might follow. The shah's small garrison could not face the
fight and fled. The Maratha chieftains took control of the
region up to the river Attock. Then, leaving behind a general
named Sahiba to consolidate their hold, they returned home.

Since I wished to describe these incidents only in brief, my   143
eloquent pen did not write all the details as to how 'Imad-ul-
Mulk became angry with Shuja-ud-Daula and how the raja
mediated between them—or how the Badakhshis behaved

از جرأت وزیر و راجه و نجیب خان؛ و رفتن وزیر به لاهور برای
ضبط اموال معین الملک که خسر او بود و برآوردن زن صوبه دار
مذکور از شهر مسطور و کشتن عاقبت محمود کشمیری؛ و کشته
شدن ستار قلی خان کشمیری؛ و خرابی شهر دهلی و بغارت رفتن
خانهای مردم از جور بی تهی چند که تازه بر روی کار آمده بودند،
و غافل بودن این خران از چوب خدائی؛ و رفتن شهزاده عالی گهر
با یکی از سرداران دکن که حالا تهمتی بادشاهت است و بدست
فرنگیان گرفتار؛ و پس از چندی آمدن او بشهر برای ملازمت پدر
و برسم پذیره رفتن راجه؛ و غدر کردن یاران و زخمی شده جان
بسلامت بردن او بجانب مشرق و لکد بخت خوردن و بادشاه
شدن؛ و قید کردن انتظام الدوله خان خانان؛ و برآوردن سلاطین
از قلعه بگفتهٔ ناکسان و باز آمدن آنها برسوائی که نانوشته به
است، قلم زبان آور من بتفصیل نه نگاشت. زیرا چه این موجز
گنجائی این همه اطناب نداشت.

۱۴۴ هنوز روزگار این همه بلاها را بتمام برنچیده بود که گردش
آسمان حقه باز فتنهٔ تازه را بعرصهٔ ظهور آورد. آشوب عجیبی
برخواست یعنی سرداری جنکو نام با فوج بسیاری از دکن رسید،
و گذار لشکرش در سواد شهر افتاد. دل اکثری از جا شد، قیامت
برپا شد. رئیسان رنگ رو باختند، شاه و وزیر باو ساختند. یاران
دتا نام سرداری که مدارالمهام آن سردارِ جگردار و جوان چارشانه

treacherously but were subdued by the bold action of the vazir, the raja, and Najib Khan—or how the vazir went to Lahore to take into custody the goods and property of Mu'in-ul-Mulk, his father-in-law, or how he brought the widow out of the city and killed Aqibat Mahmud Kashmiri—or how Sattar Quli Khan Kashmiri was killed—or how the city of Delhi was ruined and the homes of its people were pillaged due to the tyranny of a few imbeciles who had freshly come to power, and how those asses did not bear in mind God's long stick—or how Prince 'Ali Gauhar, who claims to be the emperor but is in fact a prisoner of the *firangīs*, went away from Delhi in the company of a Maratha chief—or how he returned after a while to submit himself to his father, and the raja went out to receive him—or how some of our "friends" caused trouble here, with the result that 'Ali Gauhar was wounded and escaped with his life to the east, where he suffered many blows of misfortune but eventually became the Emperor Shah 'Alam—or how Inti-zam-ud-Daula Khan-e Khanan, at the instigation of some unworthy persons, was made a prisoner—or how the princes were forced out of the citadel by some lowly people and then later returned in such an ignoble state as is best left untold.[41] My brief discourse could not contain all the details of these incidents and others.

Time had not yet brought to an end to these various calamities when the ever-turning heavens brought forth a new disaster: a Maratha chieftain named Janko arrived from the south.* As his huge army came closer to the city, an immense

144

---

* December 1758.

بود از خود کرده به نجیب الدوله که بکنار گنگ در جای قلب
ثبات قدم ورزیده تمکن داشت، دوانیدند.

۱۴۵ آنجا جنگ عظیم اتفاق افتاد. اینجا عزیزان بخانهٔ وزیر انجمن
شدند که اگر این فوج سنگین برگردد و بر ما ریزد، قیامتی برانگیزد
که عالم ته و بالا شود و شهر بغارت رود. اگر دست دهد، شریک
شده کار نجیب الدوله بسازیم وگرنه واسطه گردیده بصلح
پردازیم. هرگاه قرار یافت وزیر برآمد و آنطرف آب خیمه کرده
مکلف بادشاه گشت. او تمارض نموده جواب صاف داد. یاران
چون از بادشاه دلجمعی نداشتند، مشورت کردند که بشهر بروند
و بادشاه را از میان بردارند و انتظام الدوله را نیز زنده نگذارند.
راجه همان شب آنروی آب رفت.

۱۴۶ سفیده دم آن سیاه درونان از لشکر به شهر آمده پیش بادشاه
حاشا زدند که ما با وزیر بدیم اما زمانه سازی می کنیم. فوز
عظیمی دست بهم داده است اگر حضرت دریابند. آن ساده
لوح، فریب آن ناسرانجامان خورده، پرسید که چیست؟ گفتند،
فقیر صاحب کمالی دست از دنیا برداشتهٔ از دو سه روز در
قلعچهٔ فیروز شه وارد است. فردا خواهد رفت. آخر روز اگر
دیده شود غالب است که از دعای آن بزرگ ازین بلا رهائی
یابیم، و بر وزیر غالب آئیم. بادشاه از زبان در ته زبان داشتن
عزیزان عصر غافل بود. وعده داد که البته خواهم دید. آخر

turmoil set in. Most of the populace lost heart, while the nobles turned pale with fear. The king and the vazir made peace with him. That brave and bold chief had for his chief minister a stockily built warrior named Datta. Our "friends" conspired with him and had him attack Najib-ud-Daula, who was securely and confidently encamped at a place on the bank of the river Ganges.

A major battle took place over there,* while here in Delhi   145
the same nobles gathered at the house of the vazir, 'Imad-ul-Mulk, and took counsel. They argued, "It would be a dooms-day for us if that huge army turns around and makes us its target. The city would be totally destroyed. If at all possible, let us join with the Marathas and put an end to Najib-ud-Daula; or else we should try to mediate between the two and bring about a truce." Having reached that conclusion, the vazir came out of the city and encamped across the Jamuna. He then requested the emperor to join him. The latter feigned illness and refused. The vazir and his friends, being not sure of the emperor, decided to return to the city to get rid of him, and also not to leave Intizam-ud-Daula alive. That very night Raja Nagar Mal moved out of the city to the other side of the river.

At the white of dawn, those black-hearted people returned   146
to the city, and going to the emperor swore before him that they had not been disloyal, and that it was only for appear-ance's sake that they had been with the vazir. Then they said, "Sire, great success is at hand if you agree to help." That simple man was taken in by those scoundrels; he asked,

* Battle of Shukratal, September 15, 1759.

نزدیک بشام سوار کرده بردند. چون در قلعچه رسید، بزخم کارد
کار آن بیگناه ساختند، و مردهٔ او را پائین دیوار انداختند. بعد
از شام از آنجا برگشته در نماز رسن به گلوی خانخانان افگنده
کشیدند، و بسختی تمامش کشته لاشهٔ او را از نظر مردم پنهان
ربودند و غرق دریا نمودند.

۱۴۷   مردهٔ پادشاه تمام روز برسوائی تمام بر روی خاک افتاده ماند.
هرکه می دید بر مرتکبان این امر ناشایسته لعنت میکرد. آخر
وارثان او جگر از سنگ کرده شباشب زیر خاکش پنهان ساختند
و از هراس آن بی چشم و رویان ماتم نگرفتند. صبح دیگر آن ستم
کیشان در قلعه آمد شاهجهان نام جوانی را بر تخت نشانیدند
و نذرها گزرانیدند. مدت سلطنت عالمگیر ثانی هفت سال بود.

۱۴۸   هرگاه این زبون گیر چند از کشتن بادشاه و انتظام الدوله
فراغت کردند، وزیر را کوچ با کوچ بردند. او بعد از قطع منازل و
طی مراحل بفوج دکن پیوسته شریک جنگ شد. هفتهٔ بر این نرفته
بود که خبر رسید: فوج شاهی از اتک گذشته، صاحبا را شکست
داد. سرداران دکن جنگ نجیب الدوله را گذاشته، آسیمه سر
برای سدّ راه شدن روانه گشتند، و برابر پانی پت از آب جون
عبور نموده فرود آمدند. در اثنای راه جهانی سر سخت خورد. از
آنجا سنگ به سنگ زنان آنطرف کرنال که قصبه ایست مشهور و
آستانهٔ شاه شرف بوعلی قلندر آنجاست، خیمه گاه ساختند. شام

"How could it be?" They said, "A fakir who has renounced the world and who possesses miraculous powers has been staying for some days in the ruined fortress of Firoz Shah, but he leaves tomorrow. If you can possibly pay him a visit this evening, we strongly believe that his blessings will give us relief and make us victorious over the vazir." The emperor was unaware of the lying and deceiving ways of his nobles and promised them that he would certainly make the visit. Late that afternoon, they took him there. As they entered the fortress, they stabbed to death that innocent person, and threw his corpse below the fortress wall. Then, after it was evening, they returned to the city and strangled the Khan-e Khanan Intizam-ud-Daula as he was praying. Later they smuggled out his body and cast it in the river.*

The corpse of the previous emperor remained lying igno- 147
miniously in the dirt till the end of the day, and whosoever saw it cursed the perpetrators of that shameful act. Finally at night, his family members got up enough courage to have him buried in the dark, but they dared not raise a cry in lament out of fear of those ruthless and shameless people. The next morning those tyrants entered the citadel, where they placed on the throne a young man named Shah Jahan, and offered him homage. The reign of 'Alamgir II lasted seven lunar years.[42]

When these few evil men were done with the killing of 148
the emperor and Intizam-ud-Daula, they set off with the vazir at a rapid pace and joined with the Maratha army in their war against Najib-ud-Daula. But not even a week had

---

* November 29, 1759.

شنیده شد که لشکر شاهی بر سمت دریا سیاهی کرد. ایشان نیز سیاهی فوج نمودند.

۱۴۹ روز دیگر پیش از تیغ کشیدن آفتاب، جوانان جرار و کارگذار قریب هشت هزار سوار و یکی از سرداران جدا کرده فرستادند. وقتیکه رفتند و بروی آن فوج ایستادند، بیک تک تک پا بسیاری از پا افتادند. سخت دلان کوه پیکر بر سر سنگ نشستند، زنخ زنان را زنخدانها شکستند. خونخواران آنطرف بوضعی آویختند که خون بسا کس بیکدم ریختند. چشم لشکریان این جانب ترسید، و دل جوانان بخود لرزید. اگر خدا نخواسته آن دسته بر دائرهٔ لشکر میزد همان روزگار بتمامی کشیدی و از ما مردمان یکی بشهر سلامت نرسیدی. اینان شاخ از پشیمانی برآورده برگشتند؛ آنان سرکاوزده از آب گذشتند.

۱۵۰ هرگاه مخیم شاه [وارد] دوابه شد و نجیب الدوله ملحق گشت، دکنیان وزیر را جهت محافظت شهر لشکر دستوری دادند، و خود کنار آب گرفته آمدند و شش کروه آنطرف خیمها زدند. اینجا وزیر شهر را محکم کرده [مورچال ها] قسمت نمود، و حویلئ داراشکوه که بر دریا واقع است براجه سپردهِ بادشاهِ نو را که شاهجهان باشد دید.

164

passed when the news came that the army of the Shah 'Abdali Durrani had crossed the river Attock and defeated Sahiba. The Maratha chieftains, abandoning the siege, rushed in dismay to stop the army of the shah. They crossed the river Jamuna near Panipat and made a halt there. Everyone suffered a great deal during that journey. From there they marched with much pomp and show to a spot west of Karnal, which is a well-known town and contains the tomb of Shah Sharaf Bu-'Ali Qalandar, and set up camp.[43] In the evening the news came that the army of the shah had appeared by the river. The Marathas also got ready for battle.

The next day, before the sun drew out its shining sword, the Marathas selected some eight thousand bold and experienced soldiers and one general, and sent them forward. But when they made their attack they were instantly rebuffed and put to flight. Mighty tyrants were humbled, and the boastful had their jaws broken. Their bloodthirsty opponents fought fiercely, and killed very many in just a brief spell. Now the soldiers on this side were scared and their hearts trembled. God forbid, had that small force of the shah then attacked our camp, it would have wiped us out completely; none of us would have safely made it back to the city. Consequently, this army retreated, badly chastised, while that army, having won an easy victory, came over in entirety to this side of the river.

When the shah's camp was set up in the *doab*, Najib-ud-Daula came and joined him. Then the Marathas gave the vazir the necessary forces to protect the city, while they themselves followed the course of the river and set up camp at a distance of 6 *kurohs*. Here, in the city, the vazir strength-

۱۵۱ پس از چار روز فوج شاه و نجیب الدوله پاچفت دویده بدریا
رسید. دلاوران پیکارخو و سواران جنگجو در پی پوزمال گردیدند.
پیادگان روهیله پیش قدمی نموده هنگامهٔ جنگ را گرم ساختند،
و چنان تردد کردند که پایهای شان پوست انداختند. ازین طرف
دتا که سرکردهٔ فوج دکن بود بکارگذاران خود پهلو داده به یک
پهلو افتاد و مقابل آن فوج سنگین ایستاد. نخستین تفنگی که ازان
سو سرداده شد، تیر او به دتا رسید و به پهلو غلطید. دکنیان
دست و پا گم کرده لاش او را برداشتند و کنار آب گذاشتند.
آنان این طرف آب آمده دست جلادت کشادند. اینان سر به
بیابان هزیمت نهادند. وزیر سرداران خود را برگذاشته با فوج
دکن آمیخت. زمانهٔ غدار رنگ خرابی عالم ریخت. درانیان دنبال
گریختگان افتاده اکثری را علف تیغ بیدریغ کردند، و برگشته
انداز تاراج شهر نمودند.

۱۵۲ راجه شام از شهر برآمده قصد قلعه جات سورج مل کرد و
سلامت رفت. بنده برای حفظ ناموس خود بشهر ماندم. بعد از
شام منادی شد که شاه امان داده است، باید که رعایا پریشان
دل نگردد. چون لختی از شب گذشت، غارتگران دست تطاول
دراز نموده، شهر را آتش داده خانها سوختند و بردند. صبح که
صبح قیامت بود، تمام فوج شاهی و روهیله ها تاختند و به قتل
و غارت پرداختند. دروازه ها شکستند، مردمان را بستند، اکثری

ened the city walls and assigned garrisons at every gate and turret. Then, entrusting to the raja the mansion of Dara Shukoh—it is on the river—he himself attended on the new emperor, Shah Jahan III.

After four days, the armies of the shah and Najib-ud-Daula, marching together, arrived at the river. Fierce fighters and ferocious horsemen were determined to make a punitive strike. The Rohilla foot soldiers acted first, and launched a most fierce attempt to cross the river and attack. On this side, Datta, the general of the Maratha army, rushed to the aid of his warriors. He strove hard and pitted himself face to face against that mighty force. But the first musket shot from that side hit Datta, and he fell dead to the ground. The Marathas, in utter panic, did not even pick up his corpse and left it lying by the river. The Rohillas, crossing over to this side, started a massacre, while the Marathas ran off into the wilderness in utter rout.* The vazir, abandoning the city to the care of his officers, himself joined the Maratha army. Time, that great traitor, launched another ruination of the world. The Durranis relentlessly pursued the fleeing and killed a great many of them. Then they came back and showed signs of planning to plunder the city.

Raja Nagar Mal left the city in the evening for Suraj Mal's forts and reached there safely. I stayed behind to protect my family. At dusk it was publicly announced that the Shah 'Abdali Durrani had proclaimed peace for the city, and therefore its citizens need not worry. However, after a part of the night had passed, the plunderers stretched out

151

152

* The battle of Barari Ghat, January 9, 1760.

را سوختند و سر بریدند. عالمی را بخاک و خون کشیدند. تا
سه شبانروز دست ستم بر نداشتند. از خوردنی و پوشیدنی هیچ
نگذاشتند. سقفها شگافتند، دیوارها شکستند؛ جگرها سوختند،
سینه ها خستند. آن زشت سیرتان بر در و بام، اکابران به بی
سیرتی تمام. شیخان شهر بحال خراب؛ بزرگان محتاج دم آب.
گوشه نشینان بیجا شدند؛ اعیان همه گدا شدند. وضیع و شریف
عریان، کدخدایان بی خان و مان. اکثری به بلا گرفتار، رسوای
کوچه و بازار. بسیاری خداگیر، زن و بچه اسیر. بر سر شهری
هجوم، قتل و غارت علی العموم. حال عزیزان به ابتری کشید؛
جان بسی به لب رسید. زخم میزدند و زبان به تلخ می کشودند.
زر را می گرفتند و سلاخی می نمودند. با هرکه برمیخوردند تا
سترپوش می بردند. جهانی از جهان ناشاد رفت. ناموس عالمی بر
باد رفت. شهر نو بخاک برابر شد.

their cruel hands and set fire to the city. They burned and plundered. In the morning — which was like the morning of doomsday — the armies of the shah and the Rohilla leader Najib-ud-Daula poured in and set about looting and killing. They knocked down the doors of houses and tied up the owners, and some they burned while others they beheaded. A world was decimated. For three days and nights, they did not let up. Nothing in the way of food and clothing was spared. Roofs were dug up; walls were pulled down. Breasts were torn open; hearts were charred. Those evil ones were on every terrace and at every door, while the good people of the city had nowhere to hide. Those who had been masters were now in dire straits, and those who were once revered could not even quench their thirst. The recluses were pulled out of their corners. The notables were turned into beggars. The householders were made homeless. Noble and ignoble, all were disrobed. Most of the people suffered horribly, and were dishonored in public places. Many of them, caught in this mayhem, even had their wives and children snatched from them. A terrible host trampled the city and caused death and destruction to all and sundry. The nobility suffered; many of them faced death. The soldiers killed and wounded, and abused and cursed. They grabbed whatever riches they found, and with their words poured salt on their victims' wounds. Anyone they encountered they looted so thoroughly that he had nothing left even to cover his nakedness. Countless people departed from this unhappy world, and countless were dishonored. The New City, i.e., the walled city of Shahjahanabad, was turned into rubble.

169

روز سوم نسق مقرر شد. انزلاخان نام نسقچی باشی رسید؛
کلاهها و نیم تن مردم او کشید. باری قدغنچیان غارتگران را از
شهر برآورده باحتیاط پرداختند، و آن بیرحم مردمان بشهر کهنه
چسپیده جهانی را هلاک ساختند. هفت هشت روز این هنگامه
گرم بود. اسباب پوشش و قوت یک روزه در خانهٔ کسی نماند. سر
مردان بی کلاه، زنان بی رومال سیاه. جمعی، چون راهها قفل بود،
روزی از زخم پراگنده هم نخوردند. جماعتی را از سردی هوا دندان
بدندان کلید شد و مردند. به بی حیائی تمام تاختند. روها بر زمین
انداختند. غله ها را از گرسنه چشمی می اندوختند و بدست غربا
بطرح می فروختند. شور غارت زدگان شهر تا آسمان هفتم میرسید.
اما شاه که خود را فقیر می گرفت بسبب استغراق نمی شنید.

هزاران خانه سیاه در عین آن آتش تیز با داغ دل جلای وطن
کرده سر بصحرا زدند، و چون چراغ صبحگاهی در راه از هوای سرد
خانه روشن کردند. بی شمار بیدست و پایان را آن سیه درونان
در رکاب انداخته اسیرانه بدائرهٔ لشکر خود بردند. دست دست
ظالمان بود، دست کجی میکردند، دست پلشتی می نمودند.
دست چرب بر سر می کشیدند. دست ببازوی زنان می رسیدند.
تیغها می آختند. دستگاه می ساختند.

از دست شهریان هیچ نمی آمد. زیرا که دست و دل ایشان سرد
شده بود. کسی دست پاچه می شد؛ کسی دست بزیر سرستون می

170

On the third day, martial law was declared under Anzala   153
Khan, a member of the imperial guards. He robbed the
people of even their caps and shirts. Eventually the sergeants
at arms forced the plunderers out of the city and set about
organizing some protection. Meanwhile the savages
attacked the Old City[44] and started killing its people. That
carnage continued for seven or eight days. No household
was left with a suit of clothes or a day's food. The men lost
their caps, the women their black chadors. People could not
even go begging for food, for all the streets were blocked. A
large number of them died from the cold, their jaws locked
together. The Afghans and the Rohillas plundered without shame and paid no heed to anyone's cries. They took
away grain from the hungry and sold it at a high price to the
needy. The cries of the devastated people of the city reached
the seventh heaven. They, however, went unheard by the
shah, who remained engrossed in his own thoughts since he
fancied himself a dervish.

Thousands of wretches, in the midst of that raging fire,   154
scarred their hearts with the mark of exile and ran off into the
jungles, where, like lamps at dawn, they died in the cold air.
Meanwhile, the plundering blackguards bound up defense-
less people in large numbers and dragged them off as prisoners to their camp. It was a reign of tyrants.[45] They stole
and plundered, and enriched themselves obscenely, and did
not spare even the women. They waved their swords and
snatched away whatever they could grab.

The people of the Old City could do nothing. You could say   155
their hands and hearts had gone numb. They were stunned in
their distress. On every doorstep there stood a blackguard;

نمود. بر هر دری درون سیاهی، در هر برزنی بزن گاهی. بازاری و
گیروداری. هر طرف خونریزی؛ هر سمت بز آویزی. پاتابه پیچی
میکردند؛ بنا گوشی میزدند. غریبان از خوف خشک بودند. دیده
درایان تریها مینمودند. خانها سیاه، کوچها داغ گاه. صدها از
چوبکاری هلاک شدند، جامهٔ خون بستهٔ یکی بر سر چوب کرده
نشد. عالمی از زخم ستم جامه در خون کشید و جان داد، اما
کسی دم نزد.

۱۵۶   زمین شهر کهنه که جهان تازه اش میگفتند، دیوار صورت
کاری افتاده را مانا شد، یعنی تا هر جا که نظر میرفت سر و سینه
و دست و پای کشتگان بود. خانهای آتشزدهٔ سینه سوختگان از
تعزیت خانه ها یاد میداد، یعنی تا چشم بینندگان کار میکرد
سیه می نمود. سخت خوردهٔ که خود را بکشتن داد آرامید. چشم
خوردهٔ آنها روے بهبود ندید. منکه فقیر بودم، فقیرتر شدم.
حالم از بی اسبابی و تهی دستی ابتر شد. تکیهٔ که بر سر شاهراه
داشتم بخاک برابر شد. غرضکه آن بی مروتان تمام شهر را بار کرده
بردند. عزیزان همه ذلیل شده جانها سپردند.

۱۵۷   هنوز از نهیب و غارت دست برنداشته بودند، مشهور شد که
فوج هزیمت خوردهٔ دکن، با فوج دیگر که در نواح میوات بود
پیوست [و] ارادهٔ فاسدی دارد. شاه از استماع این خبر مهیای آن
طرف گشته، شاهجهان را، که تهمت زدهٔ چند ماهه سلطنت بود،

every street was a field of killing; and every marketplace was a scene of terror. Bloodshed went on everywhere. People were strung up everywhere. Some were cheated; others were slapped around. The poor stood stiff with fear while those impudent fellows showered abuses on them. Houses became blackened ruins. Streets were scarred. Hundreds died from the beatings they received, but not one received any justice. And thousands died at the hand of tyranny, drenched in blood, but no one said a word.

The grounds of the Old City, which used to be called a world of its own, appeared like the rubble heaps of some wall that was once painted with human figures, for wherever one looked one saw heads and limbs and torsos of those who had been slaughtered. The charred houses of those whose hearts had also been tossed into fire looked like houses of mourning, for no matter where one's eyes fell, they met only the color black. The poor wretches killed by the marauders' swords found rest, but those who fell victim only to their deviltry found no respite. I, a beggar already, became more of a beggar. I was left destitute and penniless, and my humble dwelling, which was on the main road, was leveled to the ground. In short, those shameless brutes carried away with them all that was in the city, while the notables of the city lost their honor as well as their lives. 156

The marauders had not yet finished with their oppression and pillage when it was heard that the defeated Maratha army had joined up with another army that was in the vicinity of Mewat, and they now had some hostile intentions. The shah, on receiving the news, made ready to move in that direction. 157

بدستور سابق در سلاطین فرستاد و جوان بخت پسر عالی گهر را
ولیعهد او گردانیده از شهر کوچیده و رفت. عمادالملک، همراهی
سرداران دکن گذاشته، بقلعجات سورج مل آمد و نشست.

۱۵۸ وقتیکه شاه در نواح میوات رسید و دکنیان دیدند که تیغ ما
نمی برد و چشم لشکریان ترسیده است، جنگ گریز کنان بطور
قدیم خود، تا شاهجهان آباد آمده از دریا عبور کردند. شاه نیز
متعاقب در رسید و شب در سواد شهر گذرانیده از راه پایاب
گذشت، و آنروی آب جون آب جون معسکر شد. جهان خان سردار فوج
پیش رفته، قریب سکندرآباد با فوج ملهار که احوال او گذارش
یافت درآویخت. شاه ازینجا با سه هزار غلام سوار شده در عرصهٔ
دوپاس شریک او شد. سردار آنطرف، تاب مقاومت نیاورده، دم
خود را به یکی از سران دکن سپرده، پنهان گریخت. آن سرکرده داد
دلاوری داد و کشته افتاد. کسان دیگر، دندان بحرف گذاشته، از
روبروی جراران فوج شاهی گریخته، پراگنده شدند. شاه تا کول،
که قصبه ایست معروف، تعاقب کنان رفت. گریختگان بقلعجات
سورج مل پناه برده، بعد از دو سه روز روانه پیشتر گردیدند.

۱۵۹ فوج شاه با یکی از قلعهای او که این طرف آب جون بود، چسپید،
و کار بر مردم حصار سخت گرفت. زمیندار مسطور امداد آنها
بالقوهٔ خود ندیده بدر تغافل زد. ناچار حصاریان، انتهاز فرصت
یافته، هنگام شب گریختند، و میان دار فرستاده صلح نمودند.

He dispatched Shah Jahan III back into confinement with other princelings, and after declaring Jawan Bakht, son of 'Ali Gauhar, to be the heir apparent to the throne, marched out of the city. Meanwhile, 'Imad-ul-Mulk left the company of the Maratha chieftains and took shelter in the forts of Suraj Mal.

When the shah arrived close to Mewat, the Marathas real- 158 ized that their sword would not carry the day and that their army was scared. They then began their usual hit-and-run tactics, and in that manner they came up to Shahjahanabad, where they crossed to the other side of the river. The shah too came in their pursuit, and after spending the night in the vicinity of the city, crossed the river Jamuna at a shallow spot and encamped on the other side of the river. Jahan Khan, one of the shah's generals, moved forward and, near Sikan- darabad, engaged the forces of the aforementioned Malhar Rao Holkar. Then the shah himself took to the saddle and, with three thousand slaves, reached there in six hours and joined the battle. The opponent was unable to withstand the attack and, handing over the command to another Maratha general, secretly ran away. The new Maratha commander fought bravely but was finally killed. The other chiefs, losing all hope, fled before the mighty warriors of the royal army and were scattered. The shah pursued them up to Kol, which is a well-known town.[46] The fugitives first took shelter in the forts of Suraj Mal but after a couple of days moved on.

The shah's forces then laid siege to one of Suraj Mal's forts 159 on this side of the river Jamuna and made life extremely hard for the people inside. Suraj Mal, the aforementioned *zamīndār,* saw that he did not possess enough strength to give them help and decided to ignore them. The besieged

۱۶۰ هنوز لشکر میان دو آب بود شهرت یافت که فوج سنگینی از
دکن بانداز جنگ در نواح اکبرآباد رسیده است، و زود میرسد.
نجیب الدوله سرداران سمت مشرق مثل شجاع الدوله و احمد
خان و حافظ رحمت و غیره را برای ملازمت آورد، و هر یکی را
بوعدهٔ ملکی خوشدل ساخته سراپا دهانید و آمادهٔ جنگ گردانید.

۱۶۱ درین نزدیکی بهاؤ، که سرِ سران دکن بود، بانبوه بیش از بیش
از ملک سورج مل گذشت، و وزیر و راجه را مستمال ساخته با
خود آورد و متصرف شهر گشت. یعقوب علی خان، که قرابتی با
شاه ولی خان وزیر شاه درانی داشت، و در قلعه بادشاهی بتوقع
آنکه فوج شاه آنطرف آب است کم مددی نخواهد کرد، بخود
سپرده بدست و دندان در جنگ چسپید. دکنیان محاصره نموده
ببادلیجه ها گرفتند. اکثر مکانات بادشاهی را که نظیر نداشتند
بخاک یکسان ساختند. چون دریا بسبب برشکال عسیرالعبور بود
و شاه نمی توانست گذشت، خان مذکور بدست راجه سر بسر
کرده از قلعه برآمد. نظر بر عهد و پیمان، کسی مزاحم احوال او
نشد.

people, finding an opportunity, fled at night, then sent a mediator and arranged a truce.

The army of the shah was still in the *doab* when the news   160
came that a mighty Maratha army, fully prepared for battle, had reached the vicinity of Akbarabad and would soon arrive.* Najib-ud-Daula presented to the shah the nobles from the east, such as Shuja-ud-Daula, Ahmad Khan Bangash, Hafiz Rahmat Khan, and others, and after making each of them happy with promises of additions to their territories, he had them given robes of honor by the shah and made them agree to do battle.

Meanwhile, Sadashiv Rao Bhau, who was the chief of the   161
Maratha nobles, passed through the territory of Suraj Mal with an enormous army. He won over to his side the vazir, 'Imad-ul-Mulk, and Raja Nagar Mal, and bringing them with him took possession of the walled city. Yaqub 'Ali Khan, a close relative of Shah Vali Khan, the vazir of the Durrani king, was in the citadel. He became vain, expecting that the army of the shah would not hesitate to come to his help, being just on the other side of the river, and continued aggressively to fight. The Dakhinis laid siege to the citadel and started bombarding it with their cannons. Many royal houses, matchless in beauty, were reduced to dust. But the river was impossible to ford due to heavy rains, and the shah could not come across. Consequently, Yaqub 'Ali Khan made peace through Raja Nagar Mal and left the citadel. In view of the pacts that had been made, no one bothered him.[†]

———

* June 1760.
† August 3, 1760.

۱۶۲ در این ایام، من بخدمت راجه حاضر شدم و التماس نمودم که
از گرم و سرد روزگار در آتش و آبم. میخواهم که ازین شهر برآیم
و جای دیگر بروم، شاید که آسوده شوم. ایشان رعایتی نمودند و
رخصتم فرمودند. لواحقان را همراه گرفته پیاده پا برآمدم. جای
مدنظر نداشتم، بتوکل قدم در راه گذاشتم. در تمام روز پس
از خرابی بسیار هشت و نه کروه راه طی شد. شب در سرای زیر
درختی بسر کردیم. صبح آن زن راجه جگل کشور که احوالش
نگاشته آمد، ازان راه گذشت. ما کم پایان را از خاک برداشته
همراه خود تا برسانه، که معبد هنودانست و قصبه ایست هشت
کروه این طرف قلعجات سورج مل، برد و بانواع مراعات دلدهی
کرد. سلخ ذیحجه او بکامان، که سه کروهی آن مکان شهریست
سرحد راجه جی سنگه، رفت. بنده با اهل و عیال در عشره آنجا
اقامت نمودم. فردای عاشورا قدم کشیدم و به کمهیر رسیدم.
این جا بهادر سنگه نام پسر لاله رادها کشن که پیشتر خزانچی
گری صفدرجنگ داشت و در این اوقات با راجه بود، شام آمد
و سردستی بمن گرفته آدمیانه سر کرد. احسان مند اویم که غیر
از دوست روی حقی برو نداشتم. چندی بفراغت ماندم و روز و
شب گذراندم.

۱۶۳ روزی بسبب فقدان اسباب معیشت دل تنگ نشسته بودم.
بخاطر رسید که با اعظم خان پسر اعظم خان کلان که در عهد

During this time I went to the raja and submitted to him   162
that I was in great distress due to the uncertain times and
wished to go out of the city, to some other place where
perhaps I might find some peace. The raja gave me some
token of his favor and allowed me to leave. I took all my
dependents with me and set out on foot. I had no particular destination in mind; I just placed my trust in God and
took to the road. In that entire day, with utmost difficulty,
we covered 8 or 9 *kurohs*. The night was spent under a tree
in a caravanserai. Next morning, the wife of the aforementioned Raja Jugal Kishore happened to pass through that
way. She raised us humble people from the dust where we
lay and took us with her to Barsana—a town 8 *kurohs* this
side of the forts of Suraj Mal, with a major Hindu temple—
and with many gifts and favors reduced our distress. On
the last day of Zi'l-hijja 1173 A.H.,* she moved to Kaman, a
town 3 *kurohs* from Barsana on the border of the territory
of Raja Jai Singh. My family and I stopped there to observe
the Ashura, the first ten days of Muharram, but after that we
went on and reached Kumher. Here Bahadur Singh, the son
of Lala Radha Kishan who previously had been the treasurer
of Safdar Jang and presently worked for the raja, arrived
one evening. He befriended us and treated us humanely. I
am grateful to him, for I had no claim on him but that of an
amiable acquaintance. Thus I lived, somewhat relieved of
my worries, and a few days went by.

One day, as I sat grieving over the paucity of my sources   163
for a livelihood, it occurred to me that if I were to go and

* August 12, 1760.

فردوس آرامگاه امیر شش هزاری بود و دست و دلی داشت، اگر
ملاقات کرده شود، یک دو دم خوش برآورده شود. رفتم و در
طویلهٔ سورج مل که تازه اقامت گاه خانه خرابان شهر دهلی شده
بود برخوردم. آن عزیز، خدایش بیامرزاد، لب را بخیر پرسش من
کشاد. سر رفتهٔ خود بر زبان آوردم. سامعان را از هوش بردم.
چون قهوه و قلیان بمیان آمد، این بیت آمده بر زبان آمد:

امروز که چشم من و عرفی بهم افتاد
باهم نگریستیم و گرستیم و گذشتیم

چند شعر ازین قبیل خواندم، و دو سه اشک از مژه افشاندم.
پس از نفسی چند خان مذکور را متفکر دیدم. گفتم که چه
بخود فرو رفتهٔ؟ گفت، خیر. گفتم، آخر. گفت، هرگاه شما در
شهر می آمدید، اقسام شیرینی و انواع حلویات می آوردیم و باهم
میخوردیم. امروز عجب اتفاق است که دست بر شکرِ خام هم
نداریم تا کاسهٔ شربتی برای شما بیاریم. گفتم که مولع این همه
نیستم. آنهم بر سبیل تفنن بود. صاحب خوب میدانند که گاهی
شکم را [ناف؟] سماط نکرده ام. اوقات مختلف است. آن هنگام
شربت و شیرینی بود، این موسم تلخی کشیدنست. همین گفت
و شنود بود که زنی، خوانی بر سر، از در درآمد و گفت، همسر
سعدالدین خان خان سامان دعا گفته است و قدری حلوای نزاکت

see A'zam Khan—the son of A'zam Khan Sr., a Muhammad
Shahi noble of the rank of "Six Thousand"—I would get to
enjoy a few pleasant moments, for he was both generous and
resourceful. I went and found him in the stables of Suraj
Mal, for that was the newest refuge of the ruined people
from Delhi. That noble person—may God be kind to him—
greeted me and asked about my welfare. I narrated all that had
happened to me. Whoever heard was stunned. When *qahva*
and the hookah were brought in, this verse came to my lips:

> *Today, when 'Urfi and I ran into each other,*
> *We stared and wept, then continued separately.*

I recited a few more couplets of that nature, and shed a
few more tears.

After a while I noticed that the khan seemed worried   164
about something. I asked, "Why are you so lost in thought?"
He replied, "Back in the city, whenever you visited us, we
would bring out all kinds of sweets and *halwa* and enjoy them
together. How strange that today we do not possess even
some raw sugar to make a little sherbet for you!" I said, "I
am not greedy for those things. That was just a way to divert
ourselves. You know very well that I am not a glutton. These
are changed times. That was a time for sherbet and sweetmeats; now is a time to drink the dregs." This conversation
was still going on when a maid came in through the door,
carrying a tray on her head. She said, "The wife of Sa'duddin
Khan, Khan-e Saman, sends you her 'blessings' and some
halwa-e nazākat and some consecrated sweets." When
the khan uncovered the tray and saw the richly decorated

و شیرینی شنبه فرستاده. خان چون سر خوان کشاد نگاهش بر
گل حلوا فتاد. گل گل شگفت و با من گفت که این روسیاه قدر
خود خوب میداند. عمریست که بفاقه کشی میگذراند. گاهی از
جای دم آبی لب نانی نرسیده، تا بحلوا و شیرینی چه رسد. شما
مهمان عزیزید، این اقامت شماست. حصهٔ مرا بدهید و بخانهٔ
خود فرستید. گفتم، بسیار است، من چه خواهم کرد. گفتا، بکار
میرفیض علی پسر شما خواهد آمد. غرضکه مرد خوشی بود. کاسه
بند نموده قاب حلوا و خوان شیرینی بخانهٔ من فرستاد و خندان
خندان دلم داد.

۱۶۵   دو روز بهمان شیرینی گذرانیده شد. روز سوم پسر خورد راجه
مرا طلبید و احوال گیری کرده گفت، تا تشریف آوردن ایشان
پیش من باشید. گفتم که اسباب معیشت مفقود است. گفت،
دل را جمع کنند، اینجا همه چیز موجود است. آن نوگل باغ کرم
که همیشه شاداب و خورم باشد، به شگفتگی خاطر مایحتاج مرا
میرسانید.

۱۶۶   اینجا چنان مسموع شد که بشهر شهرت گرفت که صمد خان
فوجدار سرهند با چند زمیندار و فوج بسیار می آید، و ارادهٔ لشکر
شاه دارد. بهاؤ سردار دکن، که جوان برخودچیدهٔ بود، کسی را
پیش خود وجود نمی گذاشت. اسباب زاید در قلعهٔ شاهجهان آباد
گذاشته، بمقتضای حرارت ذاتی قصد حرکت آن طرف نمود. بخاطر

halwa, his face lit up with a smile. Turning to me, he said, "I know well the worth of my wretched self. For quite some time I have lived with starvation. Never did anyone send me even a cup of water or a piece of bread, least of all *halwa* and sweetmeats. You are the honored guest. This feast is for you. Give me my small portion and send the rest to your family." I remonstrated, "But it is too much. What am I going to do with it?" He said, "It will be of use to your son Mir Faiz 'Ali." In short, that excellent man cajoled and insisted, and eventually had that dish of *halwa* and the tray of sweets sent to my place. Then he happily bade me good-bye.

We lived on those sweets for two days. On the third day, 165 Rai Bishan Singh, the younger son of Raja Nagar Mal, sent for me. After inquiring about my situation, he said, "You should stay with me until he reaches here." I told him that I had nothing to live on. He replied, "Rest assured; we have everything with us." That fresh blossom in the garden of kindness—may he always be well and happy—gladly provided me with all that was needed.

Now we heard that it was being widely said in Delhi that 166 Samad Khan, the commandant of Sirhind, was on his way together with some *zamīndārs* and a large army, and intended to join up with the army of the shah. Bhau, the Maratha chieftain, was given to self-importance and did not think much of anyone else. He left his extra baggage and equipment in the citadel at Shahjahanabad and, hot-blooded that he was, decided to proceed in that direction. He had in mind that, since the vazir had plenty of jewels with him and Suraj Mal was a major *zamīndār,* the two should be dispossessed of some of their riches at some opportune time. Raja Nagar

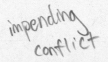
impending conflict

داشت که وزیر جواهر بسیاری دارد و سورج مل زمیندار کلانی
است، اگر زمانه فرصت دهد از ایشان چیزی بگیرد. راجه ناگرمل
بسبب ملاقات سرداران او ازین معنی خبر بود. روزی براجه پیغام
فرستاد که تصدیت ممالک محروسه باختیار شما میگذارم. این
عزیز، نظر بران معنی، گفت که از مدتی با وزیرم. مناسب نیست
که او ناکام باشد و من کار خود پیش برم. پس انسب آنست که او
را دستوری بهرت پور شود. من و سورج مل بطریق مشایعت رویم
و از سرش واکرده موافق گفته کاربند شویم.

۱۶۷   غرضکه از چرب زبانی روغن قاز مالیده روز کوچ دکنیان، خود
و سورج مل به به بهانهٔ که نگارش یافت با بهیر و بنه از لشکر آنها
بجگرداری تمام سوار شده در بلم گڈه که حصاریست محکم
دوازده کروهی شهر آمده نشستند. وزیر و اسباب و خیمها روانه
پیشتر شدند. وکلای دکنیان هرچند بسماجت گفتند، اما بشنیدن
حرف آنها نپرداختند و نسبت خود بشاه درست ساختند. رئیس
دکن که استقلال واقعی داشت و نظر بر لشکر بیشمار و آلات و
اسباب بیحد جمعیت ایشانرا بحساب نمی گرفت، چون شنید
بخود پیچید و گفت که اینها چه چیز اند. چراغ دولت اینها به
پفی دربند است. من باعتماد اینان از دکن نیامده ام. در مژگان
بهم زدن بخاک برابر خواهم کرد. تدارک این حرکت بر وقت دیگر
موقوف داشته، رفت، و قلعهٔ نجابت خان روهیله خان سرسواری

Mal, because he had contacts with his generals, was aware of the matter. One day, Bhau sent the following message to the raja: "I give you the governorship of all the imperial lands." The raja, in view of what he knew, replied, "I have been with the vazir for a long time. It does not seem proper that he should lose, while I make a selfish gain. The best thing would be to give him the authority to collect the revenues of Bharatpur. Suraj Mal and I will escort him there. Then, once we get rid of him altogether, we shall put into effect what you order." Thus he glibly kept Bhau mollified.

The day the Marathas were to set out for Delhi, the raja   167 and Suraj Mal used the already mentioned excuse and, with all their baggage and retinue, boldly left the Maratha camp and took up residence in the strong fort of Ballabhgarh, some 12 *kurohs* from Delhi. The vazir, 'Imad-ul-Mulk, with his camp and baggage, had already gone ahead. The agents of the Marathas pleaded with these men a great deal, but they did not pay any heed; instead they improved their ties with the shah. The Maratha chief was a truly resolute person; he also possessed an immense army and an enormous amount of war equipment. Consequently, he counted these men as amounting to nothing. When he heard what they had done, he swelled up with anger and vanity, and said, "They are nothing. One puff of my breath will put out the lamp of their glory. I did not come up north on the expectation of their support. I shall completely destroy them in an instant." However, he postponed that action for some later time. Instead, he proceeded to the fort of Najabat Khan Rohilla,*

* The battle of Kunjpura, October 17, 1760.

گرفته صمد خان را کشت و آن انبوه را پراکنده ساخت. چشم دکنیان از برهم زدن این فوج خیره شد. از آنجا برگشته متصل پانی پت سنگر بستند وآمادهٔ جنگ میدان شاه گشتند.

۱۶۸

وقتی که آب جون رو بکمی آورد، شاه بصد جوش و خروش با سرداران سمت مشرق از دریا عبور نموده دست جلادت کشود. چند روز پیش از جنگ صف خبر رسید که گوبند پنڈت با جم غفیرآمده است و انداز پیوستن لشکر دکنیان دارد. سرداری با فوج سنگین از لشکر شاه جدا شده دوید، وبی خبر رسیده او را بخاک و خون کشید. اسبابش همه بغارت برد. آن اجماع برهم خورد.

۱۶۹

درین ولا راجه در کمهیر که قلعهٔ سورج مل است، باو تشریف داد. منکه بحسب قسمت در آنجا بودم، رفته التماس نمودم که از چندی انتظار قدوم فرحت لزوم داشتم. اکنون اجازت شود بطرفی بروم که با روزگار ناسازگار طرف نمی توانم شد. از راه عنایتی که بحال من میداشتند، گفتند، معلوم شد که قصد بیابان مرگ شدن دارید، اما اگر من هم گذارم. همان روز چیزی جهت خرچ فرستادند و علوفهٔ من بدستور سابق دستخط کرده دادند.

۱۷۰

چون این بزرگوار بسبب آن که شاهجهان آباد خرابه بیش نمانده است و مردمان سالی دو بار خانها را بر خروس بار می کنند کسی تا کجا خانه بر دوش باشد، و درین سرزمین که

which he conquered, killing Samad Khan and scattering his forces. That victory dazzled the eyes of the Marathas. From there they proceeded onward and set up camp near Panipat and ringed it with cannons. Thus they prepared themselves to do battle with the shah in the open.

When the water in Jamuna receded, the shah, in great fury, crossed the river, along with the chiefs from the east, i.e., Shuja-ud-Daula, Hafiz Rahmat Khan, and others, and set himself up boldly. A few days before the battle proper, the news came that Gobind Pandit had arrived with a huge force and aimed to join up with the Maratha army. One of the shah's generals left with a large body of soldiers and, moving swiftly, fell upon him with total surprise. Gobind Pandit was killed, and his army was plundered and scattered to the winds.* 168

Around that time, Raja Nagar Mal paid Suraj Mal a visit at Kumher, one of the latter's many forts. Since I was there as my fate had dictated, I went to see him, and respectfully submitted, "I have been waiting for some time for Your Highness to arrive. Now please give me leave to go away, for I cannot withstand these extreme times." On account of the great kindness he felt for me, he replied, "It seems you have a wish to die in the wilderness, but that will happen only if I let you go." That same day he sent me some money for my expenses, and also signed an order for the payment of my usual salary.[47] 169

When this great man saw that Shahjahanabad was nothing but a wasteland, that people had had their houses destroyed twice in one year, that one could not go on forever living like 170

---

* December 16–17, 1760.

گوشهٔ عافیتی است و رئیس اینجا مرد آرمیدهٔ هست برخود نمی
شکند، توطن اختیار کرد، ما مردم نیز در سایهٔ دیوار او مقر خود
مقرر ساخته افتادیم.

۱۷۱   حقیقت هر دو لشکر آنکه اگر دکنیان بجنگ گریز که طور
قدیم آنها بود می جنگیدند اغلب که غالب می گردیدند.
ایشان توپخانه را گرد کرده نشستند. فوج شاهی در پی آن شد
که رسد نرسد. وقتیکه کار تنگ شد، سردار دکن مستعد حرب
گشت. سران از سنگر و سنگ چین برآمده میخ دوز ایستادند، و
جگرداران شاه میخ چشم آنها بوده بیک پهلو افتادند. کارگذاران
میدان کشیدن و برهم دگر زدن آغاز کردند. دلاوران پیکارجو
بند بر بند قبا بافته به پشت کمان گرفتند. نبردآزمایان جنگجو
بندوقها گرفته بدست و دندان چسپیدند. بر رو استادگان تیغها
آخته بر سر هم دویدند. بی دهل رقصانِ معرکهٔ کشت و خون
برکار سوار گشتند. پیش جنگان پیاده شده در آویختند و از هم
گذشتند. زخمها بجوانان رسیدند، جامه ها در خون کشیدند.
جنگ آورانِ عرصه تنگ آوران از دو طرف ریختند و تفنگها گرفته
آویختند.

۱۷۲   سردار دکن ثبات ورزیده پا بمیدان گذاشت و اکثر دستهای
فوج شاهی را از پیش برداشت. چون فتح از شاه بود از تردد کاری
نه کشود. هزار هزار بندوق می انداختند بیک نفر این طرف

a gypsy, that here was a place of refuge, and that the master of the place was not vainglorious but accommodating—he decided to settle down at Kumher. We ordinary beings also decided to take shelter in the shade of his wall and lay our burdens down.

Now the story of the two armies. Had the Marathas fought 171 in their ancient manner of "attacking and withdrawing," it is most likely that they would have won the day. But they stayed at one place and surrounded themselves with their artillery. The shah's army saw to it that they did not get any supplies. When things became too difficult for them, the Maratha chiefs decided to start the battle. Coming out from behind their guns and guard walls, they took up firm positions.* The bold soldiers of the shah, who had already been causing them much trouble, now set about it in earnest. Some warriors began repeatedly to form themselves into groups and attack. Other brave fighters formed a solid block and started to shower arrows on the enemy. Still other experienced soldiers grabbed their guns and fired incessantly. Adversaries drew swords and ran at each other. Mighty fighters attacked and killed as if in a frenzy. The horsemen of the vanguard came down from their saddles and threw themselves into the fray, only to die. So many were wounded; so many clothes were drenched in blood. Warriors who could make any battlefield uncomfortably small for their adversary poured forth from both sides and began blindly firing at each other.

Bhau, the Maratha commander, resolutely entered the 172 fray in person and drove away many of the troops of the

---

* January 14, 1761.

نمی رسید، و از دست تفنگ اندازانِ سهل مردانِ کارآمده از کار می رفتند. چنانچه در اول وهله تیر تفنگ بوسواس راؤ که ریاست بنام او بود رسید و بخاک و خون غلطید. میگویند که بهاؤ جوان غیوری بود و داد مردانگی میداد. دمی که این سانحه را بچشم خود دید، بر زبان راند که حالا روی رفتن دکن نماند. دل از جان برداشته، دندان بجگر افشرده بر قلب سپاه زد. یعنی دیده و دانسته خود را بکشتن داد. ملهار، پیر گرگ بغل زن، با دو سه هزار کس ازان مهلکه بیرون رفت و تمام لشکر غارت شد. سردارانی که زنده برآمده بودند برهنه بحال فقیران آواره شدند، و اسپ و سلاح هزارهزار سوار فرار نموده را ده ده زمیندار اطراف شهر گرفتند.

چه نویسم که چه روز سیاه بر این قوم آمد. هزاران عریان و گریه کنان از هر راهی که می گذشتند باعث عبرت می گشتند. مردم دیهات حبوب بریان کرده بهر نفر یکمشت میدادند، و احوال آنها را باحوال خود سنجیده زبانها بشکر میکشادند. شکستی این چنین کم اتفاق افتاده باشد. بسیاری از گرسنگی مردند و بسیاری از سردی هوا جان سپردند. فوجی را که در قلعهٔ شهر گذاشته رفته بودند، از خوف دست اندازی مردمان شاه هنگام شب گریخته رفت. جنس کرورها بدست لشکریان شاه و سرداران مشرق افتاد و باهم قسمت شد. توپخانه و آلات دیگر

shah who challenged him. But his efforts came to nothing, for it was the shah's destiny to win. The Marathas fired a thousand muskets, but not one person on that side was hit, while at the hands of the facile musketeers of the other side, experienced soldiers of the Marathas lost their lives. Thus, in the very first instance, a bullet hit Vishvas Rao, the Maratha prince and heir apparent, and he was fatally wounded. People say that Bhau was a man of honor and acted as his manly sense of honor demanded. On witnessing that tragic incident, he declared, "Now I do not have the face to go back home south." Renouncing all love for life and determined to take on any odds, he flung himself at the heart of the shah's army. In other words, he deliberately went forth and got killed. Malhar, that cunning old wolf, took some two or three thousand men with him and escaped from the massacre. The entire Maratha army was destroyed. The chiefs who managed to come out alive wandered around naked like beggars, while thousands of fleeing soldiers were robbed of their arms and horses by the local *zamīndārs*.

How can I describe the terrible day that these people saw! 173 As hordes of these bedraggled wretches drifted through the countryside, people could see how the mighty had fallen. The villagers gave each of them a handful of parched grain, and thanked God as they compared their condition with their own. Such a total rout has seldom occurred. So many died of hunger; so many others perished due to the cold. The force that had been left behind in the citadel of the city fled that night, fearful of the shah's men. The armies of the shah and the eastern chiefs came into possession of booty worth millions. They divided it up. Except for the cash and

حرب و فیل و گاو و شتر و اسپ سوای نقد و جنس شجاع الدوله
و غیره بپای خود گرفتند.

۱۷۴ درانیان که فقیران محضِ بودند سوار دولت گردیدند. با هر ده
باشی صدشتر بار، با یک نفر دو خروار. دولت عظیمی دست بهم
داد. هر یک کلاه کج نهاد. شاه، بعد ازین گونه فتحی که شاهان
سلف را هم میسر نه آمده باشد، با کروفر تمام داخل شهر شده
رقعها بنام سرداران اطراف و جوانب نوشت که بیایند و نوکری
نمایند. نوشتهٔ براجه نیز رسید. ایشان بگمان آنکه شاه بادشاه
هندوستان شد و ازین ملک زرخیز نخواهد رفت و ما را روزگار
باید کرد، رفتند. و نجیب الدوله پیشوا آمده برد، و ملازمت شاه
بدست شاولی خان وزیر او نمودند. صحبت بآن دستور دانشور
برآر شد. مهر خود حواله کرد و نیابت وزارت داد، چنانچه موجب
رفاه امرای عظام گشتند.

۱۷۵ وزیر یکبار گفت که پدر شجاع الدوله با شما تهدلی داشت
و این بابا طفلست و غیرِ بابائی کاری ندارد و نمی فهمد که این
شاه است. بیک پشتِ چشم نازک کردن جهانی را بر باد میدهد.
خبر شرطست. بادپرانی اینگونه بسیار بدماغش میخورد. نظر بر
رفاقت هیچ نمی گوید، لیکن برین غره نباید شد.

provisions, which the shah made his own, the rest—cannons, elephants, camels, horses, and cattle—was grabbed by Shuja-ud-Daula and others.

The Durranis, who had been mere paupers, now became 174 wealthy beyond imagination. Every sergeant had one hundred loaded camels, and every foot soldier had two asses loaded with goods. An incredible wealth fell into their hands, and every one among them became cocky and vain. After this victory, the like of which had not been gained even by ancient kings, the shah entered the city with full pomp and glory. Then royal edicts went out to all the neighboring chiefs, asking them to come and pay their respects. Raja Nagar Mal also received such a notice. He thought: *the shah has now become the emperor of Hindustan and is not likely to leave this rich land, and I'll have to serve him anyway*—and so he too went. Najib-ud-Daula came out to receive him, and had him presented to the shah through the shah's vazir, Shah Vali Khan.* The meeting with that wise minister was fruitful. He gave the raja his own seal and made him his own deputy. As a result he, the raja, was of benefit to many a grandee.

One day the vazir, Shah Vali Khan, said to the raja, "Shuja-ud-Daula's father was a good friend of yours. Shuja is still a youth, and does nothing but put on airs. He does not understand that he is dealing with a king whose merest sign of annoyance can turn the world upside down. One ought to be careful. Though his boastful ways greatly displease the shah, he does not say anything out of regard for Shuja's support. But one must not delude oneself and turn haughty.

* February 21, 1761.

بادشـــاهان و نکـــویان دو گروه عجبنـــد

که نبـــودنـــد و نباشـــــند بفـرمان کسی

بهتر آنست که شما و نجیب الدوله رفته او را معقول کنید، وگرنه
فردا جرم از ما نیست. رفتند و او را با تیغ و کفن آورده از وزیر
رخصتش گرفتند. باری صحبت کوک شد و کدورت بصفا انجامید.
من درین سفر بایشان بودم. روزی پرست زدم. راهم بر ویرانهٔ
تازهٔ شهر افتاد. بر هر قدمی گریستم و عبرت گرفتم، و چون
پیشتر رفتم، حیران تر شدم. مکانها را نشناختم، دیّاری نیافتم.
از عمارت آثار ندیدم، از ساکنان خبر نشنیدم.

از هرکه سخن کردم، گفتند که اینجا نیست

از هرکه نشان جستم، گفتند که پیدا نیست

خانها نشسته، دیوارها شکسته. خانقاه بی صوفی، خرابات بی
مست. خرابهٔ بود ازین دست تا بآن دست.

هـر کجا افتـاده دیـدم خشـت در ویـرانهٔ

بـــود فـرد دفتر احـــوال صاحب خانـهٔ

بازارها کجا که بگویم، طفلان ته بازار کجا. حسن کو که بپرسم،
یاران زرد رخسار کو. جوانان رعنا رفتند، پیران پارسا گذشتند.

۱۷۶

۱۷۷

194

The kingly and the pious, both are a strange breed:
Never subservient to anyone, nor will they ever be.

"It would be better if you and Najib-ud-Daula go to him and bring him to his senses. Otherwise, do not blame me tomorrow." The two went and brought Shuja-ud-Daula to the vazir in a submissive and penitent mood, and had the vazir forgive him. The meeting was successful, and all doubts were removed.

I was with the raja during that trip. One day, out for a walk, I happened to take the road into the newly ruined city of Delhi, outside the walled city of Shahjahanabad. At every step I shed tears and learned the lesson of mortality. And the farther I went, the more bewildered I became. I could not recognize any neighborhood or house. There were no buildings to be seen, nor any residents to speak to.

Everyone I mentioned was said to be not there anymore;
Everything I inquired about was said to exist no more.

Houses had collapsed. Walls had fallen down. The hospices were bereft of Sufis. The taverns were empty of revelers. It was a wasteland, from one end to the other.

Every brick that I stumbled upon in that ruined place
Was but a leaf torn from the book of the owner's life.

What can I say about the rascally boys of the bazaar when there was no bazaar itself? And what can I tell of my lover friends when there was nothing around of beauty? The

176

177

195

محلها خراب، کوچها نایاب. وحشت هویدا، انس ناپیدا. ربای
استادی بیادم آمد.

افتــاد گذارم چـو بویـرانـۀ طـوس
دیدم چغدی نشسته بر جای خـروس
گفتم، چه خـبـر داری ازین ویـرانه؟
گفتا، خبر اینست که افسوس افسوس!

۱۷۸ ناگاه در محلۀ رسیدم که آنجا میماندم. صحبت میداشتم،
شعر میخواندم. عاشقانه میزیستم، شبها می گریستم. عشق
با خوش قدان می باختم، ایشان را بلند می انداختم. با سلسله
مویان می بودم، پرستش نکویان می نمودم. اگر دمی بی ایشان می
نشستم، تمنا بر تمنا می شکستم. بزم می آراستم، خوبان را می
خواستم. مهمانی میکردم، زندگانی می کردم. دوست روی نیامد
که باو نفس خوش برآرم. مخاطب صحیحی نیافتم که صحبت
دارم. بازار وحشت گاهی، کوچه بصحرا راهی. ایستادم و بحیرت
دیدم. مکروه بسیاری کشیدم. عهد کردم که باز نیایم، تا باشم
قصد شهر ننمایم.

۱۷۹ هرگاه قرار یافت که شاولیخان با راجه برآید و ملک گیری نماید،
فوج شاه که از غنیمت مالامال بود بر در خانه هنگامه آرا شده
گفتند که ما بوطن خود میرویم. اگر شاه خواسته باشد بماند.

196

handsome young men had passed on. The pious old men had passed away. The palaces lay in ruin; the streets were lost in the rubble. There was desolation everywhere, and no sign of a human anywhere. This quatrain of the Master came to my mind:

> When I happened upon the ruins of Tus,
> I saw an owl where once a rooster crowed.
> "What can you tell me about this place?" I asked.
> "Alas, alas!" it replied. "Alack, alack!"[48]

Suddenly I found myself in the neighborhood where I had lived: where I gathered my friends and recited verses—where I lived the life of love and cried many a night—where I fell in love with slim and tall beauties, and sang high their praises—where I spent time with those who had long ringlets—and where I adored the beautiful ones. If I were without them for even a moment, I pined for them. This was where I had arranged joyous gatherings with beautiful people, feasted them, and lived a life worth the name. But now I saw no one familiar with whom I could spend a few happy moments. Nor did I run into anyone suitable with whom I could hold a conversation. Every bazaar was a place of desolation, and every street a track into wilderness. I stood there and gazed in amazement. I was horrified. I swore that so long as I lived I wouldn't even think of coming back to the city. 178

It was then decided that Shah Vali Khan and the raja should sally forth and bring more territory under their control. The soldiers of the shah's army—rich as they were with all the booty—gathered at the gate and began to shout: 179

مدتست که برای کار او برکار سواریم. از زن و فرزند خبر نداریم. شاه چون فکر نمود دید که بی فوج در ملک بیگانه نمی توانم بود. ناچار رفتن قندهار که دارالملک او بود مقرر گردانید. وزیر خیمهٔ برآمده را باز طلبید و از روی سرداران اینجا خجالت کشید. دو روز پیشتر شجاع الدوله و راجه را مرخص کرد و شهزاده جوان بخت را ولیعهد شاه عالم نمود، و شهر را باختیار نجیب الدوله گذاشته برخاستند. و در راه فوجدار سرهند زین خان نام افغانی را، که از قوم و قبیلهٔ آنها بود، کرده به لاهور رفتند.

۱۸۰   چون غرور این قوم از حد گذشت، غیرت الهی از دست سکهان که عبارت از ناکسان و شعربافان و ندافان و بزازان و سمساران و بذالان و نجاران و قزاقان و مزارعان و کم بغلان و پاچناریان و کلک خسپان و بازاریان و بی تهان و بی مایگان و تهی دستان آن نواح باشد، ذلیل ساخت. قریب چهل و پنجاه هزار کس گرد آمده خود را بر روی آن لشکر گران کشیدند. گاهی برنگی چهره می شدند که زخمها بر میداشتند و رو نمی گردانیدند، و گاهی طرف شده باطراف پریشان گردیده صد و دوصد را بدنبال می بردند و می کشتند. هر صبح گرد فتنه می انگیختند، هر شام از چارسو میریختند. لشکریان را سگان روی یخ ساخته بودند، یخ بسیار آب می گشت تا فرار می نمودند. گاهی سفید میشدند و بر بهیر و بنه می افتادند. گاهی سیاهی می نمودند و می استادند و بشهر

198

"We are going home. Let the shah stay on if he so desires. We have devotedly performed our duties long enough. But we haven't had any news of our wives and children." The shah thought over the matter and realized that he could not stay in a strange land without his army. Reluctantly, he decided to return to Qandahar, his capital. His vazir summoned back the camp he had sent ahead, and was thus embarrassed before the local chiefs. Two days before his departure, the shah gave Shuja-ud-Daula and the raja permission to leave, made Prince Jawan Bakht the heir apparent to Shah 'Alam, and placed the city in the custody of Najib-ud-Daula. On the way back, he appointed Zain Khan, an Afghan of his own clan, the commandant of Sirhind, then proceeded on to Lahore.*

The arrogance of these people, the Afghans, had crossed   180
all limits, and so God, in his justice, decided to humiliate them at the hands of the Sikhs—those men of no conse-quence, consisting of silk makers; cotton dressers; cloth merchants; market touts; grain dealers; carpenters; high-way robbers; peasants; lowly men of no means, name, or place; and mean, destitute, and disreputable people of that area. Some forty or fifty thousand of them came together and challenged that mighty army. Sometimes they boldly attacked and fought, and did not run away despite getting severely mauled. Other times they attacked, then withdrew in different directions, pursued by small bodies of Afghan soldiers, whom they later slaughtered. Every morning they created some new mischief, and each evening they attacked

---

* March 20, 1761. He reached Lahore on April 26, 1761.

می ریختند و سنگ بسنگ میزدند. مو پریشان و سرپیچدار در
اردو می شدند. شب، شر و شور؛ روز، عزّوگور. پیادهٔ آنها شمشیر
بر سوار زدی و قدح زین را خون ریز کردی. دست کشِ شان
قدرانداز را گرفته بردی و شست آویز نمودی. غرضکه این بی
ناموسان بی دولت آن بی حقیقتان بی مروت را آنقدر رسوا ساختند
که سرداران اطراف این صحبت را شنیده از نظرها انداختند.

۱۸۱   مقاومت بواقعی نتوانستند، سلامت رفتن خود غنیمت
دانستند. آخر سراپای نظامت آن شهر به هندوی داده راه پیش
گرفتند. این انبوه دنباله گردان، غارت کنان، سر گله زنان، تا آب
اتک رفت و شست و شوی خوبی داده متصرف آن صوبه که دو
کرور روپیه حاصل داشت، شد. بعد از چندی آن هندوی خون
گرفته شهرنشین را کشته مالک گشتند. چون وارث در میان نبود،
آن عوام کالانعام ملک را باهم قسمت نمودند و بر روی رعایا
در احسان کشودند. یعنی آگاه رسم ملک داری نبودند، هرچه
مزارعان دست برداشته دادند مفت خود شمرده گرفتند.

from every side. They sent the soldiers of the shah scurrying every which way, desperately trying to make an escape. Sometimes they suddenly appeared and pounced upon the baggage train and the people who followed the army. Other times they came in large numbers and resolutely attacking some town, turned it into ruins. With tangled beards and turbaned heads, they penetrated the camp itself. There was noise and tumult all night long, and all day long a hue and cry. Their foot soldiers attacked Afghan horsemen with swords and filled their saddles with blood; and their retainers pounced upon Afghan archers and tortured them to death. In short, these unworthy wretches humiliated those vainglorious brutes to such an extent that the chiefs of that region, on hearing of what had been happening, stopped showing the Afghans any respect.

The shah was unable to put up a real fight and decided   181
that it would be good enough if he got out of the country safely. He gave the governorship of Lahore to a Hindu and then marched off home. The Sikh horde, attacking and plundering, closely pursued him up to the river Attock. Having thoroughly punished the army of the shah, they took over that province, whose annual revenue was 20,000,000 rupees. After a while, they killed that ill-fated Hindu in Lahore and became masters themselves. Since there was no single deserving leader among them, these wild commoners divided up the country among themselves, opening the door of favors to their subjects. In other words, since they were ignorant of the ways of rulership, they accepted whatever any peasant gave them offhandedly and considered that a good enough gain.

۱۸۲ در همین سال سورج مل که زمیندار زورآوری است، آبا و اجداد او همیشه مورد عتاب بادشاهان اولوالعزم مانده اند و در حالتی که خبر بود راهداری مابین اکبرآباد و شاهجهان آباد باو تعلق داشت، در این ایام از سستی رؤسای اسلام سری کشید و متصرف اکثر محالات گردید. بسبب حرام توشگی قلعدار سیه روزگار حصن حصین اکبرآباد گرفت. شاه عالم بتحریک شجاع الدوله که حالا وزیر اوست، با لشکر بیشمار حرکت کرد. زبان زد خلق شد که برای اخراج سورج مل می آید. زمیندار مذکور جهت محافظت شهر و حصار مسطور از قلعجات خود رفته به ارادهٔ پرخاش نشست، و به راجه نوشت که آمدن شما مناسب تر است. ایشان که آشنا از چوب خشک میتراشیدند، میان دار فرستاده آن انبوه را باز گردانیدند. من باین تقریب بعد سی سال باکبرآباد رفتم و زیارات مزارات پدر و عم بزرگوار کردم. شعرای آن جا مرا سرآمد این فن دانسته اکثر ملاقات می کردند.

۱۸۳ آوازهٔ عالمی شنیدم. رفتم و دیدم. ملای قشری برآمد، یعنی بمغز سخن نمی رسید. هنوز نفس درست نکرده بودم که از بی تهی سخن سر کرد که اکثر جوانان این عهد رافضی می باشند و در حق بزرگان از سقیقه سازی چها که نمی تراشند. این تسبیح خاک امام شما که موجب غبارِ خاطرِ ما صفاپیشگانست، دلیل است که شما میل برفض دارید. اگر در واقع چنین است مرا بحال من

That same year, Suraj Mal—a powerful *zamīndār* whose   182
ancestors were always suppressed by bold and enterprising
kings, and who, while still sensible, had the responsibility
to maintain safe passage between Akbarabad and Shahjahanabad—saw the weakness of the Muslim nobles and,
rebelling, took control of large areas of land. Thanks to the
treachery of the wretched keeper of the fort of Akbarabad,
he also took hold of that fort.* Shah 'Alam, instigated by his
vazir, Shuja-ud-Daula, moved with a large army. People
began to say that he was coming to evict Suraj Mal. That
zamīndār, in order to defend the city and the citadel, came
out of his forts ready for battle. And he wrote to Raja Nagar
Mal that he had better come. The raja, who could turn even
a stiff piece of wood into a pliable ally, came, and sending an
emissary made that threatening horde turn back. Thus it was
that after thirty years I returned to Akbarabad,† and visited
the tombs of my revered father and "uncle." The poets of
that city, knowing me to be a master of the art of poetry,
frequently came to see me.

I heard high praise of a scholar and went to see him. He   183
turned out to be a mindless mulla who could never grasp
anything subtle. No sooner had I arrived than he said—
stupid that he was—"Many young men these days have
become Shia, and leave no falsehood unsaid concerning
the blessed elders. This rosary that you carry—made of the
'dust of the Imam'[49]—causes a pure-minded person like me
to be perturbed, for it strongly suggests that you might be

* June 12, 1761.
† December 1761 or January 1762.

203

واگذارید. گفتم که مرا نیز همین تردد بود. الحمدلله که صاحب
سنی برآمدند. مغزخرخورده کنایه نفهمید و بسیار خوش گردید.
چون مرا موافق یافت، پر و پوچ چندی بافت. بیمزه تر شدم و
برخاسته آمدم.

صبح و شام بر لب دریا که بسیار بخوبی واقع است، آنطرف
باغات و این طرف قلعه و حویلیهای امرای عظام، گوئی که نهر
بهشتی است، میرفتم، و چشم آب میدادم. شور بکرتراشی من
آفاق را گرفته بود. بکرنگاهان، مژگان سیاهان، خوش ترکیبان،
جامه زیبان، پاکیزه طینتان، موزون طبعتان مرا نمی گذاشتند و
بعزت میداشتند. دو سه بار سراسر شهر رفتم. علما، فقرا، شعرای
آنجا را دیدم. مخاطبی که ازو دل بیتاب تسلی شود نیافتم. گفتم،
سبحان الله! این آن شهریست که هر برزنِ او عارفی، کاملی، فاضلی،
شاعری، منشی، دانشمندی، فقیهی، متکلمی، حکیمی، صوفی،
محدثی، مدرّسی، درویشی، متوکلی، شیخی، ملائی، حافظی، قاری،
امامی، موذّنی، مدرسۀ، مسجدی، خانقاهی، تکیۀ، مهمان سرای،
مکانی، باغی داشت، اکنون جای نمی بینم که درو شادکام نشینم.
آدمی بهم نمی رسد که باو صحبت گزینم. خرابۀ وحشت ناکی
دیدم. رنجی کشیدم و برگردیدم. مدت چار ماه ازین قرار در
وطن مالوف گذارنیده وقت رفتن آب حسرت بچشم گردانیدم و
بقلعجات سورج مل رسیدم.

۱۸۴

so inclined too. If that is indeed the case, please leave me alone." I replied, "I too had my doubts. Thank God that you turned out to be a Sunni." That ass of a man did not get the point and was very pleased. Thinking that I was like him, he went on spouting more rubbish. I grew even more disgusted, and finally got up and left.[50]

Mornings and evenings I would go to the bank of the river   184
Jamuna and enjoy the sight. Such a beautiful place—with gardens on one side and the fort and the many establishments of great nobles on the other, you would say it was a river in paradise. The fame of my poetic genius had spread far and wide. Bashful beauties and those who had thick black eyelashes; those who coined fine phrases and those who dressed elegantly; and those who had a gift for poesy—all of them never left me alone and treated me with great respect. Two or three times I walked through the city from one end to the other and met with its scholars, Sufis, and poets. But I did not find any person to talk to who could comfort my restless heart. I said to myself, *Allah be praised! This is the same city where every street once had its share of gnostics, perfect masters, scholars, poets, prose writers, sages, jurists, dialecticians, philosophers, Sufis, scholars of the Hadith, schoolteachers, dervishes, spiritual mentors, mullas, Qur'an memorizers, Qur'an reciters, imams of mosques and those who called to the prayers, as well as madrasas, mosques, hospices, abodes of fakirs, inns for travelers, family homes, and gardens. But now I see not one place where I can sit and enjoy myself, and I find not one man whose company I may share and enjoy.* All I saw was a terrifying wasteland. And so I grieved and returned to where I was staying. After spending four months in the

۱۸۵ آنجا آمده شنیدم که با قاسم علی خان ناظم بنگاله و نصرانیان
تجارت پیشه که آنجا از مدت سکونت داشتند، جنگ واقع شد.
رعایا و زمینداران آن ملک از ستم بی نهایتش بجان آمده بودند،
جانب او نگرفتند. پایان کار هزیمت خورده، با لشکر شکسته و زر
و جواهر و اقمشه و امتعهٔ بسیار به عظیم آباد که این صوبه هم
باو بود آمد. فرنگیان نیز در رسیدند. خواست که شهربند شود و
بجنگد، لشکرش پشت داد. باز شکست افتاد. مال و اسباب خود
را بار نموده، با نه ده هزار کس بسرحد شجاع الدوله رسید. آنها
بالفعل دست برداشتند و قدم پیش نگذاشتند.

۱۸۶ وقتیکه متصل بنارس رسید، خیمه کرده بوزیر نوشت که من
بامید اعانت شما آمده ام. اگر سردستی بمن بگیرند و بجنگ
نصرانیان مخالف مذهب برآیند، خرچ سپاه و ملازمان حضور
متصدیان من سرانجام نمایند. ایشان نوشتند که اول شما بیائید
و ملازمت بادشاه نمائید. آنچه بحضور قرار خواهد یافت موافق
آن بعمل خواهد آمد. آن فلک کردهٔ آسمان غدار، ناآگاه از ته کار،
مع اسباب و آلات و پانصد فیل باعتماد خام دستان چند که
واسطه بودند، از آب آن رود خانه که زیر شهر مذکور واقع است
گذشته داخل لشکر شد، و دائره کرد.

city of my origin, I left it with my eyes awash with tears of longing and returned to the forts of Suraj Mal.

After arriving there I heard that a battle had occurred between Qasim 'Ali Khan, the *nāzim* of Bengal, and the Christian traders who had been settled there for some time. The peasants and the *zamīndārs* of that region— driven to despair by his endless tyranny—did not side with him. Consequently he lost and, with a battered army and plenty of gold and jewels and other rich possessions, came to Azimabad, as it was another territory that belonged to him.[51] The Englishmen also arrived there. Qasim wanted to lock himself inside the city and fight on, but his army fled and he lost once again.* He then loaded up his possessions, and with some nine or ten thousand people arrived at the border with the territory of Shuja-ud-Daula. The latter stayed put for the moment and did nothing.

When Qasim, moving forward, reached close to Benares, he set up camp and wrote to the vazir, Shuja-ud-Daula, "I have come hoping to receive your help. If you will come to my aid now and fight against the Christians, the enemies of our religion, my agents will take care of the expenses of your soldiers and retainers." The vazir wrote back, "You should first come and pay respect to the Emperor Shah 'Alam II. Whatever is decided in his majesty's presence will then be put into effect." That wretch, forsaken by fortune and unaware of the truth of the matter, took his baggage and possessions and five hundred elephants and, trusting the few greedy intermediaries, crossed the channel of the river

185

186

---

* June–September 1763.

207

۱۸۷ نظرِ تنگِ چشمان این طرف بر اسباب بادشاهانهٔ او افتاد. چشم
سیاه کردند و کهنه فعلهٔ چند فرستاده بفریب و غدر محبوسش
ساختند. بعد از دو سه روز از زرِ بسته و خرده و جواهر و اجناس
دیگر و اسپ و فیل و گاو و اشتر و خیمه و فرش هرچه داشت
وزیر بگفتهٔ آن ناماّل اندیشان پیش او هیچ نگذاشت. بدعهدان
که در میان بودند نظر به عهدنامه نداشتند. چون خامهٔ سیه رو
دندان بحرف خود گذاشتند. آمده بود که کسی دست او خواهد
گرفت، این جا انگشترِ پا شد. چون انگشت از ستم روزگار برآورد و
حلقه بر در وزیر زد، یومیه از سرکار بیگم که عبارت از مام شجاع
الدوله باشد، برای او مقرر شد. باقی داستان بفردا شب میگذارم
که افسانهٔ دیگر بر زبان دارم.

۱۸۸ جواهر سنگه پسر کلان سورج مل که سردار جگردداریست
از مدت خیال ریاست در سر دارد. چنانچه پیش ازین با پدر
درآویخته، خون بسیاری ریخته بود، و دو سه زخم دامن دار
برداشت. در این ایام به فرخ نگر که سه منزلی شاهجهان آباد
شهریست بسمت مغرب و سرحد آن بسرحد ملک پدر او پیوسته،
رفت، و با زمیندار آنجا که پدرش فوجداری گرد شهر مذکور
میکرد، آویزشی نمود و طول داد. او نیز سر فرود نیاورده در
افتاد. چون دو ماه برین گذشت، سورج مل با فوج سنگین قصد
آن طرف نموده بخانهٔ راجه برای رخصت آمد. ایشان گفتند که

that flows below the city. He then entered the vazir's camp and set up his own camp within it.*

The mean-eyed ones of the vazir's side saw his kingly possessions and became covetous. They sent to him some persons well experienced in deception, and through cunning and perfidy made him a prisoner. After a couple of days the vazir, on the advice of the reckless people around him, took away from Qasim his gold bars and gold pieces, jewels and other precious goods, horses, elephants, cattle, camels, tents and carpets—in short, whatever he possessed. Those perfidious people who had mediated between the two now ignored all that they had promised, just like the shameless pen that scratches out what it has itself written. He, Qasim, had come looking for support but found only a mirage. When he clamored for redress and petitioned the vazir, a daily allowance was settled on him by Sarkar Begum, the mother of Shuja-ud-Daula. The rest of the story I shall tell another night, for now I have another tale to relate.

Jawahir Singh, the eldest son of Suraj Mal and a brave chieftain, had long desired to be a chief in his own right. Earlier he had clashed with his father, causing much bloodshed and getting himself badly wounded. Now he marched to Farrukh Nagar, which is a city about three stages west of Shahjahanabad whose boundary touches the boundary of his father's estate. There he launched an attack on the *zamīndār* of the place, whose father used to be the commandant of that area, and let the conflict drag on. The adversary too did not give in and continued to retaliate. When

187

188

* February 1764.

شما زینهار نروید، مبادا باعث فتنه و هنگامه شوید. آنجا نجیب
الدوله هم قریب است. اگر مراعات اسلام کند، جنگ بمیان آید.
معهذا طرف ثانی قلعه دارد و صاحب الوس است، اگر سماجت
نماید و دیر شود عظم شأن شما نماند. در آداب ریاست نوشته
اند که تا کار از نفر برآید، باید که سردار به پسر نفرماید، و تا از
پسر شود، خود نرود.

۱۸۹   خاصهٔ انسانست که چون وعده قریب می شود حرف معقول
نمی شنود. گوش بر حرف ایشان مینداخت. رفت و رئیس
آنجا را اسیر ساخت. سپاهیان دست تعدی دراز نموده خانهای
شرفای آنجا را بغارت بردند. برادرانش که با نجیب الدوله بودند،
دستارها بر زمین زدند، و بی طاقتی نمودند. او برای خاطر آنها
ملتجی شد که ایشان به سزای کردهٔ خود رسیدند. اکنون از سر
تقصیر باید گذشت.

۱۹۰   نشنید و دلیرانه بشاهجهان آباد رفت. او بدر تغافل زده دروازه
های شهر را بند نمود، و سر بر نکرد. و این برخودچیده، متکبر
از آب دریا گذشته، بر سرش دوید و موجب آشوب گردید. در
آدم گری او شبه نیست. صد بار پیغام داد که من با شما سر
پرخاش ندارم، لهذا فوج خود را بر نمی آرم. غربای شهر تصدیع
می کشند. دایره کردن اینجا مناسب نیست. یک جواب آدمیانه
نداد، و بسفاهت گفته فرستاد که من فوج نواب را دیده خواهم

two months went by in that fashion, Suraj Mal decided to proceed there himself with a large army. When he came to take his leave of Raja Nagar Mal, the raja said to him, "You should not go there lest it cause greater trouble and strife. Najib-ud-Daula is close to that place. If he decides to take the side of Islam, you will have to fight him too. Besides, your adversary has a fort and also a large body of his own people—if he holds on for long, that will only diminish the awe of your name. It is written in the protocols of statecraft that a chief does not tell his son to do what might be done by a servant, and does not himself proceed with a task that might be accomplished by his son."

But when a man's time has come, he does not listen to sound 189 advice. And so Suraj Mal too closed his ears to the raja's wise words. He marched on Farrukh Nagar and took prisoner the master of that city, while his soldiers proceeded to plunder the houses of the local gentry.* The master's brothers were with Najib-ud-Daula; they threw their turbans on the ground before him to express their own abject helplessness. He, for their sake, pleaded with Suraj Mal: "Those who had erred have received their due. Now you should forgive and forget."

Suraj Mal, however, paid no heed and boldly marched on 190 Shahjahanabad. Najib-ud-Daula, anxious to overlook the matter, had the gates of the city closed and did not overtly challenge him. Suraj Mal, haughty and vainglorious, crossed the river threateningly and caused much havoc. There can be no doubt about the former's humanity. He sent word a

* December 1763.

211

رفت. اگر زود برآیند احسان است که کارهای دیگر نیز در پیش
دارم. وگرنه فوجی که در اختیار من نیست صبح و شام بشهر می
تازد. آن سردار گفت که البته صبح بر می آیم و سان فوج خود
می نمایم.

۱۹۱   شخصی که در میان بود بمن میگفت که دل شب فوج را
رخصت عبور دریا داد و خود واکشید. بعد از ساعتی چشم کشاد
و گفت که واقع عجبی دیده ام. گفتند چه طور است؟ گفت،
کلاغی بر درختی نشسته است و زاغان بسیار برو گرد آمده شوری
دارند. منکه ازان راه گذشتم، بیک تیرش بر خاک انداختم. زاغان
کشتهٔ او را دیده همه یکبارگی پریدند. غالب که فتح از من است.
انشاءلله صبح سوار میشوم و این سیاه درون را می کشم.

۱۹۲   چون صبح دمید، آسمان تیغ حادثه بچرخ کشید. جارچیان جار
زدند. خود بر فیل نشسته از آب گذشت و باستقلال تمام مقابل
گشت. حریف چون گاو چهارپهلو برخود شکسته و خر خود را
دراز بسته، صفوف فوج بر روی ایشان کشید. تفنگ چیان گرم
انداختن تفنگ؛ آزموده کاران نظر بر اسلوب جنگ. سردار این
طرف آمادهٔ کین استاده بود و پا از وضع خود بیرون نمی گذاشت.
رئیس آن طرف، دامن بالا زده، خودکشی می نمود و دست از
شوخی بر نمیداشت.

hundred times: "I have no quarrel with you, and that is why I do not come out with my army. But it is not proper for you to set up your camp here, for it causes much suffering to the poor people of the city." But Suraj Mal did not decently respond even once. On the contrary, he ignobly sent the message: "I shall leave after I have taken the measure of the nawab's army. He would do me a favor if he comes out soon, for I also have other matters to take care of. Otherwise, my soldiers are not in my control—they may attack the city anytime." Then Najib-ud-Daula responded, "Forsooth I shall march out tomorrow morning, and show you what my army is like."

Someone who was there later told me that at midnight, 191 Najib-ud-Daula ordered his army to cross the river, then lay down to catch a nap. After a while he opened his eyes and said, "I just had an amazing dream." People asked, "What did you see?" He replied, "I saw that a big raven was perched in a tree, and around it were fluttering a horde of small crows making a ruckus. I happened to pass that way and with just one shot of an arrow brought that raven down. Then the crows, seeing it dead, at once flew away. Now I'm certain that victory will be mine. God willing, I shall ride out tomorrow morning and kill this blackguard."

When dawn shone forth and the heavens unsheathed their 192 sword of contingencies, the heralds made their proclamations. Najib-ud-Daula mounted an elephant and, crossing the river, pitched himself firmly against the enemy. His adversary—fat like a buffalo, vainglorious, deluded about himself—arrayed his own army against him. Musketeers began to fire muskets. Experienced warriors began to plot strategies. The general on this side, i.e., Najib-ud-Daula,

۱۹۳ هرگاه روهیله ها سرگرم دوتیغه بازی شدند، او در دستهٔ خود را
پنهان ساخت و بالابالا رفته، غافل از این که اجل چیره دست در
کمین است، بر سپاهی که بسمت شهر بود زد. شوری برخاست.
روداران قلب بمدد آنها شتافته این بلا را برچیدند. در همان گرد
و غبار آن اجل رسیده زخمی برداشت که از اسپ بر خاک افتاد
و جامه گذاشت. اما کسی ندانست که این سورج مل است. باهم
می گفتند، وقتیکه او سمند را جلو خواهد داد، قیامت در جلو او
خواهد بود. ندانستند که جماعت دارست، و از پیش جنگی خود
را بکشتن داده است. از آن وقت تا شام باز جنگ بمیان نیامد.
آنجا کار تمام شد و اینجا هراسان که شب افتاده است، مبادا
شبخون زند و ما را بر خاک هلاک افکند.

۱۹۴ بعد شام فوجی که روبرو شده بود، پراگنده شد و رفت. تا نصف
شب مهیائی کار بر اسپ و فیل سوار استاده ماندند. اما همه
متامل که چه بلاست از آن طرف صدای بر نمی خیزد، نشود
که فوج حریف غافل بریزد و قیامت برانگیزد. جاسوسان از لشکر
برآمده دو سه کروه این طرف آن طرف کافتند. احدی را نیافتند.
قریب بشکستن شب آمده گفتند که از مردم دیهات شنیده شد
که جماعتی بسراسیمگی میرفت و میگفت، افسوس سرداری چون
سورج مل کشته شود و ما بیمروتان لاش او را بر خاک میدان
گذاشته از ترس جان برویم. ازینجا به ظهور می پیوند که او

desirous of revenge, stood firm but did not transgress his word, while the general on the other side girded his loins, strove hard, and did not refrain from mischief.

When the Rohillas engaged the enemy and hand-to-hand fighting began, Suraj Mal concealed himself in a band of horsemen, and making a furtive detour with them—unaware that ruthless Death lay in ambush for him—attacked the forces that stood closer to the city. A great cry arose. The brave fighters at the center rushed to their help and repulsed that devil. In all that tumult and dust, the man whom Death had marked received such a wound that he fell from his charger and expired.* But no one on Najib's side recognized that it was Suraj Mal. They kept saying to each other, "Beware, for when he comes riding forth our death will be marching behind him." They thought he was merely some leader of those troopers who had chosen to launch the attack and be first to die. But from that time on till evening there was no more fighting. All was over on that side. On this side, however, now that it was dark, everyone feared that Suraj Mal might make a night raid and cause much death and destruction.

As it turned dark, the opposing army scattered and disappeared. But on this side, the leaders stood alert and ready on their chargers and elephants. They were perplexed, for no sound could be heard from the enemy; they were fearful as well, lest the enemy attack them unawares and cause havoc. Spies were sent out for a few miles in every direction, but they came across not one enemy soldier. They returned near

* December 25, 1763.

در شورش آخر روز که بفوج التمش بود کشته شد، و لشکرش گریخته رفت.

۱۹۵   در این گفتگو بودند که صبح سفید شد، و سواری دست بریدهٔ آورد و گفت که این دست آن دست خشک شدهٔ اوست که جراحت داشت. دیگران نیز شناختند و کوس شادی نواختند. و چون به یقین پیوست، قدم بتعاقب کشادند و دنبال گریختگان افتادند. اگر از دریا می گذشتند باعث خرابی جهانی می گشتند. اما راجه نوشت که نواب این دولت را که عبارت از چنین فتح است از صحرا یافته باید که غنیمت بدانند، و عنان بگردانند. اینجا انبوه بسیار است. اگر استادگی نماید، باز کار دشوار است. رای درستی و قلب سلیمی داشت. نوشتهٔ ایشان را دید و بر گردید. جواهر سنگه که از استماع این خبر بفرخ نگر جان در تن نداشت و بظاهر خود را بمسمار دوختهٔ قایم بود، آمد و بر مسند ریاست نشسته در فکر گرد آوردن لشکر افتاد. در همت و شجاعت و مروت صد مرتبه از پدر خود بهتر است.

دولت ندهد خدای کس را بغلط

the end of the night and reported: "Some villagers told us that they saw a great number of people fleeing in disarray, and they were saying, 'Woe to us that a chief like Suraj Mal was killed and we faithless ones abandoned his corpse and ran away to save our lives!' It appears that he was killed in that engagement with our rear guard near the end of the day. After that his troops just ran away."

This talk was still going on when the first light of dawn appeared and a horseman arrived, bearing with him a severed arm. He said, "This is that withered arm of Suraj Mal that long ago had some surgery done." Others identified it too. They sounded the trumpet of celebration, and as their certainty increased they set off in pursuit of the fleeing army. In fact, had they then crossed the river, they could have caused tremendous damage to all and sundry, but Raja Nagar Mal wrote to Najib-ud-Daula: "The nawab should be satisfied with the victory that he has gained without any effort and should go back. Otherwise, it is a huge crowd of troops here and can cause him fresh trouble if it decides to make a stand." Najib-ud-Daula possessed a sound mind and a benign heart; he read the note and went back. Jawahir Singh, when he heard the news in Farrukh Nagar, was stunned, but made a show of holding himself together with diligence. Coming to Dig, Suraj Mal's main fort, he took his father's throne and set about the task of rebuilding the army. In aspiration, courage, and chivalry, he is a hundred times superior to his father.

Not for nothing does God give power to someone.

۱۹۶ حقیقت حال لشکر بادشاه و وزیر. حالانکه شجاع الدوله بگفتهٔ
ناکسان و ناتجربه کاران چند که در مزاجش تصرف داشتند، بطمع
صوبهٔ عظیم آباد، که اگر به یک تگ تگ پا بدست بیاید مفت
است، شاه عالم را با خود گرفته لشکر بآنصوب کشید. کشیش
عیسائیان، یعنی سردار فرنگیان شهر را محکم کرده نوشت که سر
بر سر کسیکه داشتیم او را زدیم و ازین ملک برآوردیم، با نواب
و بادشاه کاری نداریم. سبب این حرکت معلوم نمی شود که
چیست، و محرک سلسلهٔ فتنه و فساد کیست؟ اگر انقیاد منظور
است ما مطیع و منقادیم. حاجت بکشیدن این رنج بیفائده
نیست. وگر استیصال ما بگفتهٔ نوکیسه گانِ نافهم مقصود است،
گذر نداریم. مزاج بزرگان حکم سیل تند دارد؛ بهر جانب که رو
می آرد می آرد. ما خسان را چه سروسامان که سد راه توانیم شد.
طبعیت سرداران را بباد صرصر نسبت میکنند. ما که مشت
خاشاکیم چه ساز و برگ داریم که راه برتوانیم گرفت. نامعامله
فهمان حضور که بی بهره از شعور بودند، نوشتن بآدمگری آنها را
محمول بر بددلی نموده باصرار باعث کوچ شدند.

۱۹۷ هرگاه تلاقی فریقین در ظاهر آن شهر دست بهم داد، فرنگیان
بندوقها گرفته درآویختند. مغلان غیرت بحرام بر خزانهٔ آقا
ریختند. نصرانیان قدم جرأت پیش گذاشتند. عیسی نام چیلهٔ
نواب جسارتی کرد و جان داد. بادشاه چون تماشائیان ایستاده

218

Now an account of what happened in the army of the   196
emperor, Shah ʻAlam II, and his vazir, Shuja-ud-Daula. The
latter, falling for the advice given to him by some unworthy and inexperienced people who had influence over him,
took Shah ʻAlam with him and marched on Azimabad, thinking that it would be a windfall with just a little effort. The
head priest of the Christians, i.e., the chief of the *firangīs*,
reinforced the city's defenses, then wrote to Shuja-ud-
Daula: "We had our quarrel with a certain person, and so
we attacked and expelled him from this region. We have no
quarrel with either the nawab or the emperor. We do not
know what could have caused this action of yours, or who
could have sown the seeds of this strife and mischief. If you
seek our submission, we are obedient to you and submit—
you need not put yourself to trouble for nothing. But if you
seek to destroy us at the behest of certain ignorant upstarts,
then we have no choice. The mind of a lordly person works
like a fierce torrent that relentlessly proceeds in whatever
direction it takes. We are mere fallen leaves and twigs, how
can we hope to block its way? It is said that the disposition
of a chieftain is like a powerful blast of wind—we are only a
handful of dust, what means do we have to stand in its way?"
But the foolish companions of the nawab, ignorant of how
matters actually stood, mistook for cowardice the humane
words of those people, and insisted on marching on.

When the two adversaries engaged in battle at Buxar, in   197
the vicinity of the city of Azimabad, the *firangīs* grabbed
their guns and fought, while the ingrate Mughals looted
the treasury of their own master. As the Christians pressed
forward boldly, Isa, a particular slave of the nawab, fought

ماند. شکست افتاد. نواب، که بطرفی از اطراف می جنگید توقف مصلحت ندیده با معدودی راه صوبه پیش گرفت. مسافت بعیده را بیک و نیم روزی طی نموده بمقر خود رسید. از آنجا نقد و جنس و ناموس بضرورت برآورده روانهٔ فرخ آباد شد. اگرچه این عالم دارالجزا نیست اما گاهی چنین هم اتفاق می افتد، که این شکست فاحش بر این چنین لشکر گران کیفر آن بود که بقاسم علی خان کرده بودند.

۱۹۸ آنجا نصرانیان متصرف خیمه ها و آلات حرب و غیره گشته بادشاه را با خود گرفتند و بآرمیدگی عازم این طرف شدند. در عرصهٔ هشت هفت روز به اودیه که دارالقرار شجاع الدوله باشد آمده، شکرانهٔ این فتح که فوق تصور آنها بود مجوز آزار احدی نگشتند. بعد از هفته، بادشاه را دو لک روپیه ماهیانه کرده به اله آباد رخصت دادند که حضرت بطور خود باشند، ما دانیم و ملک.

۱۹۹ در خلال همین حال جواهر سنگه با لشکر غدار و ملهار که احوال او نوشته آمد، بدعوی خون پدر بر نجیب الدوله رفته به دهلی چسپیده بود. خلقی از گرانی غله بجان آمد. قتل و قتال، جنگ و جدال قریب دو ماه ماند. عمادالملک که در فکر کناره کردن بود، معه ناموس از قلعه بهرت پور برآمده مردمان زاید را بفرخ آباد فرستاد و خود شریک جواهر سنگه شد.

courageously and sacrificed his life. The emperor, all the time, stood by like a spectator, and soon a rout ensued.* Shuja-ud-Daula, who was engaged elsewhere on the battle-field, thought it better not to stay around and, accompanied by a few soldiers, took the road to his estate. Covering that long distance in just a day and a half, he arrived at his place of residence at Faizabad, took hold of whatever money, goods, and wives he needed, and proceeded on to Farrukhabad. Though this world is not the ordained world of just recompense, sometimes it does become one: the total rout of that vast army was the just deserts for what Shuja-ud-Daula had previously done to Qasim 'Ali Khan.

There in Bihar, the Christians took possession of the camp   198 and the materiel; then, holding the emperor in their custody, they marched this way at a comfortable pace. In about seven or eight days they reached Avadh, the place of residence of Shuja-ud-Daula, but in gratitude for a victory beyond their imagination, they caused no harm to any person. After a week or so, they settled on the emperor a monthly income of two lakhs of rupees and sent him off to Allahabad,† telling him: "Your majesty should now mind his own business. We shall take care of the business of the realm."

Meanwhile, Jawahir Singh, with the aforementioned   199 Malhar Rao and a huge army, had attacked Najib-ud-Daula to avenge his father's death and was holding Delhi in siege. The prices of food grains rose, and the people in the city were beginning to starve. The fighting and killing went on for

---

* October 23, 1764.
† February 1765.

۲۰۰ آخر از آمد آمد شاه که در این سال تا شاه آباد آمد و از تشویش سکهان بی سروپا برگشت، مسوده ها همه باطل شدند، و آن جنگ بصلح انجامید. عمادالملک با ملهار پیش احمد خان بنگش که ربط درستی داشت رفت، و جواهر سنگه بملک خود آمده بکارهای دیگر پرداخت. سرداران عهد پدر را که بخاطرش نمی آوردند، بعضی را کشت و بعضی را مقید ساخت.

۲۰۱ نواب عمادالملک باین سن کم یگانهٔ عصر است. اوصاف حمیده بسیار دارد. چنانچه پنج شش خط بخوبی می نویسد. شعر ریخته و فارسی هر دو بامزه می گوید. بحال فقیر عنایتی بیش از بیش می کند. هرگاه بخدمت شریف او حاضر شده ام حظی برداشته ام.

۲۰۲ تبئین مقال احوال شجاع الدوله آنکه بامید حمایت کسانیکه به فرخ آباد رحل اقامت افگنده بود، از آنها غیر از شماتت و بی مروتی ندید. ناچار با ملهار که احوال او سبقاً مذکور شد، طرح سلوک انداخته انبوهی گرد آورد و بجنگ فرنگیان برد. چون مقابلهٔ فئتین شد، بادلیجها از طرفین انداختن گرفتند. دسته های فوج دکن، برای نمود جرأت خود، بر روی توپخانه رفته نیزه بازی نمودند، و دست خونریز کشودند. عیسائیان از سنگر بآهستگی برآمده، توپ اندازان بوضعی درآمدند که چشم دکنیان ترسید و ترکی تمام گردید. آنچنان دست و پا گم کرده گریختند که گوئی

222

almost two months. 'Imad-ul-Mulk, who had been looking for some way to part company with the Jats, came out of the fort of Bharatpur with his family, then himself joined Jawahir Singh but sent the rest of his party to Farrukhabad.

Eventually, the news that the Shah 'Abdali Durrani was on his way—he came up to Shahabad, then turned back, harried by the wild Sikhs—made void all the plans of Jawahir Singh, and that campaign ended in a truce. 'Imad-ul-Mulk, with Malhar, went to Ahmad Khan Bangash, with whom he was on good terms; Jawahir Singh returned to his own territory and busied himself with other matters. Many Jat chiefs of his father's days had offered him little respect and aid, so he had some of them killed and others sent to prison. 200

Nawab 'Imad-ul-Mulk, despite his young years, is a fine and matchless person and possesses many praiseworthy qualities.[52] He writes very well in five or six different styles of calligraphy and also composes pleasing verses in both *rekhta* and Persian. To this humble person he always shows utmost kindness. I have been pleased every time I have attended upon him. 201

Now some more of what happened to Shuja-ud-Daula. He had come to Farrukhabad, and stayed there the while, hoping to obtain support from Ahmad Khan Bangash. But he received only abuse and neglect. Seeing no other recourse, he established ties with Malhar, the Maratha leader about whom we wrote earlier, and put together a joint army. He then launched an attack on the *firangīs*. When the two armies met,* their artilleries began an exchange of bombardment. 202

* May 3, 1765.

در میان نبودند. در دو سه روز بگوالیار، که سه منزلی اکبرآباد
شهریست حاکم نشین و در تصرف آنها بود، رسیدند، و حال
شکستهٔ خود را در چند روز درست کرده آمادهٔ جنگ جواهر سنگه
شدند. آنجا دعویٰ شجاع الدوله قطع شد. راضی بمرگ خود بوده،
تن تنها پیش فرنگیان رفت. آنها رو ازو گرفته دست از همه چیز
برداشتند، و صوبجات را بطور او گذاشته به عظیم آباد رفتند.
هرگاه رفع حجاب بادشاه و او شد، باز خلعت وزارت پوشیده
خلیع العذار بدارالقرار خود که اوده باشد آمد و نشست.

٢٠٣ اینجا دکنیان تیره روزگار، با فوج بسیار بسرحد جواهر سنگه
آمده، اکثر دیهات را تاختند و خراب ساختند. جواهر سنگه که
دلاور مقرریست، از قلعجات برآمده، هشت نه هزار سوار سکهان
که دران ایام دران ضلع آمده بودند، نوکر کرده رفت و چهره
شد. هنگامیکه جنگ بهم پیوست آن مدبران رو باختند، و ایشان
با سر و نهیب پرداختند. چنانچه قریب پانصد کس با سرداری
اسیر کرده آوردند، و عرض سپاهگیری آنها بردند. چون ملهار مرد
روداری بود و شکست بر شکست خورد، از فرط اندوه و غم سه
چار منزل رفته مرد.

The Maratha troops, to flaunt their gallantry, charged at the opposite cannons and with their lances killed a great many. But the Christians stealthily came out of their entrenchments and, firing their cannons, launched such an attack that the Marathas were scared witless and their arrogance turned to dust. They fled in desperation and disappeared as if they had never been there. In two or three days, they reached Gwalior, which is three days' journey from Akbarabad and a regional headquarter under their control. There they took a few days to reorganize, then got ready to attack Jawahir Singh. The ambitions of Shuja-ud-Daula came to naught. Having reached the end of his tether, he went all by himself to the *firangīs*. Embarrassed at the sight of his sorry state, they renounced their claim and returned his territories to him. Then they went back to Azimabad. After reconciliation with the emperor, Shuja-ud-Daula again received the robes of the vazir. Free of all worries, he then returned to Avadh, his permanent base, and settled down.

Here, the ill-fated Marathas came with a large army to the borders of Jawahir Singh's territory and plundered several villages. Jawahir Singh, a truly bold man, came out of his forts and took into his service some eight or nine thousand Sikh horsemen who had come into that area at that time. He then went and confronted the Marathas.* When the fighting started, the luckless Marathas lost all courage in the face of the terror and deceit employed by their opponents. They lost all taste for soldiering, and some five hundred of their men and one chief were taken prisoner. Since Malhar was a man

203

* March 13 and 14, 1766, near Dholpur.

۲۰۴ به همین نزدیکی رگهناته راؤ که سردار مقرری دکنیان است، با
فوج کثیر رسیده بیکی از زمینداران آنطرف سرحد جواهر سنگه
چسپید، و موجب فتنۀ آن ملک گردید. زمیندار مذکور بایشان
رفتگی داشت. نوشت که اگر دکنیان مرا پایمال ساختند، یقین
خاطر باشد که بملک شما هم دست تصرف دراز خواهند کرد.
آمدن بسرحد خود از واجبات است و صرفۀ من نیز درین است.
این جوان فراخ دامان با لشکر بی پایان رفته این طرف چنبل
که رودخانۀ مشهوریست، دایره کرد. دکنیان دودله شده طرح
یکدلی انداختند. هنوز هر دو لشکر محاذی بودند که خبر آمدن
شاه شایع گشت. سران دکن که از نام او آب می تاختند، جگر
درباخته رهگرای اوطان خود گشتند، و بشکستن قید اساریٰ که
در جنگ ملهار بگیر آمده بودند، صلح نمودند. این عزیز بعضی
نمک بحرامان را که با دکنیان درساخته چها که نمی گفتند،
گوشمال بواجبی داده باکبرآباد آمد.

۲۰۵ راجه از قلعه برآمده برای ملاقات او رفت. مرا زیارت مشت
خاک پدر و عم بزرگوار باین تقریب باز میسر آمد. همگی پانزده
روز آنجا مانده عنان انصراف بگرداندند. این بار هم شاه درانی تا
این طرف ستلج که رود معروف است، از دست سکهان پا در هوا
خرابیها کشید و برگشت.

of honor, he was overwhelmed with grief and dejection at these consecutive defeats, and had covered only some three or four days' journey when he passed away.

Around that time, Raghunath Rao, a major Maratha commander, arrived with an immense army and attacked a *zamīndār* who had lands bordering the lands of Jawahir Singh. Much havoc was created. Since the *zamīndār* had friendly ties with Jawahir Singh, he wrote to him, "Be assured that if the Marathas destroy me, they will stretch their hands over your territory too. You must come to the border of your estate now. Therein also lies gain for me." That noble young man marched forth with an army beyond measure and set up his camp this side of the Chambal, which is a well-known river. Now the Marathas had second thoughts about the whole affair, and started efforts to make peace. The two armies were still facing each other when the news spread that Shah 'Abdali Durrani was on his way again. The Maratha elders, who pissed in fear at any mention of his name, quickly made peace with Jawahir Singh in return for the release of the prisoners taken in the battle with Malhar, and fled home in utter dismay. Jawahir Singh, that excellent man, duly punished certain of his own men who had betrayed his "salt" and secretly conspired with the Marathas. He then turned around and proceeded to Akbarabad.

The raja left the fort he was in and went to Akbarabad to meet him.* In this manner I received a second opportunity to gain the blessed sight of the graves of my father and my "uncle." The raja stayed there for fifteen days all together,

204

205

---

* January or February 1767.

۲۰۶ درین ولا جواهر سنگه را با راجهٔ مادهو سنگه پسر جی سنگه
بر امری از امورات زمینداری ناخوشی شد، و رفته رفته بنزع
کشید. این جوان جری بخرابی ملک او کمر بسته در ظاهر ببهانهٔ
ملاقات راجه بجی سنگه پسر بخت سنگه که احوال او رقمزدهٔ
کلک سحرطراز گردید، بر پهکر که آبگیر کلانیست غیرت بحیره و
هنودان غسل آنجا را عبادت میدانند، رفت و در راه اکثر قریات
را بخاک برابر ساخت. بجی سنگه اگرچه جوان بود لیکن رای
صایبی داشت، آمده برخورد، و واسطهٔ صلح شد. عهد و پیمان
بمیان آمد. چون جواهر سنگه برگشت، سرداران راجه مادهو
سنگه نقض عهد نموده آمادهٔ پیکار شدند. تا دوپهر جنگ تیر و
تفنگ در میان ماند. آخر راجپوتان جهالت کیش از اسپان فرود
آمده دست بشمشیرها زدند. پای ثبات اکثر از جا رفت. این
جوان دلاور داد داد جوانمردی داده این چنین بلائی صعب را برچید.
چون شام افتاد بر هر دو لشکر شکست افتاد. آتش تیز کین از هر
دو سو زبانه کش است و رعایا مثل خس و خاشاک می سوزد. باید
دید که از پردهٔ غیب چه ظهور میرسد.

۲۰۷ چون جواهر سنگه بقلعجات آمد و نشست، فوج راجپوتان
بخیرگی تمام دست تاراج بدیهات نواح دراز کردند، و باستظهار
دکنیان آبادیها را خراب نمودند. درین ایام انبوهی از سکهان
آنطرف آب جون بود. رئیس این طرف بآنها مستظهر شده،

then returned. This time too, the Durrani king came up to this side of the well-known river Sutlej, but then, having greatly suffered at the hands of the worthless Sikhs, he went back home.

Meanwhile, Jawahir Singh had a quarrel with Raja Madho   206
Singh, son of Jai Singh, on some matters of *zamīndārī* that gradually grew worse. This bold young man decided to destroy the territory of that raja and, under the pretense of going to meet Raja Bijai Singh, son of Bakht Singh— the latter's story was described by my magic-creating pen earlier—marched to Pushkar, a lake big enough to shame a sea and where the Hindus consider it a religious duty to bathe, ravaging many a village on his way. Bijai Singh, young but right in thinking, came and met him, and became a mediator. Mutual promises were then made. But when Jawahir Singh was on his way back, the chieftains of Raja Madho Singh broke their promise and attacked.* A battle of bullets and arrows raged for six hours. Finally, the barbaric Rajputs got down from their horses and drew swords. Many people lost courage and fled. However, this bold man, Jawahir Singh, proved true to his mettle and remained steadfast against such heavy odds. Now fires of enmity blaze on both sides, and the common people burn like dry leaves and twigs. Let us see what appears from behind the veil of the Unseen.[53]

When Jawahir Singh returned to his forts and settled   207
in, the Rajput army, with utmost treachery, began to ravage the countryside and, with the aid of the Marathas, plundered many villages. At that time, there was a large

---

* December 14, 1767.

طرف گشت. کشت و خون بمیان آمد. عالمی تلف گشت. آخر
فوج حریف را از ملک خود بدر کرده سرداران سکهان را بر روی
آنها دوانید، و رفتن خود مصلحت ندید. این قوم دغلی باآنها
درساخت، و باین سردار بد باخت. هرگاه بدعهدی این بی سر و
پایان دید، کار بسیار به بی مزگ کشید. در همین حال اقبال یاوری
کرد که راجه مادهو سنگه بسبب بیماری که داشت درگذشت.
سرکردگان آن فوج ناچار سربسر کرده برگشتند، و سکهان بی ته از
همان راه گذشتند.

٢٠٨   سانحهٔ عظیمی آنکه درین نزدیکی جواهر سنگه باکبرآباد رفت
و از دست ناکسی به یک زخم شمشیر جهان فانی را پدرود نمود.
ریاست به راؤ رتن سنگه برادر او رسید. این سیه کار مدام شراب
میخورد، و بر خلق خدا جفا از حد می برد. چنانچه در ریاست
ده ماه با کس و ناکس بد باخت. آخر مهوسی بزخم کارد کار
او ساخت. سرداری بنام پسر او کیهری سنگه مقرر شد. اختیار
بدست نوکران افتاد، کار ابتر شد. اکنون کارپردازان، نول سنگه
پسر چارمین سورج مل را که در عرصه نبود، به نیابت آن طفل
برداشته اند. اگر از آب خوب بر می آید خوبست، وگرنه کار بسیار
بی اسلوب است.

band of Sikhs on the other side of the river Jamuna. The chief on this side, i.e., Jawahir Singh, made them his allies and launched an attack on the Rajputs. A bloody battle ensued, and innumerable people were killed. Eventually he managed to push the enemies out of his territory; then, considering it prudent not to go himself, he sent the Sikhs in further pursuit. Those treacherous Sikhs secretly made peace with the Rajputs and began to conspire against Jawahir Singh. The latter was greatly irritated when he learned of the treachery of those worthless people. But then his good fortune came to his aid: Raja Madho Singh of Jaipur succumbed to the illness that he had.* Consequently, his generals made peace with Jawahir Singh and returned home, whereupon the worthless Sikhs followed suit and left Jawahir Singh's territory.

A major tragedy followed when Jawahir Singh went to   208
Akbarabad and some wretched man there dispatched him from this mortal world with just one stroke of the sword.†
The estate then devolved to his brother, Rao Ratan Singh.
That wicked man was always drunk, and ordinary people suffered beyond limits at his hands. In just ten months of his rule he made everyone his enemy, high and low. Finally a demented man stabbed him to death. His son, Kheri Singh, was named the new chief; power passed into the hands of the subordinates; and the affairs of the state fell into disrepair.
At present, they have made Nawal Singh the regent of that child; he is the fourth son of Suraj Mal but is not a contender

* March 1768.
† August 1768.

٢٠٩ وقتیکه نفاق این قوم به طول کشید و نوبت کارپردازی ملک
به سفها رسید، نول سنگه و برادر خورد او رنجیت سنگه که قلعهٔ
کمهیر باو تعلق دارد، هر دو بجنگ برخواستند. قریب پانزده
شبانروز جنگ توپ و بان و تیر و تفنگ در میان ماند. چون قلعه
استحکام واقعی داشت، ناچار نول سنگه بدر صلح زد و گذاشت.
هرچند در میان هر دو برادر بظاهر صلح و صفا شد اما کینه باطنی
را چه علاج؟ جیارام که سرکردهٔ فوج رنجیت سنگه و مدارالمهام
بود در لشکر دکنیان، که در آن ایام چار پنج منزل آن طرف می
گشتند، رفت. سرداران را ترغیب نموده در ملک خود راه داد.

٢١٠ همین ها که حالا گوشهٔ کله به آسمان هفتم میرسایند، بحال
خراب باو آمده زیر دیوار قلعهٔ کمهیر دایره کردند. آنقدر دل
باخته بودند که از هر کس می پرسیدند، فوج نول سنگه چه قدر
است و چه قسم می جنگد. اگر نول سنگه از جای خود حرکت
نمی کرد کار او باین خرابی نمی کشید، و دکنیان هم بطریق
ضیافت چیزی گرفته میرفتند. چنانچه حرکت بجانب متهرا کرده
بودند، که هنگام شب ناآزموده کاران نول سنگه قریب گوردهن
که آن هم معبد هنودانست آمده پریشان جنگیدند. صد این جا
و دوصد آنجا، هزاری این جا و پانصدی آنجا، ازین جهت هرکه هر
جا بود همان تنها بود. کسی بداد کسی نرسید. نسیم فتح و ظفر بر
پرچم علمهای دکنیان وزید. اسپان و فیلان و شتران و آلات حرب

it seems like religious conflict is starting to stir up

himself.[54] It would be nice if some good comes of it, otherwise things are in very bad shape.

When the Jats' internecine conflict was prolonged and affairs of state fell into the hands of foolish people, Nawal Singh and his younger brother Ranjit Singh, master of the fort at Kumher, engaged in mutual hostilities. For nearly fifteen days there was a fierce battle of guns and cannons and rockets and arrows. But the fort was truly strong, and Nawal Singh had to make peace and withdraw. There was now an apparent peace between the two brothers; but is there a cure for ingrained animosity? Jiya Ram, the commander of Ranjit Singh's army and his chief minister, went to the camp of the Marathas, who happened to be in that area in those days at a distance of some four or five days' journey. He made promises to their chiefs and invited them into his own territory. {209}

The Marathas, who presently show themselves so high and mighty, came with him in a wretched state and set up camp under the walls of the fort at Kumher. They were so scared that they would ask everyone: "How large is Nawal Singh's army? How is it in battle?" Had Nawal Singh not stirred from his place, his fortune would not have declined as it did—the Marathas would have accepted some money as "a gift to guests" and moved away. In fact, they had started to march toward Mathura when the inexperienced warriors of Nawal Singh haphazardly attacked them one night near Gowardhan—it too is a sacred place for the Hindus. A hundred here and two hundred there; a thousand at this place and five hundred at that place—this is how they were, each for himself. None came to the help of the others. Consequently, the breeze of victory unfurled the Maratha {210}

بسیار این طرف بدست قلقچیان آنطرف افتاد. بر چنین شکست
هم نتوانستند که بقلعجات نول سنگه بچسپند. غنیمت شمرده
از رودخانهٔ جون گذشتند و میان دوآب خیمه گاه ساختند.

چون اقامت ایشان بامتداد کشید، نجیب الدوله که از حزم
بهرهٔ وافی داشت، با خود سنجید که این بلا بالابالا نخواهد رفت.
مبادا که آسیبی بشهر رسد. با پسر و برادر و فوجی که همراه بود
توکل کرده پیش سرداران آمد. تا جان در تن داشت نگذاشت که
دکنیان رو بسوی شهر کنند. وقتیکه او از مرض مزمنی که داشت
از میان رفت، سرداران بر امری از امورات سهل ناخوشی بضابطه
خانِ پسرِ او در میان آوردند. آخرالامر او واسوخته بسکرتال رفت،
و ایشان قریب شهر آمده خیمها زدند.

چون بدپردازی و ناسازی جائان از حد گذشت و لطف باش
و بود بالکلیه رفت، راجه ناگرمل با بست هزار خانهٔ مردم دهلی
که آنجا بسبب این مرد آباد شده بودند و اکثر وابستگی بدامن
دولت این داشتند، برخاستن مقرر کرد، و اجازت از سرداران آنجا
خواست. آن بی چشم و رویان که هنوز در کمین آزار مردمان اند،
بلیت و لعل گذرانیده خواستند که در بنای عزم این سرکرده خلل
انداز شوند، و بآهستگی دست تطاول کشایند. هرگاه بیقین پیوست
که اینها نمی گذارند بلکه سد راه می شوند، راجه نظر بر خدا
کرده، آنچه لازمهٔ سرداریست بکار برده با هر دو پسر بجرأت تمام

banners,* and many horses, elephants, camels, and tools of war of this side fell into their hands. However, despite such a victory, they did not dare to attack the forts of Nawal Singh. They thought it better to be satisfied with what they had gained, and crossing the Jamuna set up camp in the *doab*.

When their stay in that area continued for too long, Najib-ud-Daula, a wise and vigilant person, concluded that "the plague" was not going to disappear quietly. Lest it reach the city itself, he took his son and his brother and the army that was with him, and confidently came to the Maratha chiefs. So long as he lived he did not let them move toward the city. But when he died of the chronic illness that he had,† the chiefs quarreled with his son Zabita Khan over some insignificant matter. He was greatly peeved and went off to Sakar Tal; meanwhile the Marathas came and set up camp near the city.

When the nasty intrigues and ill behavior of the Jats went beyond all limit and life became entirely unpleasant, Raja Nagar Mal decided to leave, along with some twenty thousand families from Delhi who had settled there on his account and of whom most were dependent upon him. He asked permission of the chiefs of that place. The wretches, being bent upon harming people—as they are even now—delayed him with one pretext or another, wishing to defeat him in his purpose and gradually expand their own dominance. When it became obvious that they were not going to let him leave—and in fact, might block his way—the raja put his trust in

211

212

—————

* April 6, 1770.
† September 30, 1770.

سوار شد و بیرون قلعه آمده چنان همت بامداد غربا گماشت که
ناموس نفری هم آنجا نگذاشت. از لطف دادار بیهمال و بیمن
نیت خوب بخیر و خوبی در دو سه روز معه این قافلهٔ گران داخل
کامان، که شهر سرحدی راجه پرتهی سنگه پسر مادهو سنگه است
و حالا رئیس او را قرار داده اند، گشت. ما تلخ کامان نیز بسبب
علاقهٔ نوکری و وابستگی درین شهر اقامت گزیده ایم. می بینم که
آبشخور چندی اینجا نگاه میدارد یا جای دیگر می برد.

۲۱۳

درین ایام مشهور شد که رایات اقبال بادشاهی بفرخ آباد سایه
افگن گشت. راجه مرا پیش حسام الدین خان که در مزاج بادشاه
تصرف داشت، فرستاد. رفتم و عهد و پیمان درست کرده آمدم.
این جا پسر خورد او که با من خوب نبود، از آن سبب که من با
برادران کلانش ربط گونه داشتم، علی الرغم به پدر فهمانید که
پیش دکنیان رفتن اولی است. چنانچه به لشکر بادشاه نه رفتند
و عازم شهر گشتند. ناچار من نیز معه لواحقان خود برسوائی تمام
با ایشان شدم. چون بشهر رسیدم، زن و فرزند را در سرای عرب
گذاشته از درِ ایشان برخاستم. بعد از دو سه روز با رای بهادر
سنگه برخورده حقیقت حال همه بیان نمودم. آن بابا موافق
مقدور خود در پرداخت احوال شکسته ام تقصیری نکرد.

God and did what is required of a chief. With his two sons, he boldly rode out of the fort and provided such earnest assistance to the poor refugees that not one family was left behind. Thanks to the mercy of the Matchless Dispenser of Justice and the blessing of his own good intentions, the raja and his huge train of followers safely reached Kaman in just a couple of days. It is a city that borders upon the territory of Raja Pirthi Singh—son of Madho Singh—who has now been made the ruler of Jaipur. We, the long-suffering people, being employed in his service and dependent on him, are also staying in this city, waiting to see if destiny keeps us here for a while or takes us elsewhere.[55]

At that time it was widely reported that the banners of the emperor's glory were fluttering over Farrukhabad.* Raja Nagar Mal sent me to Husamuddin Khan, who was close to the emperor. I went and exchanged pacts and promises, then came back. In the meantime, the youngest son of the raja—he did not like me because I was especially close to his older brothers—persuaded his father that it was best for him to go to the Marathas. Consequently, they did not go to the royal camp and instead set out for the city, i.e., Delhi. I had no choice but to go along ignominiously, together with my dependents. When we reached the city, I left my wife and son at "Sarai Arab,"[56] and parted company with the raja at his mansion. A few days later, I attended upon Rai Bahadur Singh, the eldest son of Raja Nagar Mal, and told him the full story. The young man did all that was in his power to help us in our plight.

213

* July 1771.

۲۱۴ درین ولا سندهیا، که یکی از سرداران کلان دکن است، پیشوا رفته بادشاه را با خود آورد و داخل شهر کرد. چندی برین نرفته بود که سرداران باهم قرار دادند که بادشاه را با خود گرفته بر ضابطه خان پسر نجیب الدوله مرحوم باید رفت. هرچند بادشاه تعلل ها بمیان آورد، فائده نکرد. باین تقریب من با هم با رای بهادر سنگه همراه لشکر بادشاهی روانهٔ آنطرف گشتم. رفتند و ضابطه خان را بی جنگ گریزانیده اموال و اسباب و خانه و ناموس او بتصرف درآوردند. بادشاه را غیر از دوصد اسپان لاغر و چند خیمهٔ کهنه نه دادند. بادشاه ازین حرکت بسیار بی مزه ماند. اما چه فائده که دکنیان مغتر و اینجا نه زور و نه زر.

۲۱۵ چون زور بآنها نرسید، متصدیان حضور بضبط جاگیرات اعزهٔ اینجا پرداختند، و بسا عزیزان را ذلیل و خوار ساختند. ازین جهت رای بهادر سنگه را نیز دستی نماند. من بگدائی برخاسته بر در هر سرکردهٔ لشکر شاهی رفتم. چون بسبب شعر شهرت من بسیار بود، مردمان رعایت گونه بحال من مبذول داشتند. باری بحال سگ و گربه زنده ماندم و با وجیه الدوله وجیه الدین خان برادر خورد حسا م الدوله ملاقات نمودم. آن مرد، نظر بر شهرت من و اهلیت خود، قدری قلیلی معین کرد و دلدهی بسیار نمود.

۲۱۶ القصه چون بادشاه از سرکشی رئسیان دکن دل خوشی نداشت، بی مرضی آنها روانهٔ شهر شده داخل قلعه گشت. اینجا آمده،

238

Meanwhile, Sindhia, who is one of the senior chiefs of the   214
Maratha, went out to receive the emperor, Shah 'Alam II, and
escorted him into the city.* Not many days later, the Maratha
chiefs mutually decided to take the emperor with them and
attack Zabita Khan, the son of the late Najib-ud-Daula. The
emperor put up many excuses, but to no avail. I too at this
time, in the company of Rai Bahadur Singh, went with the
royal army. Zabita Khan fled without putting up a fight, and
all his wealth and goods and even the members of his household fell into the hands of the Maratha chiefs. They gave
nothing to the emperor except two hundred decrepit horses
and some old tents. The emperor was highly displeased but
could do nothing. The Marathas were vain and bold, while
the emperor had neither power nor gold.

When they could do nothing to the Marathas, the emper-   215
or's retainers turned to confiscating the estates of some of
the local nobles, and thus robbed and dishonored many of
them. As a result, Rai Bahadur Singh too lost his wealth. I
went around like a beggar to the tent of every chief in the
royal army. Since I was well known for my poetry, they
treated me kindly enough, and I survived for a while living
like a dog or a cat. Eventually I met Vajihuddin Khan Vajih-
ud-Daula, the younger brother of Husam-ud-Daula. That
man, taking into consideration my fame and his resources,
reassured me much and fixed a small salary for me.

To make the story short, the emperor, peeved at the   216
perversity of the Maratha chiefs, left the camp for the city

* January 6, 1772.

نجف خان که خود را در لشکر بادشاهی سپاهی میگرفت، بادشاه
را ناسنجیده و نافهمیده برین پله آورد که محالات متعینه جاث
را متصرف باید شد. آخر باصرار تمام اجازت این امر عظیم، بی
مشورت حسام الدوله که با سرداران دکن ربط تمام داشت، گرفته
ده پانزده هزار مردم مفلوک شهر و بیرونجات گرد آورد و شروع در
آن مهم نموده دوازده محالات نزدیک شهر را متصرف شده طرف
کلاه برشکست. چون کم سن و نادیدهٔ روزگار بود، بگفتهٔ سفیهان
ناماّل اندیش از جای رفته مستعد حرب دکنیان گردید.

۲۱۷ آنها با خود مشوره کردند که هنوز بادشاه مانا بگداست، باین
زور و طاقت ارادهٔ مقابلهٔ ما کرده است. اگر زور واقعی بهم خواهد
رسانید، کار بر ما تنگ خواهد کرد. بهتر آنست که از دوآبه کوچ
بطرف شهر نمائیم و فرصت نداده کار او بسازیم. اگر در جنگ از
میان برود رفته باشد، وگرنه سرجنگی زده انبوه کذائی را پراگنده
سازیم، و خودش را بحال فقیران نگاه داریم که بنان و نمک معاش
می کرده باشد و دست نگر ما باشد.

۲۱۸ هرگاه این مشوره قرار یافت، ضابطه خان را، بوعدهٔ بخشی گری
و سهارنپور که از تصرف او برآورده ببادشاه داده بودند، خوشدل
ساخته رفیق نمودند. فوج جاث را نیز برین منوال همراه گرفته،
از میان دوآب بتریهای تمام در عرصهٔ یک هفته برابر فریدآباد
آمده عبور دریا پایاب کردند.

against their wishes, and took up residence in the citadel.* Here Najaf Khan, who considered himself a warrior of note, began to persuade the emperor—without due thought or consideration—to confiscate the districts that had been assigned to the Jat leader. Eventually, after much persistence and without the advice of Husam-ud-Daula—who had close ties with the Maratha chiefs—he received permission to undertake that enormous task. He gathered together some ten or fifteen thousand destitutes from the city and elsewhere, launched the campaign, and took possession of twelve districts close to the city. This greatly turned his head. Young in age and inexperienced, he got carried away by the advice of some foolish and reckless people, and now made plans to take on the Marathas.

The Marathas, on their part, took counsel among themselves: "The emperor is still a beggar, and yet he makes bold to challenge us. If he becomes really strong, he will make our lives difficult. We had better leave the *doab* immediately, march on the city, and make short work of him. If he escapes, we shall let him go; otherwise, after our victory, we shall scatter his horde but keep him like a destitute under our control, obliged to subsist on our charity."

Once they had agreed on that plan, the Marathas won over to their side Zabita Khan, son of Najib-ud-Daula, by promising him the rank of *mīr bakhshī* and the territory of Saharanpur that they had earlier snatched from him and given to the emperor. Similarly, they induced the Jat forces to come along with them. Then they left the *doab* and, causing much

217

218

---

* July 9, 1772.

۲۱۹ دو سه روز زد و خوردی ماند. آخر روزی جنگ بمیان آمد. ازین
طرف هم نجف خان و بلوچان و موسی مدک فرنگی که باغوای
نجف خان از نوکری جات دست برداشته ملحق این فوج فلک زده
گشته بود، پای جلادت به میدان معرکه فشردند. چون سیاهی
فوج دکنیان دیدند، مغلان حرام توشه پشت داده روسیاهی
گزیدند. اجل رسیدگان چند که جامه هم بر تن نداشتند، مفت
زخم هائی دامن دار برداشته بوادی عدم شتافتند. دستهٔ آن طرف
میدان را خالی یافته بی محابه به شهر درآمد. فیلان بادشاهی و
یراق بسیاری را بر سر گریختگان گذاشته با خود برد. پریشانی چند
که جمع شده بودند، بیک چشمک زدن از میان رفتند.

۲۲۰ تا یکپاس شب گذشته حسام الدین خان با معدودی چند
در ریتی استاده ماند، و باز برخاسته پیش بادشاه رفت. قریب
نصف شب نجف خان نیز مظلومان چند را بکشتن داده داخل
حویلی خود شد. شهر کهنه که جسته جسته آبادی داشت، در
این سانحه از سر نو بغارت رفت. ما غربا را حافظ حقیقی در حفظ
خود نگهداشت.

۲۲۱ صبح جراران این طرف تاب مقاومت نداشتند که بمیدان
برآیند. مورچال برابر دیوار شهر پناه درست کرده بجنگ بادلیجها
آن روز گذارنیدند. اقبال بادشاهی کار کرد وگرنه آنها قلعهٔ مبارک
را هم می پرانیدند. سلیقهٔ جنگ و استعداد این طرف همان روز

distress on the way, reached Faridabad in one week, where they crossed the river Jamuna.

After minor skirmishes for a couple of days, there was 219 finally a decisive battle.* On the emperor's side, Najaf Khan, the Baluchis, and M. Madec,[57] the *firangī*—he had been seduced by Najaf Khan into leaving the service of the Jats and joining his ill-fated army—stood firm on the battlefield. But the treacherous Mughals turned tail when they saw the huge Maratha army and fled ignominiously. A few wretches whose time had come were fatally wounded for nothing, and shuffled off to the vale of nonexistence. Whereas some troops of the other army, seeing the field clear, rode unchallenged into the city and took away the royal elephants as well as huge quantities of weapons and goods, loading the loot on the fugitives from the field. Thus the motley crowd that had come together disappeared in the twinkling of an eye.

Until the first watch of the night, Husamuddin Khan, 220 together with some soldiers, remained standing on the sandy plain below the ramparts; then he retreated and attended upon the emperor. Near midnight, Najaf Khan, after ordering the execution of a few hapless people, also returned to his mansion. The Old City that had human habitation only here and there was ravaged once again. The True Protector, however, looked after us helpless people.

Next morning, the stalwarts of this side did not have the 221 courage to return to the battlefield. Instead, they set up embankments beside the city wall and spent the day firing off cannons. The emperor's glorious fortune worked in his favor,

---

* December 17, 1772.

معلوم شده بود که چون آمدآمد فوج دکنیان شد هوش اکثری
رفت، و مردم توپ خانه برای تیاری آلات حرب مثل توپ رهکله
و [جزائیل] افتاده و سرب و باروت و بان و غیره عرضی بحضور
اقدس کردند. متصدیان صد روپیه به میرآتش، که از برف خنک
تراست، تنخواه کردند. هیئت و سبلت او اگر بینی دانی که
مردمان چنین می باشند. آنچنان در کنجی خزید که تا جنگ در
میان بود او را کسی ندید. آخر روز سوم حسام الدوله سوار شده
رفت و صلح دلخواه آنها کرده آمد. باری شهر نو سلامت ماند.
اکنون باشارهٔ مختار دکنیان در پی برآوردن نجف خان و مغلان
حرام کوزه اند. به بینم که چنان صورت میگردد. این ادباززدگان
چه طور از شهر بر می آیند و بکجا میروند.

۲۲۲   القصه سندهیا که سردار سیومین دکنیان بود بطرف جی پور
رفت. سرداران دیگر ارادهٔ آن طرف آب دارند، غالب که از راه
فرخ آباد به جهانسی بروند، و از آنجا سبب آشوب ملک شجاع
الدوله شوند.

۲۲۳   چون زبان زد مردم شهر بود که نجف خان و غیره سرداران
و مغلان شوره پشت دعوی تنخواه در سر دارند، هرگاه دکنیان
کوچیده میروند، این جم غفیر بر درِ بادشه نشسته متصدیان را
تنگ کرده زرِ طلب خود خواهند خواست. لهذا حسام الدوله به
دکنیان گفت که اینها نمک بحرام و هنگامه پردازند. بهر طوریکه

otherwise they might have sent flying to bits the royal citadel itself. The talent and fighting ability of these warriors had become apparent the day the news came that the Maratha army was on its way. Most of these men lost their wits right away. The men in charge of the artillery petitioned the emperor for money to get their tools of war ready—such as different kinds of cannons and muskets, lead, gunpowder, rockets, et cetera. His accountants assigned 100 rupees as salary to the chief of the artillery. Though called "Master of Fire," he is colder than ice, even if on seeing his build and whiskers you might exclaim, "Ah, that is how a man should look." He crept away into some corner so carefully that no one saw him during the entire engagement. Finally, on the third day, Husam-ud-Daula rode out and made peace with the Marathas on their terms. At least the New City, i.e., Shahjahanabad, remained safe. At present, at the instigation of the mukhtar, Husam-ud-Daula, the Marathas are deter-mined to have Najaf Khan and the treacherous Mughals expelled from the city. Let us see how things develop, how these woe-stricken people leave the city, and just where they finally go.[58]

In the event, Sindhia—the third-ranking Maratha chief—went off to Jaipur. Now the other chieftains are thinking of going across the river. Most probably they would go to Jhansi via Farrukhabad, and from there cause havoc in Shuja-ud-Daula's territory. 222

It was on everyone's lips that Najaf Khan and other mili-tary commanders—as well as the refractory Mughals—were determined to recover their wages, and that, once the Marathas packed up and left, a mob of these men would 223

دانند همت بر اخراج ایشان بر گمارند. حالا حسب الاشارهٔ او
سرداران جنوب در پی آنند که آن قوم را از شهر برآرند. چنانچه
قدغن است که که مغلی در شهر نماند.

۲۲۴ وقتیکه این گفتگو بطول کشید و متصدیان حضور در قلعه رفته
نشستند و مردم شهر را بند کردند، در ظاهر آن گروه بی شکوه
تا لاهوری دروازه [مورچالها] بسته آتش فتنه و فساد برکردند،
و بباطن با دکنیان که بالقوه روکشی آنها نداشتند درساختند.
چون از هنگامه آرائی کار پیش نرفت و دیدند که در استادگی
کشته خواهیم شد، ناچار مهیای برآمدن شده با جنوبیان عهد و
پیمان نمودند. بعد از دو سه روز نجف خان و دیگر سرکردهای
مغلان با همه یاران خود در لشکر آنها رفته فرود آمدند. اهل
دکن که صاحب سلوک اند و مراعات ظاهر را در هیچ وقت نمی
گذارند، در عزت این ازدحام نافرجام تقصیری نکردند. اما آن
عزت که در نوکری پادشاه بود معلوم. در چند روز این جماعت
بی حقیقت پراگنده می شود. هر کس بطرفی خواهد رفت. و همین
مشهور است که بالفعل دکنیان این هئیت مجموعی را تا اکبرآباد
با خود می برند و از آنجا اجازت خواهند داد که هر کس هر جا که
خواسته باشد برود.

۲۲۵ الحاصل مغلان شرارت بنیاد و جنوبیان سراپا فساد قریب
است که بروند، و حضرت ظل سبحانی بذات قدسی صفات با دو

(handwritten annotation at top: expulsion of Mughals from Maratha held city)

gather at the emperor's door, pester the account keepers, and demand payment of their promised wages. Consequently, Husam-ud-Daula, the mukhtar, said to the Marathas, "These men are treacherous and troublesome. You should endeavor to expel them any way you can." And so presently, at the suggestion of that nawab, the Maratha chieftains are bent on expelling them, and an order has been issued that no Mughal should remain in the city.[59]

When the matter dragged on and the emperor's account keepers holed themselves up inside the citadel and closed its gates on the city's people, that worthless mob set up battle lines up to the Lahori Gate, and began to create much mischief. But that was only on the surface; at heart they knew they did not have the strength to fight the Marathas, and so quietly began to make a deal with them. When their mischief won them nothing and they realized that they would be slaughtered in any battle, they agreed to leave the city. After a couple of days, Najaf Khan and other Mughal chiefs—together with their followers—went to the Maratha camp. The latter are a hospitable people and never fail to show courtesy in public; they received that good-for-nothing crowd with due honor. Of course, the honor they had in the service of the emperor was something else. In a few days, this worthless mob will be scattered—they will all go their separate ways. It is widely reported that for the moment the Marathas will take them to Akbarabad with them, but on arrival give them permission to go wherever they wish.

In sum, the mischief-mongering Mughals and the evil-incarnate Marathas are about to go away, while His Majesty,

(margin note: 224)

(handwritten annotation at right: mughals — now "good for nothing")

(margin note: 225)

سه محرر در قلعهٔ مبارک بی تشویش آینده و رونده تشریف دارند. اگر روزی صد بار بر کنگرهٔ حصار جهت سیر برآیند، کیست که حجاب او مانع شود. وگر به بازار پیاده پا برآیند حاجب کو که دورباش نماید. اسلوب چنین به نظر می آید که اهل حرفه سر بصحرا زنند، و سپاهی پیشگان بگدائی دست دراز کنند. هر کسی راه خود گیرد؛ شهر رونق بسیار پذیرد.

۲۲۶ تازه آنکه چون جنوبیان نجف خان را همراه گرفته رو بآن روی آب آوردند، وزیر حال از صوبهٔ خود باستظهار نصرانیان یلغار کرده به فرخ آباد رسید و روکش گردید. چون سرداران جنوب خود را در آن مرتبه نیافتند که حریف آنها شوند، قریب سه ماه به قیل و قال گذارنده خواهان صلح شدند. وزیر که دلاور مقرری بود غنیمت دانسته قبول این معنی نمود. آخرالامر نجف خان را مختارکار حضور کرده روانهٔ صوبهٔ خود شد. دکنیان هم جواب و سوال خود باو سپرده به مکان های متصرفه رفتند.

۲۲۷ چون نجف خان داخل شهر گردید، رنگ از روی حسام الدوله پرید. دو سه روز در خانه نشست، بعد ازان پادشاه در قلعه طلبداشته کاغذ حساب چند سالهٔ خود را طلب کرد و همان جا نگاهداشت. مجدالدوله عبدالاحد خان پسر عبدالمجید خان مغفور که از کارپردازان مقرری پادشاهی بود، از تغیر راجه ناگرمل خلعت دیوانی خالصه پوشید و به کاروبار پادشاهی پرداخت. پایان

the Shadow of God, resides by his angelic self in the Blessed Fort with a couple of scribes, and has no worry as to who comes or goes. If he were to come out a hundred times a day to stroll on the ramparts and enjoy the scenery, there is none whose presence might give him pause. And if he were to walk out into the marketplace, there is none who would keep people away from him. It seems that all the artisans and tradesmen will abandon the city and take to the wilderness, and the men of soldiery will make the rounds as beggars. Each man will go his separate way—and the city will gain more glory![60]

Here is the latest. When the Marathas, taking Najaf Khan with them, set out to cross into the *doab,* the present vazir, Shuja-ud-Daula, with the support of the Christians, marched forth from Avadh. Arriving at Farrukhabad, he stood ready to face any attack. When the Marathas found they were in no position to challenge him, they dilly-dallied for almost three months, then eventually expressed a desire to make peace. The vazir, being truly bold, accepted that as good enough. He made Najaf Khan the regent for all imperial affairs and returned to his own place. The Marathas too gave Najaf Khan the authority to settle their claims and went back to their own territories.

When Najaf Khan returned to the city,* Husam-ud-Daula turned pale with fear and did not stir out of his house for a few days. Then the emperor summoned him to the citadel and, after asking him to submit the accounts for the previous few years, had him held in custody there. Majd-ud-Daula

226

227

* May 1773.

کار بادشاه حسام الدین خان را که مختارالملک بود مجبور ساخته بابت زر پادشاهی و تنخواه مغلان بعوض هشت لک روپیه حوالهٔ فتح علی خان درانی و غیره نمود. او از قلعه بخانهٔ خود برد. حالا مغلان مختار اند خواه بکشند و خواه بگذارند:

این شامت اعمال قیامت بسر آورد

آنچه ظاهر است حسام الدین خان در حقیقت از میان رفت، چراکه بدست دشمنان جانی افتاده است. تا مقدور زنده نخواهند گذاشت. پیشتر اختیار خداست که او بر همه چیز قادر است.

احوال فقیر از سه سال آنکه چون قدردانی در میان نیست و عرصهٔ روزگار بسیار تنگ است توکل بخدای کریم که او و رذاق ذی القوةالمتین است کرده بخانه نشسته ام. ظاهر اسباب ما اعزه چند مثل ابوالقاسم خان برادر خورد عبدالاحد خان مجدالدوله و وجیه الدین خان برادر حسام الدین خان و بیرم خان صاحب خلف الصدق بهرام خان کلان که در آدمی روشی یکتای روزگار خود اند، و قطب الدین خان پسر سعدالدین خان خانسامان، اگرچه سنش کم است اما فهم درستی دارد و خالی از سعادتمندی نیست، و قاضی لطف علی خان که او میانه میزید، گاه گاه ملاقات کرده می آید. خواه از دست ایشان انتفاعی برسد یا نرسد مایهٔ توکل این هما صاحبان اند. و گاهی اینچنین هم اتفاق میشود که کسی فقیر

'Abdul Ahad Khan, son of the late 'Abdul Majid Khan who was a devoted servant of the emperor, was given the robes of the revenue minister of the crown lands—in place of Raja Nagar Mal—and began to take care of the emperor's affairs. Eventually, the emperor, holding Husamuddin Khan, the former Mukhtar-ul-Mulk, responsible for the royal income and for the salaries of the Mughals, extracted 800,000 rupees from him, then handed him over to Fateh 'Ali Khan Durrani and others.[61] The latter took him from the citadel to his own house. Now the Mughals are in full control—they might kill him or they might let him go.

His misdeeds brought him this day of doom.

Obviously, Husamuddin Khan can be said to be dead already, for he is in the hands of his mortal enemies. If at all possible, they shall not let go of him alive. It is all in God's hands, of course, for he has power over one and all.[62]

As for the life of this humble man over the past three years: since connoisseurs are not to be found and times have become extremely hard, I have stayed home, placing my reliance on God, the Magnanimous, for he is the most powerful Provider. In appearance, though, support has come to me from some of the nobles, such as Abul Qasim Khan, the younger brother of 'Abdul Ahad Khan Majd-ud-Daula; Vajihuddin Khan, the brother of Husamuddin Khan, and Bairam Khan Sahib, the eldest son of Bahram Khan Sr.—they are all unique in their humanity. And from Qutbuddin Khan, the son of Sa'duddin Khan, the Khansaman, who is young but wise and does not lack in felicitous behavior; and

228

251

و شاعر و متوکل دانسته بطریق نذر چیزی میفرستد. محل شکر
است. اکثر قرضدار میباشم و بعسرت تمام بسر میکنم.

۲۲۹ درین مدت کم، این یک یک قطرهٔ خون که دلش می نامند انواع
ستم کشید، و همه خون گردید. مزاج ناسازی داشتم؛ ملاقات
همه کس گذاشتم. اکنون که پیری رسید، یعنی که عمر به پنجاه
کشید، اکثر اوقات بیمار می باشم. چندی درد چشم کشیدم.
ضعف بصر بچشم خود دیدم. عینک خواستم و دست بهم
سودم. نظر بر این شعر ترک نظربازی نمودم:

دیده چون محتاج عینک گشت، فکر خویش کن
بــر نفــس دارنـــد روز واپســـین آئینـــه را

از وجع الاسنان خود چه گویم؛ حیرانم که چاره تا کجا جویم:

روزی خــود را بـرنج از درد دندان میخـورم
نان بخون تـر میشـود تا پارهٔ نان می خـورم

غرضکه از ضعف قویٰ و ناتوانی، و بی دماغی، و دل شکستگی، و
آزرده خاطری معلوم میشود که دیر نخواهم ماند. زمانه هم قابل
ماندن نمانده است. دامن باید افشاند. اگر خاتمه بخیر شود
آرزوست، وگرنه اختیار در دست اوست.

from Qazi Lutf-e 'Ali Khan, who leads a most decent life and frequently comes to see me. Whether they help me or not, they are all upon whom I now depend. It also happens sometimes that someone, believing me to be a fakir and a poet and resigned to God's will, sends me something as a pious offering. That too is something I should be grateful for. More often I am in debt and live in great poverty.

During this brief spell of time, that drop of blood that people call "heart" suffered many a torture. Having a discordant disposition, I stopped meeting with people. Now that old age is upon me, i.e., I am fifty, I frequently fall ill. For some time I had trouble with my eyes, and realized that my sight was growing weak. I needed spectacles, and eventually obtained a pair and felt better. But then, in view of the following couplet, I gave up "the game of glances." 229

> *Think of your end when your eyes begin to need glasses,*
> *   for it is*
> *on the deathbed they check for your breath with a looking*
> *   glass.*

And what should I say of the pain in my teeth—I am at my wits' end. How long must I go on treating them?[63] (Author's verse:)

> *My aching teeth! It's an agony to eat my daily bread.*
> *Each morsel needs my blood to make it soft to swallow.*

In short, the decline of my powers, my irritability, the loss of strength, my despair and despondence—they tell me that

۲۳۰ عبدالاحد خان که دیوان خالصه شده بود و در مزاج بادشاه
دخل تمامی کرد، مختار گشت و هرچه میخواست میکرد.
کسی را یارای دم زدن نبود. فوج بادشاهی باحال تباه، بادشاه
بیدستگاه. بر سایر شهر و چند ده گذران معلوم. جاٹ که
عبارت از اولاد سورج مل باشد تا درگاه حضرت خواجه قطب
الدین بختار کاکی که از شهر سه چهار کروه است، متصرف بود.
نجف خان پیش بادشاه عرض میکرد که حضرت، زندگانی باین
قسم ظاهر است. اگر این ملکی که در تصرف جاٹ است بدست
بیاید، نصف دل خوش بسر می توان کرد. بادشاه میگفت،
مگر خواب می بینید. سخن که از دهن خود خود زیاده باشد چرا
باید گفت. او می گفت، گر چنین اتفاق شود، حضرت مرا چه
میدهند. بادشاه گفت، سوم حصهٔ از ملک من بگیرم، باقی بخش
شماست.

۲۳۱ چون ادبار آن قوم نزدیک شد، روزی فوج آنها بمیدان گرهی که
قریب درگاه خواجه مسطور علیه الرحمه است، آمد و آغاز شوخی
کرد. نجف خان با مردمی که یراق هم نداشتند حرکت مذبوحی
کرده بروی آنها دوید. آنها که مغرور بودند، بخاطر نیاورده
زودبودی نمودند. چون جنگ بمیان آمد صورتی که متصور نبود
جلوه گر شد. یعنی تا شام آن جنگ زدند. مردمان پادشاه شب
بزراعت خام معاش کرده هم آنجا اقامت انداختند، و کوس

the end is not far. The times too are not fit to live in. It would behoove me to withdraw and take my leave. If my end is well I shall get what I desire, but otherwise too it is all in God's hands.[64]

'Abdul Ahad Khan, who had become the *dīwān* of the crown lands and had much influence over the emperor, became the master of everything and did as he pleased. None dared to complain. The imperial army fell into disrepair; the emperor himself had no power. His only income was from the city octroi and a few villages. The Jats, i.e., the descendants of Suraj Mal, held sway over the environs of the city up to the *dargāh* of Khwaja Qutbuddin Bakhtiyar Kaki—it is about six or eight miles from the city itself. Najaf Khan would often say to the emperor, "Your Majesty, we know what life is now like. If we take possession of the land that is presently under the control of the Jats, we might then at least have a halfway decent life." The emperor would reply, "You must be dreaming. Why talk of that which is beyond your means?" To which Najaf Khan once responded, "What will you give me, sire, if it actually comes about?" The emperor said, "I shall take one-third of the land; the rest will be all yours."

Since bad days had come for the Jats, a force of theirs arrived at Maidan Garhi, near the *dargāh* of the said khwaja, "May God bless him," and began to do their mischief. Najaf Khan put his life on the line, and taking some troops that didn't even have the necessary weapons, went out and confronted them.* The Jats, being arrogant, did not think much of him and showed little concern. But when the

230

231

* September 1773.

شادی نواختند. صبح آن قدم پیش گذاشته، به بلم گَدَه که حصار مضبوط آنها بود بفاصلهٔ دوازده کروه از شهر، رفته چسپیدند.

۲۳۲ چند روز جنگ توپ و رهکله در میان ماند. سردار آنجا گفت، از گرفتن حصار جنگ جاثان تمام نمی شود. پیشتر بروید. جنگی که با سرداران است، آن جنگ را بزنید. این حصار را با من بی جنگ خالی کرده خواهم داد. نجف خان باین سن کم سردار سخن شنو بود. دست از آن حصار برداشته، همان سردار را آنجا گذاشته، ارادهٔ پیشتر نمود. چون قریب هورل که قصبهٔ متصرفه جاثان بود، رسید، کار بدشواری کشید. یعنی فوج سنگین از آن طرف آمده، بر رو استاد. کار کلانی بر سر افتاد.

۲۳۳ سردار جاثان که نول سنگه نام داشت، با لشکر گران و توپخانهٔ بسیار آمد و چهره شد. هنگامهٔ جنگ گردید. فلک جامه های بسا کس بخون کشید. رفته رفته زمین به تنگی گرائید. پرخاش به یراق کوتاه انجامید. مردمان پادشاهی، از کثرت فاقها تباهی، دست ازجانها برداشته پای ثبات افشردند و سخت خوردند و مردند. چون فتح به ادبار آن قوم بود، سرداران پیاده شده کار را پیش بردند. آن فوج گران هزیمت خورده برگشت. سمرو نام فرنگی که توپ و رهکلهٔ آن طرف داشت بجرأت تمام دیری ایستاده ماند، آخر روز آن هم رو بفرار نهاد.

256

actual battle started, something happened that no one had imagined: the battle went on the whole day. The emperor's men made a meal of the unripe grain standing in the fields and spent the night on the battlefield. And they sounded their trumpets of victory. The next morning, they marched forward and laid siege to Ballabhgarh, a strong fort of the Jats, some 12 *kurohs* from the city.

For a few days there was a war of artillery, then the commander of the fort sent a message: "Your war with the Jats will not end with the capture of this fort. You should move on and take the war to the chiefs. As for this fort, I would then give it up without a fight." Najaf Khan, despite his young years, was a thoughtful person; he raised the siege, left the commander in control of the fort, and continued onward. But when he reached near Horal—a town controlled by the Jats—things became difficult. A large army of the Jats blocked his way. Now he was forced to face a much greater task. 232

The Jat chief, Nawal Singh by name, came with a huge 233 army and numerous cannons and launched an attack. A major battle ensued. The turning heavens dragged many a man through a tide of blood, and for many the earth became too narrow a place. Eventually, a hand-to-hand fight with small arms started. The men of the royal army, having seen days of starvation, gave little thought to their lives and stood firm; they suffered a great deal and lost many lives. But the adverse fortune of the Jats dictated the victory of the royal army. Its commanders got down from their chargers and continued to fight. They won the day, while the other army, badly defeated, fled. Somru, the *firangī* who had commanded

۲۳۴ نجف خان که این کار بزرگ بسرداری او سرانجام یافت، کلاه
کج کرد. هرکه این ماجرا شنید خیلی متعجب گردید. سردار
جائان بحصار خود رفت و بر بستر افتاد. اینجا بر نجف خان مردم
بسیاری گرد آمدند. رئیس کلانی شد. چون زر پیش خود نداشت،
مردمانرا بزبان نگاهداشته نمی گذاشت. هر کسی که می آمد نوکر
میشد. در چند روز لشکر حکم دریائی بی کران پیدا کرد. اگرچه
کنار خشک داشت اما بترزبانی کار خود میکرد. چون دید که
بسخنهای دروغ فوج نمی ماند، جگر کرد و سرداران را بمحالات
جاث فرستادن آغاز کرد. آخر این نقش درست بنشست. خودش
رفته بحصار ڈیگ که از آنجا دوازده کروه بود چسپید. سردار آن
طرف که بیمار بود قضا را درگزشت. آنها رنجیت پسر چهارم
سورج مل را برداشته همت بر جنگ گماشتند. داروغهٔ توپخانه
آن قلعه بسرداران این طرف سازشی کرده راه درآمد حصار نشان
داد. مردمان یورش نموده درآمدند، و بغارت شهر منتفع شدند.
هر کم بغل دو بغل تاژ بادله آورد. اسباب بسیار و توپخانهٔ بیشمار
بدست نجف خان هم آمد. قلقچیان این فوج مالدار شدند.

۲۳۵ بعد غارت هفت هشت روز آن قلعه را حوالهٔ سرداری کرد و
قدم پیش کشاد. کمهیر که حصار دیگرش بود، قصد آنجا نمود.
رنجیت که سردار آن قوم شده بود، آن قلعه را خالی گذاشته و
آلات جنگ یکشاخ افگنده، به بهرت پور که حصار محکمیست،

258

the other side's artillery, stood firm for a long time, but at the end of the day he too ran away.

Najaf Khan, under whose command that major victory 234 had been achieved, puffed up with pride. Whoever heard of the events was greatly amazed. The Jat chief fled to his fort and took to bed, while here a host of people gathered around Najaf Khan. He became the most important noble. Since he had no money in hand, he kept everyone happy with promises. No one was turned away; whoever came was taken into service. In a short time, his army was vast like an ocean. With empty pockets but a glib tongue, he achieved his purpose. But when he saw that lying would not help him retain his army, he acted boldly and started sending out his commanders to raid the Jat territories. It turned out to be the right move. Then he himself sallied forth and laid siege to the fort at Dig, 12 *kurohs* away. It so happened that the Jat chief, who had been ill, passed away. The Jats made Ranjit Singh, the fourth son of Suraj Mal, their new chief, and girded themselves for battle. The chief of the artillery of that fort conspired with the commanders on this side and showed them the breach in the fort's wall. This army rushed into the fort and plundered it to its maximum profit.* He who had nothing to show for himself now had two mules loaded with riches. Enormous amounts of goods and innumerable cannons fell into Najaf Khan's hands, and even the servants in his army became men of wealth.

That pillage lasted some seven or eight days. Then Najaf 235 Khan, placing the fort under the command of one of his

---

* April 1776.

رفت. ایشان متصرف این شهر نیز شدند، و مال بسیاری بدست
سپاهیان آمد. ناچار جاثان پیغام صلح دادند، و کشوری که مادر
رنجیت باشد و از شعور بهرهٔ داشت، آمد و آشتی خواست. نجف
خان بهرت پور را باینها داده و کار بر وقت دیگر گذاشته باکبرآباد
که دارالسلطنت مقرریست و جاثان متصرف بودند، رفته مهیای
جنگ آن قلعه شد.

٢٣۶   چون اقبال یاور بود، در اندک فرصت نقب داده بدست آورد.
سرداریکه از طرف جاثان دران تمکن داشت، بوعده و وعید بدر
کرد. با مردمان آنجا سرکرد، و تمام آن صوبه را متصرف گشت.
بهرکه میخواست محالات آنجا تنخواه میکرد. در چندی مالک
تمام آن ملک شد. راجها و زمینداران همه سر حساب شدند. اگر
جاثان حرکت مذبوحی میکردند، بیک سیلی زدن باز روی اینطرف
نمی آوردند.

٢٣٧   هرگاه نجف خان مالک این همه ملک شد و کار او بالا گرفت،
و در حضور عبدالاحد خان لکد برابر زد یعنی مدار سلطنت بران
قرار گرفت، بادشاه از نجف خان موافق وعده سوال حصهٔ سیوم حصهٔ
ملک نمود. او در حضور آمده گفت که این همه فوج که با من
است ملک [را] تنخواه مردمان کرده داده ام. حضرت زر سوم
حصهٔ ملک از من میگرفته باشند. بادشاه از زبان زیرِ زبان داشتن
او اطمینان نداشت. گفت، این قدر ملک باید گذاشت. کش زدن

generals, moved onward to Kumher, another fort of the Jats. Ranjit Singh, who had become the chief of those people, vacated the fort, and abandoning much of his accoutrements of war escaped to Bharatpur, which is a mighty fort. Najaf Khan took possession of Kumher, and a great bounty fell into the hands of his soldiers. The Jats were forced to seek a concord. Kishori, who is the mother of Ranjit and a most wise person, came and asked for peace. Najaf Khan gave Bharatpur to her and Ranjit Singh, deciding to settle the matter another time, and went on to Akbarabad. It has long been a capital city, but was in the possession of the Jats at that time. Arriving there, he began preparations to attack that fort.

His good fortune favored him. In a very short time he   236
managed to make a breach in the fort, and took possession of it. He then got rid of the Jat commandant by making all kinds of promises to him, and treated the people of the city with much kindness. Next he took possession of the province of Akbarabad* and assigned villages to whomsoever he chose. In just a short time he became the master of that entire land. All the rajas and *zamīndārs* were now put on notice. And if the Jats ever acted belligerently, he made them retreat with a flick of his wrist.

When Najaf Khan became the master of this vast territory,   237
and his successes increased, and he turned boastful in the presence of 'Abdul Ahad Khan—as if the state depended upon him alone—the emperor asked him to render to him one-third of the land as he had promised. He came before the

* February 1775.

مردانۀ او پیش زورآوری عبدالاحد خان پیش رفت نشد. ناچار
محالات سیوم حصۀ ملک بطور مختار جدا کرده داد. خلعت
میربخشیگری عطا شد و امیرالامرا شد. بعد از چندی از حضور
رخصت خواسته باکبرآباد رفت.

اینجا عبدالاحد خان سکهان را از خود کرده هرچه بالقوه داشت
بآنها داد. باعتماد آن جم غفیر بادشاهزاده فرخنده اختر را گرفته
براجه پیّاله لشکر کشید. ته دلش این که اگر اتفاق شود سکهان
را بروی نجف خان باید دوانید. آن طرف میرفت و خیال این طرف
داشت. رفته رفته کار بآنجا کشید که مردم بسیاری، از لشکر
امیرالامرا جدا شده، ملازم مختار گردیدند. چون ملک دار نبود
و تدبیر ریاست خوب نمی دانست، کارها را ناتمام میگذاشت.
چندی بسر کرد و بمشورت سکهان با راجه سربسر کرد. زریکه
داشت بخرج آمد. چیزی از بادشاه خواست. شاه از طلب کردن
زر بی مزه شد و نوشت که بهر طوریکه باشد آنجا باشند، من زر
ندارم.

۲۳۸

emperor and said, "This large army that is with me—I have
set aside this territory for the payment of its salaries. Your
majesty may take from me one-third the income from this
land." The emperor was not satisfied by his duplicitous talk,
and said, "You must let go of so much land." Najaf Khan's
audacious ploy did not succeed against 'Abdul Ahad Khan's
strong actions, and he perforce had to relinquish one-third of
the villages as dictated by the mukhtar. He then received the
robes of the office of *mīr bakhshī* and also the title of Amir-
ul-Umara.* A short while later he took leave of the emperor
and went off to Akbarabad.

Here, in Shahjahanabad, 'Abdul Ahad Khan conspired   238
with the Sikhs and gave them whatever he had within his
grasp. Then, placing his trust in that large mob and taking
along with him Farkhunda Akhtar, the emperor's son, he
attacked the Raja of Patiala. But secretly he wished to let
loose the Sikhs against Najaf Khan whenever any opportunity arose. Thus he went in one direction but kept thinking
about the other. By and by, a large number of men left the
army of the Amir-ul-Umara, Najaf Khan, and took service
with 'Abdul Ahad Khan, the mukhtar. The latter had never
possessed a territory and had little understanding of statecraft; consequently he was in the habit of leaving tasks
unfinished. Now too he persisted for a while and then, at
the advice of the Sikhs, made peace with the Raja of Patiala.†
Since whatever money he had with him was now used up,
he asked the emperor for more funds. The request did not

---

* May 1777.
† November 1779.

۲۳۹ وزیر اعظم امیر معظم نواب شجاع الدوله که سر بفلک داشت،
بجنگ حافظ رحمت روهیله که باو دم همسری میزد و خصومت
می کرد، برآمد. حریف از راه خصومت بفرنگیان اکثر می نوشت:
وزیر، که این همه فوج نگه می دارد، سر بر سر شما دارد. چنانچه
گورنر بهادر که صاحب است، بارادهٔ پرخاش پیشتر آمده بود.
نواب وزیر، که مراعات این قوم غالب بیش از بیش می نمود،
تنها پیش آنها رفت و گفت من پاس شما میکنم، و از کسی دیگر
فروتنی نخواهم کشید. درین هرچه خواسته باشد بشود. یا مرا
همراه به کلکته ببرند، یا ملک را بطور من گذارند. فرنگیان سلوک
وزیر دیده دست از همه چیز کشیده، کژه و اله آباد را هم حواله
کرده، رفتند.

۲۴۰ سپهر کاسه باز چرخ زدن آغاز کرد و زمانهٔ دیگر گشت. هرگاه
وزیر از آنجا برگشت، اکثری از فرنگیان مقدمة الجیش وزیر شده
جنگ را بطور خود مقرر کردند. چون چشم روهیله ها ازین لشکر
گران که حکم دریائی بیکران داشت ترسیده بود، ضابطه خان
و سرداران چند به جمعیت ده دوازده هزار کس، الف بر زمین
کشیده، اظهار این معنی نمودند که ما مردم دولت خواهانیم.
سرتابی نمی توانیم کرد. وزیر اعظم نظر بر فضل نامتناهی الهی
گفت که پس پشت فوج استاده باشند. اگرچه بعضی از سرکرده
ها گفتند که این قوم غدار است، رو نباید داد. مبادا در وقت

please the emperor, who wrote back, "Stay there in whatever manner you can, but I have no money."

The great vazir, the most exalted noble, Nawab Shuja-ud-Daula, a man of towering dignity,[65] now decided to wage war against Hafiz Rahmat Khan, the Rohilla, who boasted of being the nawab's equal and held him in enmity. The enemy, as was his wont, used to write to the *firangīs*: "The reason the vazir has assembled such a large army is that he is plotting against you." Consequently, Governor Bahadur, who is the overlord, had come forth with warlike intentions. The nawab, who had always displayed the greatest consideration toward these triumphant people, went to them all alone and said, "I hold you in respect, but I will not humiliate myself before anyone else. In the matter at hand, do as you decide: either take me with you to Calcutta or leave the territory to my judgment." The *firangīs*, having experienced the nawab's generosity, forsook their claims, and in addition gave the nawab the territories of Kara and Allahabad.* Then they left the area.

The heavens—that great juggler—started a new turn, and times changed. When the vazir returned home, many of the *firangīs* formed his vanguard and made plans for the coming battle in their own way. The Rohillas, on seeing this vast ocean-like army, were filled with fear. Consequently, Zabita Khan and some other chieftains, together with some ten or twelve thousand men, came abjectly to seek forgiveness and said, "We are your humble servants and constantly pray for your greater glory. We can never dare to disobey you." The vazir, confident of God's endless bounty, told them, "Go and

239

240

* September 1773.

جنگ موجب تشویش شوند. چون وزیر جگردار واقعی بود، پشت
چشم نازک کرده گفت که زور اینها را در نظر دارم. به یک تگ
تگ پا بخاک درآرم.

۲۴۱ صاحبزاده آصف الدوله بهادر که حالا وزیر اعظم است، در تردد
کارزار سرگرم بسیار. بهر طرف که رو می آورد گرد می انگیخت.
زنجیرهٔ توپ خانه بزور تیغ می گسیخت. وقتیکه هنگامهٔ جنگ
گرم تر شد، حریف که غرق آهن بود از موم نرم تر شد. گوله
ها باین بسیاری می رسیدند که بسیاری را بخاک و خون می
کشیدند. چون زمین تنگ شد، حریف دید که گذر و گریز نیست.
ناچار جگر از سنگ کرده در میدان باستاد، و دل از جهان برداشته
تن بمردن داد. زد و بردی بمیان آمد. انبوه آن طرف بجان آمد.
هوش از سرِ دلاوران پرید. گوله بسینه اش رسید. صفوفها برهم
خوردند. سر دشمن چون گوئی بردند. هرگاه در این لشکر ظفراثر
آوردند و نمودند روهیله ها زبان به تصدیق کشودند که هر عمل
را جزای و هر کرده را سزای است.

۲۴۲ چون یقین شد که او کشته افتاد، شکرانهٔ این فتح وزیر سر
بسجده نهاد. لشکرش بغارت رفت، و ناموس بگیر آمد. ملک
سیرحاصل او و همه در تصرف وزیر آمد. نجف خان که درین جنگ
از اکبرآباد آمده ملحق لشکر وزیر شده بود، رخصت شده باز
باکبرآباد رفت.

stand at the back of my army." Some of his commanders said to him, "They are a treacherous people. Do not put trust in them, lest they cause problems during the battle." But the vazir was truly bold; he remarked with disdain, "I know just how strong they are. A wave of my hand and they will be rolling in the dust."

The prince, Asaf-ud-Daula Bahadur, who is now the vazir [241] himself, was highly active in conducting the battle, and raised a storm whichever direction he turned to. With the strength of his sword he cut asunder the chain of the artillery. As the flames of combat arose high, the enemy, though clad in steel, turned soft as wax. There was such a cannonade that thousands were laid down in dust and blood. The world became too small for the enemy, and, seeing that there was no way to escape, he stood firm and fought, resigned to his death. A fierce battle raged.* The opposing army was almost wiped out, and even brave men went witless with fright. Then a cannonball hit Hafiz Rahmat Khan on the chest. The ranks were trampled down and the vazir's soldiers carried away the enemy's head like a ball in a game. When it was brought into the victorious army and showed around, the Rohillas attested to the matter and declared: "Every deed has its recompense, and every misdeed its punishment."

When it was confirmed that the Rohilla leader had been [242] killed, the vazir prostrated himself before God in gratitude. The enemy's camp was plundered, and his family made prisoners; his vast territory came entirely into the possession of the vazir. Najaf Khan, who had come from Akbarabad

---

* The battle of Katra Miranpur; April 23, 1774.

۲۴۳ فقیر در آن ایام خانه نشین بود. بادشاه اکثر تکلیف کرد، نرفتم. ابوالقاسم خان پسر ابوالبرکات خان که صوبه دار کشمیر بود و بنی عم عبدالاحدخان مختار است، مراعات گونه بکار می برد. گاه گاه باو ملاقات می شد. گاهی بادشاه هم چیزی بچیزی می فرستاد.

مصرعی گاه گاه می گویم
کار دنیای من همین قدر است

۲۴۴ بعد این فتح عظیم، وزیر اعظم امیر معظم بشکوه تمام داخل صوبه شد. چون چشم سپهر بدنبال اهل روزگار میباشد، گوئی که چشمی باین انبوه پرشکوه رسید. یعنی دستور جگردار کلان کار بسبب آب گردش بیماری بهم رسانید که تدارکش دشوار بنظر می آمد. هرچند اطبا و فرنگیان بمعالجه سعی نمودند، اما فایده مترتب نشد. از هشیارسری چون دید که بیماری بطول کشید، خلف الصدق آصف الدوله بهادر را که شایستهٔ کار و جرار و عالم مدار و مدوارِ فیض و احسان است، بر مسند وزارت نشاند و از جهان فانی دامن افشاند. در ماتم آن امیر بزرگ عالمی سیاه پوش گردید. عجب سانحه بظهور رسید. اگر هزار سال چرخ چرخ میزند تا این چنین جوان سرداری، همه تن جرأت، سراپا مروت، بهم می رسد.

268

during that campaign and joined the vazir's camp, now took his leave and went back to Akbarabad.

This humble man, during that time, stayed at home in Shahjahanabad like a recluse. The emperor often sent for me, but I did not go.[66] Abul Qasim Khan—the son of Abul Barkat Khan, who had been the governor of Kashmir, and a cousin of 'Abdul Ahad Khan, the regent—showed me much kindness, and we met a few times. The emperor too sent me something every so often.

243

I compose a line every once in a while—
That is all that happens in my world.

After this great victory, that premier noble, the vazir, returned to his estate with pomp and glory. The jealous heavens, however, are always bent upon destroying great men of affairs, and their evil eye struck him too. In other words, that bold and brave vazir, affected by the rigors of that travel, became severely ill. His recovery seemed impossible. The local practitioners of medicine, as well as the *firangis*, strove to cure him, but none had success. When he saw that his illness was drawing long, the vazir, being a farsighted person, placed on his seat of authority his son, Asaf-ud-Daula Bahadur, who is an able, brave, distinguished, and generous man. Then he himself cast aside this mortal world.* All humanity dressed itself in black, mourning for that eminent noble. What a terrible loss! The heavens must turn for a thousand years to bring forth a chieftain like him,

244

* January 26, 1775.

۲۴۵ بعد از چندی مختارالدوله که اختیار کاروبار وزارت و صوبه
داری داشت، زمانه اش فرصت نداد و نگذاشت. از دست
خواجه سرائی بسنت نام کشته افتاد و سر بوادی عدم نهاد.
نوبت نیابت به حسن رضا خان سرفرازالدوله بهادر رسید. و این
سرداریست باتمکین، متواضع، متصف به حسن خلق، صفت کرم
بر صفت های حمیده اش غالب، دلجوئی وضیع و شریف را به
حسن سلوک طالب، الطاف عمیمش مراچه اکثری را در می یابد.
خداش سلامت دارد.

۲۴۶ بادشاه از طلب کردن زر مختار بی مزه شده به نجف خان
ذوالفقارالدوله نوشت که خود را بهر طوریکه داند اینجا رساند.
او بایمای بادشاه شیرانه و دلیرانه روانهٔ حضور گردید. از استماع
این خبر که امیرالامرا می آید، سرکن پرکن با بنوه سکهان معه
بادشاهزاده، عبدالاحد خان باَهو سوار شده دو روز پیشتر از
نجف خان مسطور داخل شهر گشت و در قلعه بندوبست کرده
نشست. شوری برخاست که ذوالفقارالدوله آمد. بادشاه همین
مختار را برای پذیراشدن گفت. بتزک تمام رفت و ملاقات کرد.
وقت سوارشدن هر دو بر یک فیل نشستند. نجف خان عبدالاحد
خان را دورو و منافق دانسته، بزبان داشته تا دروازهٔ قلعه بنرمی
تمام آمد. ازینجا اشارتی به مردمان خود کرد که توپ و رهکله
و فوج من بلاتحاشا اندرون قلعه بروند و جابجا ایستاده شوند.

an embodiment of courage and chivalry.

After some time, destiny caught up with Mukhtar-ud-Daula, who had charge of the affairs of the *wizārat* and the *sūba;* he was struck down by a eunuch named Basant and dispatched to the land of nonexistence. The responsibilities were now transferred to Hasan Raza Khan Sarfaraz-ud-Daula Bahadur. He is a nobleman of dignity, and modest and pleasing in behavior. Generosity is the greatest of his virtues. With kind deeds, he constantly seeks to comfort all people, noble and plebeian alike. His boundless favors benefit not only me but also so many others. May God preserve him![67]

The emperor, being displeased at the mukhtar's demand for money, wrote to Zulfiqar-ud-Daula Najaf Khan to come to Delhi any way he could.[68] The latter, understanding the emperor's purpose, boldly and courageously set out. When 'Abdul Ahad Khan heard that the Amir-ul-Umara, Najaf Khan, was on his way, he too took off in haste and, with his mob of Sikhs and with Prince Farkhunda Akhtar in tow, arrived at Delhi two days before Najaf Khan. He then entered the citadel and settled there fully prepared.* When the cry went up that Zulfiqar-ud-Daula had arrived, the emperor ordered the same mukhtar to go out and receive him. The mukhtar went with much pomp and met him. When it was time to leave for the citadel, the two men rode on the same elephant. Najaf Khan considered 'Abdul Ahad Khan a two-faced hypocrite, so he beguiled him with soft words until they reached the gate of the citadel. There, he signaled his own commanders to rush in with troopers and

245

246

---

* November 1779.

271

هرچند تفاوت میان هر دو یک پشت کارد بود، اگر میخواست کار مختار می ساخت، اما نظر بر بندگی بادشاه که این هم بندهٔ است، مرضی بادشاه را اول دریافت کنم، بعد ازان هر چه خواهد شد خواهد شد.

۲۴۷ چون باین هنگامه پیش بادشاه آمد و ملازمت کرد، دید که آقا دل پری دارد، میخواهد که این را نگذارد. از آنجا برگشته در میان بازار ایستاد و عرضی فرستاد که من از لحاظ حضور دست انداز نشدم. اکنون تا ازینجا عبدالاحد خان را با خود نبرم، نخواهم رفت. بادشاه در ظاهر گفت و شنود بمیان آورد و بباطن گفت که بهر طوریکه باشد این را باید برد. چون مردمان مختار مجبور شده رفته بودند و سکهان یکسو شدند، ناچار قول و قسم بمیان آورده که نجف خان با من بد نکند و خواهان عزت من نباشد. بادشاه گفت، من ضامن شما؛ بی اندیشه بروید. چون چاره ندید و زمانه را بطور دیگر یافت، آخر روزی بر یک فیل سوار شده از قلعه برآمد.

۲۴۸ امیرالامرا که در بازار انتظار می کشید، خود هم سوار شده فیل این را برابر فیل خود کرده بخانه برد، و آنجا نگهداشت. چند روز به لیت و لعل گذرانید که امروز پیش بادشاه میروم، فردا می برم. بعد ازان گفت که آنجا رفته چه خواهند کرد؟ بهتر اینست که پیش من باشند. لیکن بر مال و اموال او دست انداز نشد. بیست

272

big and small cannons, and take up positions everywhere inside the citadel. Though the two men had been seated so close that only a knife's breadth was between them, and had he so desired he could have killed the mukhtar, Najaf Khan showed regard for the fact that he and the mukhtar both were servants of the emperor. He decided, *Let me find out what the emperor wishes. Then shall happen whatever is to happen.*

When in that tumultuous manner he arrived before the emperor and made his obeisance, he saw that the master was highly displeased with the mukhtar and desired that he should not go unpunished. On his return from the audience, Najaf Khan stopped in the marketplace and sent a petition to the emperor: "Out of regard for your majesty, I did not lay a hand on him; but now I shall not leave without taking 'Abdul Ahad Khan with me." The emperor made a show of negotiation, but secretly sent him the word to take away the mukhtar by any means possible. The mukhtar's own men, being pressed hard, had already left him, and the Sikhs had stepped aside. Seeing that he had no choice left, the mukhtar begged for a promise that Najaf Khan would not harm or dishonor him in any manner. The emperor told him, "I stand guarantee. Go without fear." Now he had no option; and so, recognizing that the times had changed, he one day seated himself on an elephant and rode out of the citadel.

Amir-ul-Umara Najaf Khan, who had been waiting for him in the bazaar, also got on an elephant and, riding beside the mukhtar, took him home and detained him. A few days went by in idle excuses: "I am going to the emperor today, but I shall take you to your place tomorrow." Then he said

247

248

روپیه روز از خانهٔ خود کرده و چند خدمتگار پیش او گذاشته
خود بامورات ملکی و مالی حضور مشغول شد.

۲۴۹ رفته رفته کار بجای کشید که سر بفلک رسانید. بسبب
مرجعیت و علو مرتبت امیران وقت مجرا را بدست نمی آمد.
روزی که بحضور می آمد دربار می شد، وگرنه بادشاه با چند
مصاحب بسر می کرد. چون جوان بود و شاهجهان آباد طلسم
خانهٔ، یاران بعیش و عشرتش مایل کردند. باستعمال منهیات و
تماشای زنان چنان پرداخت که قوت از بدن زایل شد. آخر بمرض
سل گرفتار شد. اطبا کوشش بسیاری در علاج او بکار بردند اما
فایدهٔ مترتب نشد. چون مایوس شد بحسرت می گفت که من
هیچ نمی خواهم جز این قدر که زنده بمانم. در بیماری او زمانه
رنگ دیگر گرفت.

۲۵۰ فقیر که خانه نشین بود خواست که از شهر بدر رود، وز جهت
بی اسبابی حرکت متعذر بود. برای نگهداشت عزت من در خاطر
نواب وزیر الممالک آصف الدوله بهادر آصف الملک گذشت که
اگر میر پیش من بیاید بطلبم. نواب سالارجنگ پسر اسحاق خان
موتمن الدوله و برادر خورد نواب اسحاق خان نجم الدوله که
خالوی وزیر اعظم می شوند، نظر بر ربط قدیم که خالوی من [را]
بایشان بود، گفتند، اگر نواب صاحب از راه عنایت، جهت زاد
راه، چیزی عنایت نمایند، میر البته بیاید. اشارتی رفت که چنین

to him, "What would you do there anyway? It's better that you stay here with me." But he did not lay a hand on his property and possessions. In fact, he assigned him 20 rupees per day from his own pocket, and also provided him with some servants. Meanwhile he busied himself with all the political and financial matters of the emperor.

Gradually Najaf Khan came to be the most important person and source of all powers, so much so that other nobles could not find time to go and pay their respects to the emperor. The imperial audience occurred only when he came to the court; otherwise the emperor spent his time in the company of just a few ordinary courtiers. Since Najaf Khan was young and Shahjahanabad a "house of enchantment," people soon had him pursuing a life of luxury and sensuous delights. He used intoxicants and spent time with women to such an extent that soon his body lost all strength. Eventually he fell ill with consumption. The doctors tried hard to cure him, but to no avail. When he had lost all hope, he would say piteously, "I desire no riches; I only wish to stay alive." During his illness the times put on a different aspect.

This humble man had taken to staying at home and desired to leave the city for good. But having no means, I was helpless to do so. God wished to protect my honor, and so it occurred to Nawab Vazir-ul-Mamalik Asaf-ud-Daula Bahadur Asaf-ul-Mulk that if Mir would come to him, he would invite him. Nawab Salar Jang—the son of Ishaq Khan Motaman-ud-Daula and younger brother of Nawab Ishaq Khan Najm-ud-Daula—happens to be the maternal uncle of the vazir. On account of the old ties that my maternal uncle Sirajuddin 'Ali Khan, Arzu, had with him, he said to the vazir, "If the

249

250

باشد. ایشان چیزی از سرکار گرفته خطی بمن نوشتند که نواب والاجناب شما را می خواهند، باید که بهر طوریکه دانند خود را اینجا برسانند. من که دل برداشته نشسته بودم، بمجرد دیدن خط برخاستم و روانهٔ لکهنؤ شدم.

۲۵۱ چون ارادهٔ الهی متعلق بود، بی یار و یاور و بی قافله و رهبر، در چند روز از راه فرخ آباد گذر افتاد. مظفرجنگ که رئیس آنجا بود، هرچند خواست که چندی پیش من بمانند، دل من آنجا آب نخورد. بعد از یک دو روز روانه گردیده بمنزل مقصود رسیدم. اول بخانهٔ سالارجنگ رفتم. ایشان را خدا سلامت دارد، عزت بسیاری نمودند و آنچه می بایست بجناب بندگان عالی گفته فرستادند.

۲۵۲ پس از پنج چار روز اتفاقاً نواب جناب عالی بتقریب جنگانیدن خروس تشریف آوردند. منکه آنجا بودم، ملازمت حاصل نمودم. از فراست دریافته فرمودند که میر محمدتقی است. بعنایت تمام بغل گیر شده با خود در نشینه بردند، و شعرهای خود مخاطب نموده خواندند. گفتم، سبحان الله، کلام الملوک ملک الکلام. از فرط مهربانی مکلف من هم گردیدند. آنروز چند شعر غزل التماس نمودم. وقت برخاستن نواب، سالارجنگ گفتند که حالا میر حسب الطلب آمده است. بندگان عالی مختار اند. جای برای ایشان نمایند، و هر وقتیکه خواسته باشد طلبداشته

nawab would kindly grant some funds for his travel expenses, Mir would definitely come." The nawab indicated his assent. Salar Jang then obtained some money from the treasury and sent me a letter, saying, "The exalted nawab has asked for you—it would be appropriate for you to get here any way you can." I was sitting at home, disgusted with life. When I read the letter I immediately set out for Lucknow.

God's will was in my favor. In a few days—with no friend or protector, without any guide or companion—I reached Farrukhabad. Muzaffar Jang was the lord of that city. He tried much to have me stay with him for a while, but my heart did not take to the place. I left after a couple of days and finally reached my destination.* Right away I went to the house of Salar Jang, may God protect him. He received me with much honor, and sent word to the nawab as it was due and proper.

251

After four or five days, it so happened that the nawab came to the mansion of Salar Jang to enjoy a round of cockfights. I was present and paid my respects. He intuitively recognized me and said, "You must be Mir Muhammad Taqi." He then embraced me with utmost kindness, took me with him to where he was to sit, and addressing me recited some of his own verses. I responded, "Praise be to God. 'A king's verse is the king of verses.'" Out of extreme kindness, he then pressed me to recite some verses too. That day I recited only some couplets of a *ghazal*. At the time of the nawab's departure, Salar Jang said to him, "Now that Mir has come here at your command, you are his master. You may assign him a

252

* Sometime between mid-January and mid-March, 1782.

277

صحبت دارند. فرمودند، من چیزی معین کرده پیش صاحب می
فرستم. بعد از دو سه روز یاد فرمودند. حاضر شدم و قصیدهٔ که
در مدح گفته بودم خواندم. شنیدند و بلطف تمامم در سلک
بندگان منسلک گردانیدند، و عنایت و مهربانی بحال من مبذول
دارند.

۲۵۳   بعد از آمدن من از این طرف، آنجا که نجف خان بر بستر افتاده
بود، فوت کرد. کاروبار حضور درهمی پذیرفت. غلامان او مثل
نجف قلی خان، و افراسیاب خان، و دیگر سرداران، هر کسی
بطرف خود کشید. چندی کشاکش در میان ماند. آخر مرزا شفیع
که از برادران او بود و برای تنبیه سکهان فوج کشی میکرد، باشارهٔ
حضور حاضر شد و عبدالاحد خان را عموی خود قرار داده از قید
رها کرد و دیوانی خالصه دهانید، و خود بر مسند ریاست نشست.

۲۵۴   چون سفاک و جرار بود، هر یکی ازو خطرمند می ماند. از سرکشی
غلامان نجف خان بی مزه شده در شهر طرح جنگ انداخت، و
نجف قلی خان را اسیر ساخت. افراسیاب خان آمده در ظاهر به
مرزای مذکور پیوست. چون دولت این بابا مستعجل بود، چند
روز نکشید که لطافت خواجه سرای که از طرف وزیرالممالک
بحضور می بود و فی الجمله زوری همداشت، و فرنگی از اقربای
سمرو فرنگی، باهم ساخته هیچگاه او را یافتند رو ازو برتافتند.
بادشاه را نیز فهمانیدند که این عزیز بی تمیز است. چون آش او

position, and send for him to keep you company whenever you wish." The nawab replied, "I shall fix a salary and let you know." After a couple of days, the nawab sent for me. I went and presented myself and read the panegyric I had written in his praise. He listened to it and, most graciously, accepted me into his service. And he showers on me much kindness and consideration.[69]

After I arrived in Lucknow, there in Delhi Najaf Khan, who had been lying ill, passed on.* The affairs of the state fell into disarray. His slaves, such as Najaf Quli Khan and Afrasiyab Khan, and other deputies each tried to gain the emperor's favor, and the tussle continued for a while. Finally, Mirza Muhammad Shafi, who was one of Najaf Khan's brothers and had been campaigning against the Sikhs, came to the emperor at his invitation. Shafi declared 'Abdul Ahad Khan to be an uncle of his and set him free. He also made him the revenue administrator for the crown lands, and himself occupied the seat of authority and became the de facto mukhtar of the emperor.

253

Since Shafi was a belligerent and ruthless man, everyone felt threatened by him. Angered by the rebellion of Najaf Khan's slaves, he set up battle lines within the city and took Najaf Quli Khan into custody. Then Afrasiyab Khan arrived and pretended to side with him. However, the days of glory for that young man were limited, and not many had passed when the eunuch commander Latafat 'Ali Khan, who was the vazir's representative at the royal court and indeed possessed much power, joined with a *firangi*

254

* April 6, 1782.

پختند، او هم خبر شد، و یک آش پختن صبر نکرده از شهر بدر
زد، و عبدالاحد خان را با خود برد. تا خبردار شدند خبر او نیافتند.

بادشه شقه ها به مردمان شهر و اطراف نوشت که هر جا که
بیابند نگذارند و بحضور بیارند. نوشتهٔ بسردار بلم گژه نیز رسید.
اتفاقاً این آنجا رفته فرود آمده بود. سردار آن قلعه نوشته را نمود.
مضطرب گردیده عبدالاحد خان را پیش او گذاشت، و خود راه
گریز اختیار کرد. یک منزل دو منزل پیش رفته متوقف گشت.
در اکبرآباد، که احمد بیگ همدانی تسلط داشت، باو عهد و پیمان
درست نموده بجنگ یاران حضور مستعد ساخت. او با بست هزار
کس همراه او شده روانه گشت. اینجا فرنگی و خواجه سرا و دیگر
اعزه بادشاه را از شهر برآورده خیمه بر لب دریا استاده کردند، و
غافل از ریسمان تابیدن او که تا قتل همراه است بطنطنهٔ تمام
قریب رسیدند.

بادشاه چون دید که کار او بالاست، لطافت علی خان خواجه
سرای و فرنگی را برای آوردن او پیش فرستاد. آنها دویدند؛ خواجه
سرا را گرفتند و فرنگی را کشتند. بادشاه بجرأت تمام خود را
نگهداشت. زور آنها نیز پیش نرفت. بجواب و سوال پرداخته
بسیار کسان را به وعده وعید از خود ساختند. هرگاه دیدند که
بادشاه بی جنگ و جدل بدست نمی آید، عبدالاحد خان را در
میان داده قول و قسم بکار بردند، و اظهار رسوخ و بندگی نموده از

relative of "Somru the *Firangī*" in a conspiracy against him.[70] They began to oppose him at every chance. They also convinced the emperor that Shafi was an uncouth man. As the conspiracy grew thicker, he got wind of it, and not wasting a moment left the city, taking 'Abdul Ahad Khan with him. By the time his enemies got the news, they could find no trace of him.

The emperor sent letters to the notables of the city and the   255
neighboring regions that they should not let him get away, that if they found him they should bring him to the emperor. A letter also went to the chief of Ballabhgarh, where Shafi, it so happened, was staying. The chief showed Shafi the royal order. He panicked and, leaving 'Abdul Ahad Khan there, fled. But after traveling one or two stages, he stopped and, by making promises to Ahmad Beg Hamadani—who held Akbarabad—made a pact with him to challenge the supporters of the emperor. Hamadani took twenty thousand men and set out with him for Delhi. Here in Delhi, the *firangī*, the eunuch commander Latafat 'Ali, and other nobles took the emperor with them out of the city and set up camp by the river. Then they marched forward with great pomp, oblivious to what pursues all men till their end.

When the emperor saw that he, Mirza Shafi, had the   256
upper hand, he dispatched the eunuch commander Latafat 'Ali Khan and the *firangī* ahead to bring him to him. Their opponents, however, rushed upon them, took the eunuch captive, and killed the *firangī*. The emperor, with great courage, protected himself. His opponents too were unable to prevail, and negotiations were set afoot. Shafi and Hamadani won over to their side many people by making illusory

خیمه بقلعه آوردند. نجف قلی خان و افراسیاب خان و عبدالاحد خان یکدل شده بکار بادشاهی دخل کردن آغاز نهادند. با همدانی که مرزا شفیع وعده وعید داشت، هیچ نداد. او چند توپ و رهکله گرفته روانهٔ اکبرآباد گردید.

۲۵۷ اینجا بعد چند روز افراسیاب خان به محالات خود رفت و مرزای مذکور با نجف قلی خان در شهر جنگیده او را بدست آورد. پیش بیگم که همشیرهٔ نجف خان است فرستاد. عبدالاحد خان از خانهٔ خود آمده به چرب زبانی باز کارِ خود را پیش برد. بیگم مسطور شفیع شده نجف قلی خان را وارهانید و بجائیداد او روانه ساخت.

۲۵۸ رفته رفته تسلط مرزا شفیع خوب شد. بیرون شهر آمده متوجه ملک گیری گشت. چون همه ها ازو دلجمعی نداشتند، افراسیاب آمده همدانی را آورد، و مقرر کرد که مرزا برای دلدهی همدانی بخیمهٔ او بیاید. آوردند و بغدر او را کشتند. بعد کشته شدن او، دور دور افراسیاب خان شد. کار ریاست باو رسید. همدانی باز بمکانهای خود رفت. ایشان در حضور امیرالامرا شده بکار بادشاهی مختار گشتند.

promises to them. But when they saw that the emperor could not be taken hold of without a fight, they used 'Abdul Ahad Khan as a mediator, made promises and took oaths of sincerity, and after putting on a display of loyalty escorted the emperor back from the camp to the citadel.* Now Najaf Quli Khan, Afrasiyab Khan, and 'Abdul Ahad Khan joined hands and began to assert themselves in the affairs of the state. The mirza, having made false promises, gave nothing to Hamadani, who then grabbed some large and small cannons and started back for Akbarabad.

A few days later, Afrasiyab Khan went off to his own 257 assigned territories while the mirza fought with Najaf Quli Khan within the city, took him prisoner, and sent him to Begum Khajista Sultan, the sister of Najaf Khan. 'Abdul Ahad Khan came out of his house and won his way again by using his glib tongue. The begum interceded on Najaf Quli Khan's behalf and got him freed; she then sent him off to his own place.

Gradually the authority of Mirza Muhammad Shafi 258 became well established. He ventured out of the city and set about recovering possession of the lands. Since everyone was still mistrustful of him, Afrasiyab Khan returned and also brought Hamadani with him. He then demanded that the mirza should visit with Hamadani in order to reassure him. Thus they brought him to their camp and deceitfully killed him.† After the mirza's death, the star of Afrasiyab Khan rose high, and the affairs of the state fell into his hands.

---

* November 24, 1782.
† September 23, 1783.

اینجا وزیر اعظم امیر مکرم، برای پذیره شدن گورنر بهادر که از
کلکته حسب الارشاد می آمد و غالب این تمام ملک او بود، روانه
شدند. گرد فوج تا آسمان می رسید؛ این سفر تا اله آباد کشید.
ز آمدِ آمدِ صاحب مسطور، سرداران این ضلع همه سرحساب
شده مهیای دیدن او شدند. یک منزل پیشتر، با نواب گردون
جناب ملاقات شد. از آنجا با خود در لکهنؤ که محل سکونت
است آوردند. و در هر منزل ضیافتی جدائی اتفاق می افتاد. خیمه
هائی نو و طعامهائی خوب. اسپان ترکی و تازی، و فیلان کوه پیکر.
کشتی های پوشاک و جواهر بیش بها. شربتهای خوشگوار و میوه
جات لایحصیٰ. تحفه های نغرِ اینجا. شمشیرهای جنوبی و مغربی
و کمانهای چاچی.

هرگاه در دارالقرار لکهنؤ آمدند و داخل دولت خانه شدند،
فرش بوقلمون هر روز، در گوشهایش طلای لخلخه سوز. اطراف
مکان گلاب پاشیده، بستر خواب عطرمالیده. لباس بوی خوش
برداشته، فروش مخمل پانگذاشته. دیوارهای سیم گل کرده،
ایوانهائی مرتب بچغی و پرده. بهارعنبر طرفه بساطی گسترده،
مکان گرو از بهاربند برده. پسته و بادام بوداده، نقل فرنگی برای
تنقل نهاده. شبها رقص زنان پری وش، نی نی از حوران بهشتی هم
دلکش. گلدانهای شیشه و چینی بسلیقه چیده، طاقها پر از میوه
های رسیده. رقص فرنگچی، تماشای خوشی. خانه جای خوشی،

۲۵۹

۲۶۰

Hamadani once again returned to his own place, while Afra-siyab Khan became the Amir-ul-Umara and began to act as the mukhtar of the emperor.

Here in Lucknow, the vazir, the benevolent noble, set out to receive with honors the governor general,[71] who was coming from Calcutta at the nawab's invitation, and who is the overlord of all his lands. The dust raised by the nawab's army reached the sky as he suffered the hardship of the journey up to Allahabad. All the chiefs of the surrounding region had been alerted about the coming of the aforementioned sahib, and they assembled to see him. The meeting with the mighty nawab took place one day's journey before Allahabad.[72] From there the nawab escorted him personally to Lucknow, his own place of residence. At every stage of the journey, a different feast was offered in new tents and of elegant dishes. And presents were offered: Turkish and Arab horses; towering elephants; trays of precious robes and jewels; delightful drinks; various fruits of the best kind; fine gifts of local specialties; southern and western swords and bows from Chach.

When they entered Lucknow,* the nawab's permanent abode, and took up residence in the palace, new carpets of manifold hues were laid out every day with a golden incense burner placed on each corner.[73] The area surrounding the house was sprinkled with rose water, and attar was rubbed in the beds. Everyone's clothes were fragrant with perfume.[74] Velveteen carpets were spread out such as none had ever stepped upon. Walls glittered like silver. Elegant pavilions

259

260

* March 1784.

هوای خوشی. شام سیم بندی کرده آتش بازی می آوردند. ستاره و هوائی سر بفلک میزدند. تماشای چراغان دل از دست ربودی، مهتابی شب را روزی نمودی. سائبان زربفت بدین خوبی کشیده که دیدهٔ خورشید مثل او ندیده. امیران سرگرم پاسداری، راجه ها در خدمت گذاری. مدح خوان شاعران مربوط ، حاضران جوانان مضبوط. در هر خانه داریست خوب، ظل ممدود و ماء مسکوب. نرگس دانهای برابر جلوه پرداز چون باغ نظر. برف به از سیم مذاب، خوبی برآمد از آب. گلهای فالودهٔ الوان، شربت آن شیرهٔ جان.

اقسام نان در وقت طعام: نان بادام، بنزاکت تمام؛ شیرمال و باقرخانی، بر خورشید گرم نواخانی. نان جوان به آن گرمی و خوبی بود که پیر از خوردن آن پیرافشانی می نمود. نان ورق چنان که اگر وصفش کنم دفتر شود. نان زنجبیلی که ذائقه از ادراکش محظوظ تر شود. انواع قلیه و دوپیازه در میان نهاده؛ نان مهمانان همه بروغن افتاده. اقسام کباب بر دستار خوان کشیده: کباب گل بخوبی و تازگی رسیده؛ کباب خوش نمک هندی دلها را از دست می برد؛ کباب قندهاری امزجه سوئی خود می آورد؛ کباب سنگ از سختی کشیدگانِ راه کوفت زایل میکرد؛ کباب ورق عجب نسخهٔ برشتهٔ بود که طبایع را مایل میکرد؛ کباب هائی متعارف همه بامزه و بانمک، قابها ده ده گذاشته پیش یک یک. پلاوها انواع و آشها اقسام؛ عجب آش در کاسهٔ، «سبحان ذی الجود والاکرام».

were set up in gardens and decorated with screens and curtains. The sweet smell of amber spread everywhere, creating a unique effect. The houses put to shame the homes for spring. Roasted almonds and pistachios and *firangī* tidbits were laid out for munching. At night, there were dances by women who were like fairies—nay, they were more attractive than the houris of paradise. Flower vases of crystal and porcelain were carefully arranged. Shelves and niches in the walls were filled with choice fruit, perfectly ripe. A *firangī* dance was held, a lovely scene—a house of joy, filled with joy. In the evening, they had elaborate illuminations and set off fireworks. The starbursts and rockets touched the sky. The sight of the illuminations stole the hearts of the spectators. The flares turned the night into day. A pavilion of gold brocade was set up—of such beauty that not even the sun had seen its like. The nobles were busy, offering hospitality; the rajas went about, offering their services. Excellent poets sang their praises. Young stalwarts stood by to tend to their needs. Every house was finely prepared, with shady nooks and channels of flowing water. Vases that held bunches of narcissus flowers seemed like the "Garden of Nazar." Ice, more pleasing to sight than molten silver, was a beauty garnered from water. Bowls of sweet noodles of many hues and kinds were offered, their sherbet sweeter than the nectar of life.

As for the kinds of breads served at the meals: "Almond 261
Bread" of utmost delicacy; Shirmal and Baqarkhani, their tops painted with saffron, that would put the sun to shame; "Youthful Bread," so soft and warm that if an old man were to eat it he would act like a youth; "Paper Bread," of such

287

۲۶۲ مهمانی باین وفور، میزبانی همچو دستور. مهمانی باین شوکت،
میزبانی باین دولت. مهمانی باین حسن اخلاق، میزبانی باین ریاست
آفاق. مهمانی باین خوبی و خوش معاشی، میزبانی چون خورشید
باین زرپاشی. مهمانی باین عقل کامل، میزبانی باین لطف شامل.
چشم روزگار ندیده، و گوش عقلا نشنیده. بدین گونه روز و شب
تا شش ماه گفت و شنود و باهم معاش و مشورت و صحبت بود.

۲۶۳ هرگاه این خبر بحضور رسید، هر یکی از امرایان آنجا بفکر خویش
افتاد. عبدالاحد خان کسان را اینجا فرستاد و با فرنگیان ساخت.
افراسیاب خان و غیره را گمان شد که فرنگی اینجا خواهد آمد.
چون زبردست است، بادشاه را بطورخود نگاهداشته آش ما
خواهد پخت. بهتر آنست که پادشاه را باکبرآباد ببریم و مردمان
را گرد آوریم. و مرهٔ که متصرف رانائی گوهد واله است، از آن
خود کرده پیغام با فرنگی کنیم. اگر جنگ اتفاق افتد، افتد، وگرنه
از بُن دبدبه همانجا باشند. چنانچه بادشاه را برآورده به اکبرآباد
رفتند، و در راه عبدالاحد خان را محبوس ساختند.

quality that I could fill a book with its praise; "Ginger Bread," so flavorful that the palate grows zestful thinking of it. In the middle were placed varieties of *qaliya* and *do-piyāza*, such rich stews of different kinds that the guests were all delighted and satisfied. And the kababs that were laid out on the long tablecloth: "Flower Kababs," full of bloom and flavor; "Indian Kababs," perfectly salted to steal people's hearts; "Qandahari Kababs" attracted all and sundry; "Stone Kababs" brought relief to those who were tired from the hardships of the journey; "Paper Kababs," so amazing in recipe they delighted men of every taste; and all the more common kababs, spicy and flavorful. Ten large serving plates of kebabs were placed before every single guest. Then there were pilafs of every variety and wonderful soups of all kinds. "Praised be the One, who is bountiful and generous!"[75]

What a splendid guest! What an exemplary host! A grand 262 guest; a glorious host—a guest of wonderful disposition, a host of the greatest eminence—a guest, so refined and elegant; a host, sun-like in his munificence—a guest, perfect in sagacity, a host, the embodiment of hospitality. The likes of them had never been seen by the eyes of the ages, nor had the ears of the sages heard of them. In that manner the two continued to meet, converse, and consult, day and night, for six months.[76]

When the news of the visit reached the court at Delhi, 263 every noble there began to worry about his own future. 'Abdul Ahad Khan sent some men to Lucknow and established ties with the *firangīs*. Afrasiyab Khan and others thought that the *firangī* lord might come there and, being so powerful, take the emperor under his own wing and "cook

۲۶۴ وقتیکه به شهر مسطور رسیدند، پادشاهزاده جوان بخت از
آنجا گریخته پیش نواب وزیر و فرنگی آمد. مضطرب با مرهش
عهد و پیمان درست کردند. او جانب ایشان گرفته گفت و شنود
فرستادن شهزاده در میان آورد. اینجا فرنگی بزبان نگه داشته
که کار ملک خود که کلکته باشد مدّنظر داشت. بعد چندی
پادشاهزاده را همراه گرفته از وزیرالممالک رخصت شد و رفت.
هنگام وداع بمردمان صاحب نواب والاجناب چنان انعام بی
احصا مبذول داشت که در قیاس نگذرد. بهر کس اسپ و فیل و
قبای، بهر بی سروپا سراپای.

۲۶۵ چون صاحب از راه دریا متوجه شد و وزیر بدارالقرار خود
آمد، مرهش و افراسیاب خان با محمد بیگ همدانی ارادهٔ پرخاش
کردند. او هم سر فرود نیاورده بجنگ اینها ایستاد. در همین اثنا
کس میر زین العابدین، برادر مرزا شفیع، خنجری بافراسیاب خان
حواله کرد. بعد از دوچار روز مرد. حالا سرداری درحضور نیست،
بادشاه بی زور است. غالب که دوردور مرهش شود.

their goose." They decided that it would be better for them to take the emperor to Akbarabad, gather some troops, win the support of the Maratha who lords over the Rana of Gohad, and then contact the *firangī*. If it came to war, they would fight; otherwise they would remain there on the basis of their existent awe and power. Consequently, they took the emperor out of the city and set off for Akbarabad, and on their way made 'Abdul Ahad Khan a prisoner.

When they reached Akbarabad, Prince Jawan Bakht 264 fled from them and came to the nawab and the *firangī* at Lucknow.* Those men in Akbarabad became extremely agitated and quickly made a deal with the Maratha to win him over; he took up their cause and began negotiations to have the prince sent back. Here the *firangī* kept everyone happy with sweet words, saying that he had the affairs of his own state—that is, Calcutta—on his mind. But a while later, he took leave of the Vazir-ul-Mamalik and left, taking the prince with him. At the time of his departure, the exalted nawab gave gifts to the sahib's men in such numbers that none could even imagine. Every person of any note was given a horse, an elephant, and a fine robe, and every man of no means received a full suit of clothes.

When the sahib left by the riverine route and the vazir 265 returned to his capital, the Maratha and Afrasiyab Khan made plans to attack Muhammad Beg Hamadani. He was not intimidated and firmly faced their challenge. Meanwhile, some man of Mir Zainul Abidin, the brother of Mirza Muhammad Shafi, stabbed Afrasiyab Khan, who died after

* May 1784.

۲۶۶ بعد این سانحات فوج مرهش و احمد بیگ همدانی باهم
جنگیدند. چون دست بر او نیافتند، غدر کرده همدانی مذکور
را بگیر آوردند. اینجا صاحب که بادشاهزاده را با خود برده بود
رخصت کرد. چنانچه برگشته آمده اند. یا در اطراف می مانند، یا
پیش بادشاه می رسانند. بالفعل سایهٔ دولت نواب عالی جناب عالی می
گیرند. آنچه ایشان می گویند، می پذیرند.

۲۶۷ اینجا فقیر با نواب عالی منزلت است. در دعاگوئی ایشان بسر
میکند. بندگان عالی برای شکار تا بهرائچ رفتند. من در رکاب بودم.
شکارنامهٔ موزون نمودم. باری دیگر باز برای شکار سوار شدند. تا
دامن کوه شمالی تشریف بردند. اگرچه مردمان از نشیب و فراز
این سفر دوردراز سخت خوردند لیکن شکار چنین و فضائی چنین و
هوائی چنین ندیده بودند. بعد از سه ماه بدارالقرار خود آمدند. فقیر
شکارنامهٔ دیگر گفته بحضور خواند. دو غزل از غزلهای شکارنامه
انتخاب زده خود بدولت مخمس کردند، بخوبی که می بایست، و
در زمین غزل پسند افتاده غزل دیگر فرمایش نمودند. آنهم از فضل
الهی گفته شد. زبان مبارک به تحسین کشادند و داد سخنوری
دادند. درین ایام بسبب آبگردش بعد عشرهٔ محرم انحرافی در مزاج
عالی ظاهر شد. استعلاج نمودند. نصیب اعدا بطول کشید. عالمی
از خیر و خیرات بهره اندوز شد، و هر کسی دست بدعا افراشت.
حکیم مطلق و شافی برحق شفا داد، و بر ما عالمیان منت نهاد:

a few days.* Presently there is no preeminent noble at the court. The emperor is powerless. Most probably the Maratha will come to have the upper hand.

After these events, the Maratha's army fought the army   266
of Muhammad Beg Hamadani and, unable to gain a victory, took him prisoner through deception. Here, the sahib who had taken the prince with him sent him back. So now the prince has returned to Lucknow. He may stay here, or he may be sent back to the emperor. For the time being, he rests in the shade of the nawab's glory and does whatever the latter asks.[77]

Here this humble man is with the exalted nawab and   267
passes his days in grateful prayers. His Excellency went on a hunting trip to Bahraich; I accompanied him and composed a poem about the hunt. Later, he went hunting a second time, up to the foot of the northern mountain. Those who went with him suffered a great deal from the hardships of that long and arduous journey, but they had never before seen such wonderful hunting and scenery. The nawab returned to the capital after three months.† This humble man composed another poem and read it before him. He selected two *ghazals* from those included in it and himself turned them into two *mukhammas* in a most excellent manner.[78] Further, liking the *zamīn* of one *ghazal*,[79] he asked me to compose one more *ghazal* in the same manner. By the grace of God, that too was accomplished. The nawab was pleased, and praised it as was its due. Then, after the tenth of Muharram, he fell

---

* November 2, 1784.
† The two hunts of 1782.

«الهی تا جهان باشد تو باشی».

۲۶۸ چون در حضور بادشاه از غلامان نجف خان که مسلط بودند
کسی نماند، مرهثہ که قریب بود تسلط بهم رساینده کوس لمن
الملک زد. بادشاه مرهثہ را مختار ساخت، و روهای مردمان نجف
خانی بخاک انداخت. اکثر مشوره باو دارند، و امورات را بطور
او می گذارند. فوج مرهثہ به شاهجهان آباد هم رفت. زبان زد
است که تسلط یافت. سکهان که اطراف شهر را می تاختند حالا
سرحساب شده اند، چرا که کمان دکنیان نمی توانند کشید و
بگرد میدان داری اینان نخواهند رسید. بادشاه بیرون شهر اکبرآباد
خیمه داشت. پس از چند روز روانهٔ دهلی شدند. عبدالاحد خان
را در علی گڈہ، که در تصرف همشیرهٔ نجف خان است و اکثر
مردمان نجف خان در آن قلعه جمع اند، فرستاده مقید ساختند.

۲۶۹ مرهثہ مالک الملک است. هرچه میخواهد می کند. بادشاه
را چیزی دست برداشته میدهد، و هر جا که میخواهد می برد.
چنانچه در شهر یکماه ماند و به علی گڈہ برد. ده پانزده روز
بجنگ کشید. آخر بعهد و پیمان بیگم را برآورده ازو چیزی از
مال نجف خان گرفت و گذاشت. از آنجا بادشاه را بر راجپوتان
برد. آنها استادگی کردند. بعد از چند روز صلح از راجپوتان نموده
بادشاه بشهر دهلی آمد، و مرهثہ در شهر اکبرآباد ماند. چون خیال

294

ill, affected by all the "changes of water" during the hunting expedition. He sought treatment, but the illness lasted a long time. The moneys given away in charity benefited millions. Everyone raised his hands in prayer for his cure. God, the true and perfect healer, rid him of his sickness, and made me and millions eternally bound to him in gratitude.

May God that you live so long the world lasts.

When there remained with the emperor none of the slaves 268 of Najaf Khan who had become masters of the state, the Maratha leader Mahadji Sindhia, being close by, gained power and took over all authority. The emperor made him his regent, and all the men from Najaf Khan's days fell into disgrace.* The emperor consults with him frequently and decides on matters as he advises. The Marathas' army also went to Shahjahanabad and is said to be in full control. The Sikhs, who used to plunder the environs of the city, have now been put on notice. They have neither the power nor the ability to challenge the Dakhinis on the field. The emperor had his camp outside the city of Akbarabad; after some days, he and Sindhia set out for Delhi. They sent 'Abdul Ahad Khan to prison in Aligarh, which is occupied by Najaf Khan's sister and where many of his men have also gathered.

The Maratha commander Sindhia is the master of the 269 land and does what he desires. He offhandedly gives some money to the emperor and takes him with him wherever he wishes. And so he stayed in the city for a month, then took

* December 1784.

راجپوتان در سر داشت، باز فوج کشی کرده به آن طرف رفت.
راجه ها همدانی را، که سردار نجف خانی بود، طلب داشته رفیق
خود کردند.جنگ بمیان آمد. همدانی جرأت نمود و کشته شد.

۲۷۰   سرداری بجای او مرزا اسمٰعیل که همشیره زادهٔ او بود یافت.
این بابا بجسارت تمام جنگیده بلای مرهٹه را برچید. شکست
فاحشی شد. آلات جنگ و اسباب مرهٹه بالکل رفت. جان خود را
غنیمت دانسته گریخت و به اکبرآباد آمد. آنجا هم مرزا اسمٰعیل
رسیده ازان شهر برآورد و قلعه را خود چسپید. جنگ قلعه بطول
کشید. مرهٹه صرفهٔ خود بطرف دیگر دید. بادشاه از شهر برآمده
به نجف قلی خان که جانب حصار بود رفت. آنجا جنگ بسیار
شد. آخرالامر از نجف قلی خان چیزی گرفته بشهر رسید.

۲۷۱   درین حال پسر ضابطه خان که غلام قادر نام داشت و بعد
از پدر خود متصرف سهارنپور و غیره بود، زوری بهم رسانیده و
فوج سکهان را همراه گرفته آمد. اکثر محالات پادشاهی که میان
دوآبه بودند ضبط کرد. قریب رسیده از بادشاه چیزی خواست.
بادشاه جواب داد. او آنروی آب مورچال بسته مهیای جنگ شد.
چنانچه یک ماه کسری زیاده جنگید. بادشاه اگرچه فوج و زوری
نداشت، به دندان چسپیده آن بلا را برچید. آن از آنجا برخواسته
تا گرد اکبرآباد تسلط کرد. اینجا که مرزا اسمٰعیل بیگ در شهر
بقلعه چسپیده بود، زور آنرا دیده دستار بدل شد. و عهد و پیمان

the emperor with him to Aligarh, where hostilities lasted ten or fifteen days. Finally, making pacts and promises, he made the begum come out of the fort; he then grabbed from her some of Najaf Khan's property and let her go. From there he took the emperor with him against the Rajputs. They stood firm, and after some days he made peace with them. Then the emperor returned to Delhi, while the Maratha remained in Akbarabad. But he still had the Rajputs on his mind. Once again he launched an attack on them. The Rajput rajas sent for Muhammad Beg Hamadani—the Najaf Khani commander—and got him to fight on their side. When the battle took place, Hamadani showed much bravery and was killed.*

Then his sister's son, Mirza Isma'il, took command. That young man fought most boldly and removed the Maratha evil. The Maratha, badly defeated, lost all his goods and materiel. Grateful to escape alive, he fled to Akbarabad. Mirza Isma'il followed him there and forced him to leave. He then himself laid siege to the fort. The siege grew long. The Maratha realized that his interests lay elsewhere than with the emperor. Meanwhile, the emperor marched out of Delhi on a campaign against Najaf Quli Khan, who was in the region of Hissar. A major battle occurred there. Eventually the emperor extracted some money from Najaf Quli Khan and returned to Delhi.† 270

Just then, Ghulam Qadir, who was the son of Zabita Khan and, after the father's death, had gained control of Saharanpur and other places, gathered more power and set out, 271

---

* July 27, 1787.
† March 1788.

بمیان آمد که با مرهڻ ما و شما بالاتفاق خواهیم جنگید. بعد از چند روز مرهڻ که ارادهٔ آن طرف چنبل داشت، یلغار کرده رسید. درین روزها اینجا شاهزاده صاحب عالم بود، لیکن تغافل کرد. تنها جنگ بر سر مرزا اسمٰعیل افتاد. آن بابا پای جسارت افشرده این جنگ را هم زد. مرهڻ گریخته آن طرف گوالیار که در تصرف او بود اقامت کرد. بعد از چندی فوج دیگر طلبداشته سرگرم پرخاش شد. ده پانزده روز در ظاهر اکبرآباد جنگ شد. آخر شکست مرزا اسمعیل اتفاق افتاد. غلام قادر خان تماشائی ماند. مرزای مذکور فرار کرده پیش غلام قادر آمد. این را که دید که در احتیاط خود است و بکار من نمی پردازد. ناچار پیش او ماند، و بعد از چند روز ارادهٔ ملک خود نموده روانه شد.

accompanied by an army of Sikhs. He took possession of most of the crown lands in the *doab* and arrived close to Delhi, where he made demands upon the emperor. When the emperor refused, Ghulam Qadir set up his artillery on the other side of the river and launched an attack. The hostilities continued for a little more than a month. The emperor did not have an army or any other power, but he fought back resolutely and extirpated that affliction. Ghulam Qadir withdrew from Delhi and took possession of the lands up to Akbarabad. When Mirza Isma'il Beg, who was in Akbarabad investing the fort, saw how strong Ghulam Qadir was, he met him and exchanged turbans with him as a token of deep friendship. The two made a pact to fight against the Maratha jointly. After some days, the Maratha leader, who had planned to go to the other side of the river Chambal, instead launched a sudden rapid attack on Akbarabad. Although the prince was there at the time, he neglected to act, and the burden of battle fell entirely on Mirza Isma'il. That young man boldly fought back and again won.* The Maratha fled and encamped beyond Gwalior, in the area under his control. Some time later, he summoned another army and launched another attack. For some ten or fifteen days, the two sides fought outside Akbarabad. Finally Mirza Isma'il was defeated.† All that time, Ghulam Qadir remained a mere spectator. The mirza fled to him but discovered that the latter had only his own interest in mind and was not going to help. Caught in a bind, he stayed on with him, but after some time, expressing

---

* December 1787.
† June 1788.

۲۷۲ ناظر پادشاه که غلام قادر را پسر خوانده بود، نوشت که شما اینجا بیائید. گفتهٔ من پادشاه نمی شنود، یعنی طرف مرهٹه نمی گذارد. ایشان هر دو بشهر رفتند. پادشاه خود زوری نداشت. به مشورت ناظر نمک بحرام بندوبست در قلعه کرده بادشاه را برداشت، و سلوکی که نمی بایست، کرد. و تمام قلعه را غارت کرد. و با پادشاهزاده ها آنچه نه کردن بود کرد. زر بسیاری بدستش آمد. چشم پادشاه برآورد، و پادشاه دیگر کرد. چون تسلط کلی یافت، ناظر را نیز قید نمود و بر شهر هم کار تنگ گرفت. چون غلبه از حد افزون گشت، از مرزا اسمعیل پی هیچ بی مزه شد، و در چیز دادن کوتاهی کرد. آن عزیز با مرهٹه صلح کرد.

۲۷۳ درین هنگام فوج مرهٹه قریب رسید. بعضی از سرداران داخل شهر شدند. روهیله قلعه بند گشت، و هنگام شب از راه خضری دروازه معه فوج و اسباب و زر و مال خود و پادشاهزاده ها و ناظر و لواحقان او را نیز همراه برده نزد شاهدره با فوج سنگربسته استادگی کرد. آخرالامر مرهٹه ها بی حیائی او دیده آن روی آب رفته مقیّد جنگ شدند. گاهی ایشان غالب می آمدند و گاهی آن ملعون.

a desire to return to his own territory, left.

The *nāzir* of the emperor had earlier called Ghulam Qadir   272
his son; he now wrote to him, "You must get here. The
emperor does not listen to me. He is not willing to give up
siding with the Maratha chief." The two, Mirza Isma'il and
Ghulam Qadir, went to the city. The emperor was powerless.
Ghulam Qadir, in consultation with the traitor, the *nāzir,*
took hold of the citadel, deposed the emperor, and did to him
what should never be done.[80] He plundered the entire fort
and treated the princes and princesses in the most improper
way. A great deal of wealth fell into his hands. He pulled out
the eyes of the emperor and then placed another person on
the throne. When he had gained control over everything,
he imprisoned even the *nāzir.* Now the city too began to
suffer at his hands. When his dominance became total, he
quarreled with Mirza Isma'il over some insignificant matter
and stopped sharing the loot with him. The latter then made
peace with the Maratha.

In the meantime, the Maratha army came very close, and   273
some of its commanders entered the city. The Rohilla, i.e.,
Ghulam Qadir, shut himself in the citadel. Then, at night,
he slipped out through the Khizri Gate, taking with him
his troopers, his bag and baggage and all the wealth, as
well as the royal children, the *nāzir,* and the *nāzir's* relatives. Setting up his camp near Shahdara, he prepared with
bastions and trenches to repulse any attack. On seeing his
impudent belligerence, the Maratha chief crossed the river
and started hostilities. Sometimes he gained the upper hand,
other times that accursed person did.

When that had gone on for almost a month, a commander   274

۲۷۴ چون قریب یک ماه کشید، علی بهادر نام سرداری از دکن آمد
و گرم جنگ روهیله شد. بعد از دو سه جنگ بجرأت تمام او را
اسیر کردند. مال و اسباب معه پادشاهزاده ها ازو گرفتند و قید
داشتند. و پادشاه همان شاه عالم کور را مقرر داشتند. قلعه را
حواله جاثان نمودند. و صد روپیه روز به پادشاه می دهند، و بر
تمام ملک متصرف اند. آن ملعون را بخواری تمام کشتند. حالا
مرهٹہ پادشاه است، هرچه می خواهد می کند. باید دید که چنین
تا کجا خواهد بود.

۲۷۵ القصه جهان عجب حادثه گاهیست. چه مکانها خراب گشتند؛
چه جوانان از هم گزشتند؛ چه باغها ویرانه شدند؛ چه بزمها
افسانه شدند. چه گلها افسردند؛ چه خوبان مردند. چه مجلسها
برشکستند؛ چه قافله ها رخت بستند. چه عزیزان ذلت کشیدند؛
چه مردمان بجان رسیدند. این چشم عبرت بین چها دید، و این
گوش شنوا چها شنید:

by the name of 'Ali Bahadur came from the south and joined the fight against the Rohilla.* After two or three battles, Ghulam Qadir was finally taken prisoner. They confiscated all his wealth and rescued the royal children. Then they put the blind Shah 'Alam on the throne and placed the citadel under the Jats. Now they, i.e., the Marathas, give the emperor 100 rupees per day for his expenses and hold power over the entire land. They also killed that accursed person Ghulam Qadir in a most debasing manner.† Presently, the Maratha, i.e., Sindhia, is the "king" and acts as it pleases him. Let us see how long things last in this fashion.[81]

In short, the world is a place of strange happenings. What houses there were that crumbled down! What young men there were who gave up their lives! What gardens that are now a wilderness! What joyous assemblies that now seem fantasies! What lovely flowers that withered away! What handsome men who passed on! What friendly gatherings that were tossed to the wind! What caravans that loaded up and disappeared! What honorable men there were who suffered ignominy! What bold men there were who tasted mortality! These eyes have seen everything, and these ears heard everything.

275

* November 1788.
† March 1789.

هر کاسهٔ سر ز افـسری مـی گـوید

هر کهنه خـرابه از دری مـی گـوید

دنیاست فسـانه، پارهٔ ما گفتیم

وآن پارهٔ که ماند دیگری می گوید

۲۷۶ حالیا خامه لطایف چند بر زبان دارد، و برای خاطر دوستان می نگارد.

۲۷۷ (۱) میر سید شریف و ملا سعدالدین تفتازانی که از علمای قرارداده بودند اکثر باهم شوخی می نمودند. میر ظاهر خوبی داشت. یکی از گرد راه با رخسار گردآلود رسید. ملا گفت، یا لیتنی کنت تراباً. میر گفت، بلی، «یقول الکافر یا لیتنی کنت تراباً».

۲۷۸ (۲) یکی مولانا روم و ملا صدرالدین در مسجد شام وقت شام وارد شدند و اقتدا به پیش نماز آنجا کردند. هیبت هر دو بزرگ بر او غالب آمد. در هر دو رکعت سوره «قل یا ایها الکافرون» با سوره فاتحه ضم نمود. چون رو برای سلام گردند، شیخ بجانب مولانا دید و دوش زد، یعنی ضم کردن یک سوره دو بار چه معنی دارد. مولانا خندید و گفت که معقولست. یک خطاب بشما بود و یک بما.

۲۷۹ (۳) دو فاضل راه میرفتند. یکی خراسانی بود و یکی خواندساری. دیدند که خرسی را کشته و بر خر بار کرده می آرند. خراسانی به خواندساری چشمک زد.او بتفرس دریافته گفت، هنوزمردهٔ من

304

This bowl of a skull speaks of some mighty man;
And the crumbling ruins tell of a mansion grand.
This world is a lengthy tale—we told a tiny part;
Now someone else will tell the part that remains.

Now the pen has on its tongue some witty tales, and lays them out for its friends' sake:[82]

    276

(1) Mir Sayyid Sharif and Mulla Sa'duddin Taftazani were acknowledged scholars; they also used to jest with each other. The mir was handsome in looks. Once he arrived with his face covered with the dust of the road. The mulla said to him, "Woe unto me! Would that I were dust." The mir responded, "Indeed, the unbeliever will say at the end: 'Woe unto me! Would that I were dust.'"[83]

    277

(2) Once Maulana Rum and Shaikh Sadruddin arrived at the Syrian mosque when it was the time for the evening prayers.[84] Accordingly they took their places behind the imam of the mosque. The imam was so awed by the presence of these two revered men that in his confusion he repeated the same *sūra*, "Say: Oh you Unbelievers," in both parts of the prayers—something that should never be done. When the prayers ended, the shaikh looked questioningly toward the maulana, as if to ask: why did the man repeat himself? The latter smiled and said, "It was only reasonable. The first time he addressed you, and the second time me."

    278

(3) Two scholars were on a journey together. One was from Khurasan, the other from Khundsar. They came upon some people who had killed a bear and were carrying it away on an ass. The Khurasani gave the Khundsari a nudge, who intuitively grasped the situation and said, "My 'dead' still tops

    279

305

زندهٔ ترا بار است. لطف این لطیفه اینست که خر از خراسان می
آرند و خرس از خواندسار.

۲۸۰ (۴) روزی ملا باقر مجلسی از راه میگزشت. پایش بنجاست
درآمد.چون آب حاضر نبود ملا حیران شد. لوطی دید و گفت،
اخوند چه بخود فرو رفتهٔ؟. ملا تر آمد و بهمان حال رفت.

۲۸۱ (۵) یکی حکیم خاقانی از سواد شهر می آمد. دید که خری آلت
تناسل برآورده از شدت شبق هر طرف می دود، و زنی نشسته می
بیند و گریه میکند. پرسید که سبب گریه ات چیست. گفت
برای شوهر میگریم که از مدت مدید در سفر است. گفت، ای
کس فراخ، اگر آن دور رفته تریاکی خواهد آمد این قدر گنده و
دراز خواهد آورد؟ برو، سر خود گیر.

۲۸۲ (۶) دو کس باهم رابطه داشتند. خواهران هر دو نامزد هم
بودند.اتفاقاً باتفاق نجومیان ساعت تزویج هر دو شخص یک
برآمد. ملا محمد باقر مجلسی را برای خواندن نکاح خواندند. او
بسبب ضرورتی تعلل کرد و همشیره زادهٔ خود ملا محمد سعید
اشرف را فرستاد. این بابا بسیار شوخ طبع بود. آمد و نکاح هر دو
خواند. چون عقد تزویج بسته شد و فراغت کرد، گفت، حالا چرا
نشسته اید، بر خیزید و بکس خواهر همدیگر بزنید.

۲۸۳ (۷) عمادالدین مشهور بعمادِ لُر، ملازم خواجه شمس الدین
محمد، شطرنج خوب باختی و خواجه با او ظرافت کردی. روزی

your 'living.'"[85] The fun here lies in the fact that asses come from Khurasan and bears from Khundsar.

(4) One day Mulla Baqir Majlisi was walking down the road when he stepped into some excrement.[86] Since there was no water to clean with, he stopped and stood there at a loss. A *lūtī* saw him and said,[87] "Teacher, sunk deep in our thoughts, aren't we?" The mulla was so embarrassed that he walked away just as he was.

(5) Once Hakim Khaqani was coming back to the city when he saw an ass—its penis fully extended—running wildly in lust, while a woman sat nearby, watching the ass and crying.[88] "Why the tears?" Khaqani asked. "I'm crying for my husband," she replied. "He has been away on a journey for a long time." "You 'wide cunt,'" the hakim retorted. "If that opium-eating milksop comes back, you think he would bring you something that thick and long? Get up and go home!"

(6) Two men were close friends; they were also engaged, each to the other's sister. By chance the astrologers set the same day and time for the two weddings. Mulla Muhammad Baqir Majlisi was invited to perform the weddings but, due to another obligation, he excused himself. Instead he sent his nephew, Mulla Muhammad Ashraf, who was of a jocular bent of mind. Mulla Ashraf came and performed the two ceremonies. He then turned to the two grooms and said, "Why are you still sitting here? Go and start poking into each other's sister."

(7) 'Imaduddin, more famous by the name "'Imad the Lur,"[89] was in the employment of Khwaja Shamsuddin Muhammad;[90] he also played chess rather well. The khwaja used to make fun of him, and one day said to him derogato-

خواجه این دشنام داد که ای کون زنت فراخ. عرق لری عماد

بحرکت آمد و این رباعی بداهته گفت:

هــرچنــد سخنهای چــو دُر میگوئی

هشــــدار که بــعمادِ لُر مــــیگوئی

عیب تو همین است که اندر شطرنج

ای کــونِ زنت فـراخ پُـر مــیگوئی

(۸) روزی انوری بر دوکانی نشسته بود. تابوتی میرفت. ورثۀ آن ۲۸۴

مرده مویه کنان میرفتند و میگفتند که ترا جای میبرند که تنگ و

تاریکست. چراغی ندارد، مونسی نیست. انوری میدود و میگوید

(کذا) مگر بخانۀ من میبرند. این لطیفه ببادشاه وقت رسید.

مکان وسیعی عنایتش کرد.

(۹) لوطی ماده خری را میگائید. شخصی دید و پرسید که این چه ۲۸۵

عمل است. گفت، برو! تو چه دانی که مردان خدا در چه کار اند؟

(۱۰) مرزا ابرهیم ادهم مهمان گشت. خدمتگارش خوشرو بود. ۲۸۶

چشم برو سیاه کرد و شب هنگام از فرش خواب برخاسته سرگرم

تلاش او شد. رفت و پای یکی کشید. او گفت که مرزا مگر خیر

است؟ شرمنده شده برگشت. بعد ساعتی باز برخاست و در فکر

همان عمل افتاد. اتفاقاً پای همان کس بدست آمد. گفت، مرزا

این چه حرکت است؟ باز خجالت کشید و برگردید. همین قسم

rily, "Hey, you with a fat-assed wife!" That aroused 'Imad's wild streak, and he responded with this impromptu quatrain:

> *You may spout words as fine as pearls*
> *But watch out, for you speak to 'Imad the Lur.*
> *It's your fault when during the chess's strife*
> *You shout so often, you with a fat-assed wife.*

who is Anvari?

(8) One day Anvari was seated at a shop when a funeral procession came by.[91] The relatives of the deceased were crying and wailing: "Woe that they are taking you to a dark and narrow place ... where there is no light ... where there is no one to comfort you." Anvari ran after them, exclaiming, "They must be taking him to my house." This amusing incident was reported to the king, who gifted Anvari a spacious residence. 284

(9) A rogue was busy fucking a she-ass. Someone saw and exclaimed, "What are you doing?" "Move on!" the rogue replied. "How would *you* know what task 'God's men' are engaged in?" 285

→ what do these anecdotes say about Mughal society

(10) Mirza Ibrahim Adham was a guest at someone's house. The host's servant was good-looking, and so the mirza took a fancy to him. That night, when everyone stretched out on the floor and went to sleep, the mirza got up and went looking for the youth. Making a guess in the dark, he shook someone's foot. The man asked, "Mirza! Are you all right?" Embarrassed, the mirza went back and lay down. After a while, however, he got up and again went on his quest. By chance, he again grabbed the foot of that same man, who exclaimed, "Mirza! What are you doing?" Once more, highly 286

was gay interest normalized ???

چند بار در اماکن مختلفه پای همان کس بدستش افتاد. آخر بیدماغ شد و گفت، هرجا که دست می اندازم پای تو بدست می آید، گیدی مگر هزار پائی.

۲۸۷ (۱۱) یکی با خالهٔ خود سری داشت. فرصت وقت یافته از وطن جای دیگرش برد. در اثنای راه زیر درختی تنه کرده گائید. لته که ازان عضو مخصوص را پاک ساخته بود بر آن درخت انداخته پیشتر رفت. چون آن درخت بر سر راه واقع شده بود هرکه از آن راه گزشت لتهٔ بتقلید برو انداخت. رفته رفته شجرِ فاضلی شد. بعد مدتی که برگشت و در سایهٔ آن نشست، لته های بسیار برو دیده قیاس برخود نمود و گفت، الله! زیر این درخت چقدر خاله ها گائیده اند.

۲۸۸ (۱۲) مرزا صائب در قهوه خانه با یاران نشسته بود. قزوینی هم آمد و نشست. چون قزوینیان احمق و بدقافیه می باشند مرزا بر سبیل ظرافت ازو پرسید که در قزوین شما قرمساق هم می باشند. او طبعیت شوخی داشت. گفت، چرا نمی باشند؟ قزوین شهر کلانیست. اما اینقدر نیست که صف بسته می نشینند.

۲۸۹ (۱۳) از سخنان سادات بارهه که خالی از لطف نیستند و بر السنهٔ هندیان بسیاراند، ازان جمله دو سه بیاد داشتم نگاشتم. سیدی مفلس جلای وطن کرده جهت تلاش معاش بشاهجهان آباد آمد، و از فاقه کشیها ضعیف و نحیف شد. سورهٔ «قل یا

310

mortified, the mirza went back to his place. In that manner, he repeatedly went groping but somehow always found the same man's foot. Finally he lost his temper and cried out, "No matter where I put my hand it always lands on your foot! What are you, you blockhead—a centipede?"

(11) A certain man lusted after his aunt. After some time he had to take her to another city. On the way, stopping under a nice big tree, he fucked her. Afterward he wiped himself clean with a piece of cloth, threw it into the branches, and continued onward. As the tree was by the roadside, everyone who later came by and saw that rag followed the example by throwing a piece of cloth into the branches. By and by, it became a *fāzil* tree.[92] Then after a long time, that first man, returning home, again stopped in its shade. When he saw those numerous strips of cloth in its branches, he recalled his own experience and exclaimed, "God Almighty! How many aunts have been fucked under this tree!"

(12) Mirza Sa'ib was seated with some friends in a coffee shop.[93] A Qazvini also came in and took a seat. Since the people from Qazvin are considered to be foolish and ignorant, the mirza jokingly asked the man, "Do they have pimps in that Qazvin of yours?" The man was quick-witted; he replied, "Certainly. Why not? Qazvin is a big place. But they aren't so many that they must sit in rows."[94]

(13) Indians have many stories about the sayyids of Barha that are not devoid of fun.[95] Of these, I now write a few that I recall. An indigent sayyid left home and came to Shahjahanabad to find a living. But instead, he was forced to starve and became quite lean and thin. Earlier at his native place

ایها الکافرون » را در وطن بر لوح طفلی بخط جلی نوشته دیده بود. اتفاقاً گذرش بر مکتبی افتاد. آنجا سورهٔ مسطور را بخط خفی دید. گفت، سبحان الله! گردش ایام بیچاره «قُلیا» را هم بحال او نگذاشت. آنچنان لاغر شده است که شناخته نمی شود.

(۱۴) سیدی پسری آورد. گفتند چه نام کردهٔ. گفت، ابوجهل، اگر خدا هم جهالت او نصیب این بکند.

(۱۵) از سیدی پرسیدند که بارهٔ شما از کدام مدت آباد است. گفت، پنجهزار سال شده باشد. گفتند، سیادت از پیغمبر علیه السلام اعتبار می کنند. مدت عهد آن برگزیدهٔ آفاق مشهور آفاقست. گفت، ایشان سادات دیگراند و ما سادات دیگر.

(۱۶) الف ابدال موزون طبعی بود. الف تخلص میکرد و رندانه بسر می برد. مدعیان بشاه عباس گفتند که این عزیز متمول است، چیزی ازین باید گرفت. شاه بحضور خودش خواند و گفت، شنیده ام که زر سرخ و سفید بسیاری داری. گفت، قربانت شوم، شنیدهٔ که زر دارم، نشنیدهٔ که الف هیچ ندارد. شاه خندید و سرخ و زرد گردید.

(۱۷،) قزوینی پیش میرزا صائب آمد و گفت مشتاقِ زادهٔ طبع شریفم. میرزا که اخلاق پسندیده داشت شعرهای که طرف وقوع داشتند خواند و متوقع تحسین و آفرین شد. گفت، قرمساق، هرچه می بیند می بندد و خود را شاعر میگردد؟؟

۲۹۰

۲۹۱

۲۹۲

۲۹۳

he had once seen the Qur'anic verse—"*Qul yā ayyuh-al-kāfirūn …*"[96]—written out in big letters on a child's school tablet. Now in Delhi he happened to pass by another school, where he saw the same verse written out on a tablet in very small letters. The man exclaimed, "Allah be praised! These grinding times haven't spared even the '*Qulya*.' It's become so thin, it can hardly be recognized."

(14) A sayyid from Barha had a son. People asked him, "What have you named him?" He replied, "Abu Jahl—now if God would also bless him his *jahālat*."[97]

(15) People asked a sayyid from Barha, "How long has it been since you sayyids settled at Barha?" "Five thousand years," he replied. They said, "But 'sayyidness' is traced from the Prophet, peace be upon him, and the whole world knows how long ago that most select of men had lived." "He was a sayyid of one kind," the fellow replied, "and we are of another."

(16) Alif 'Abdal had a poetic bent of mind; he had taken Alif for his *takhallus* and lived the life of a carefree person. His enemies said to Shah Abbas, "Alif is a man of much wealth. You should extract some from him." The shah summoned him and said, "I hear you have plenty of gold and silver." "May I die for you," Alif replied. "You heard that I have plenty of gold, but haven't you heard that *alif* has nothing?"[98] The shah laughed and felt embarrassed.

(17) A Qazvini came to Mirza Sa'ib and said, "I'm most eager to hear your verses." The mirza, being a polite and cultured man, recited a few topical verses and waited for some words of praise.[99] Instead the man said, "You pimp! You write only what you see—and yet you call yourself a poet?"

313

۲۹۴ (۱۸) مخفیای رشتی مخفی تخلص مخلص مصاحب حاکم
شیراز بود. چون کوکنار بسیار میخورد بغایت نحافت بدن
داشت. روزی حاکم مذکور گفت که مخفی استخوانی بیش
نمانده، از کوکنار دست بردار.گفت، تقصیر کوکنار نیست. این
تاثیر نفرین مردمانست. گفت، چه معنی دارد. گفت، هرکه می
نویسد اول می نویسد که مخفی نماند. من ام که اینقدر هم
مانده ام. اگر بجای من دیگری می بود کی ها از میان می رفت.

۲۹۵ (۱۹) امردی لفظ «نفس» را نوشته پیش خوشنویسی برای
اصلاح آورد. او لفظ مسطور را خود هم نوشت باو نمود که اینقسم
بایستی نوشت. امرد زیاده سر گفت که هیچ تفاوت نیست؛ من
هم خوب نوشته ام. خطاط که طبعش مایل بظرافت بود گفت،
در خوبی نوشتهٔ تو حرفی نیست، لیکن اینقدر هست که این اندکی
تندوتیز است.

۲۹۶ (۲۰) روزی حکیم شیخ حسین شهرت که شهرت دارد بخانهٔ
خواجه سرای بادشاهی رفت. آنجا شخصی فتق داشت، رجوعی
کرد. حکیم گفت، علاج خود سهل است، لیکن خایه درین خانه
یمن ندارد.

۲۹۷ (۲۱) نجم الدوله اسحاق خان اکثری برای فردوس آرامگاه طبخ
نظر میکرد و می فرستاد. روزی پادشاه فرمود که دل و جگر تیار
کرده بفرست.آنعزیز بخانه آمد و گفت که از قصابان جگر چند

(18) Makhfiya-e Rashti, whose *takhallus* was Makhfi, was a courtier to the ruler of Shiraz. Since he habitually consumed a great deal of opium, he had become thin and weak. One day the ruler said to him, "Makhfi, give up the opium. There is nothing left in you now except skin and bones." "It's not the opium's fault," Makhfi replied, "it's the effect of the people's curses." "What do you mean?" the ruler asked. Makhfi said, "When anyone writes anything he always first writes: *makhfī na-mānad*.[100] At least I have managed to last this long. Had it been someone else, he would have succumbed long ago."   294

(19) An adolescent boy wrote out the word *nafs*—"man's lower self"—and brought it to a calligrapher for correction. The calligrapher wrote the word himself and said, "Now that's how you should write it." The lad began to insist that there was no difference, that he too had written the word quite nicely. The calligrapher, having a playful nature, responded, "I don't question the loveliness of your *nafs*; it's just that it's a bit too headstrong and aggressive."   295

(20) Once the famous physician Shaikh Husain Shuhrat went to the house of the royal eunuch.[101] A man there was suffering from a hernia in the scrotum and asked the physician's advice. Shuhrat replied, "The treatment is easy enough, but in this house no testicle can ever be safe."   296

(21) Najm-ud-Daula Ishaq Khan often had some special dish prepared and sent to the palace for the enjoyment of the late Emperor Muhammad Shah. Once the emperor asked him for some grilled liver-and-heart. He came home and ordered his servants to get some hearts and livers from the butchers and bring them before him. When they did, he   297

معه دل بگیرند و پیش من بیارند. آوردند و بحضوراو بردند. اتفاقاً جگری برآمد که با او دل نبود. روی درهم کشید و سوی بکاول بخشم دید. آن مرد ظریف بود. گفت، تقصیر من نیست و قصابان هم بیگنه اند. این جگر مرزا بیدل است.

۲۹۸ (۲۲) علوی خان حکیم کلانی بود. از کمال شهرت محتاج تعریف نیست. ندیمی داشت میرمعصوم نام. روزی او دیر حاضر شد. گفت، ای میرمعصوم، کجا رفته بودی؟ گفتا، امروز برای سیر سواد شهر رفته بودم. گفت، هان چه دیدی؟ گفتا، تا نظر کار میکرد الواح مزارات بود، و بر آنها نوشته بودند: عمل علوی خانصاحب، عمل علوی خانصاحب. گفت هنوز از مزاح دست برنمیداری. گفتا، محل شکر کردن است نه مقام بد بردن. نام خدا، یمن دست نوابصاحب را زیاده بر پدر مرحوم نواب می بینم.

۲۹۹ (۲۳) شبی در ایوان کیف مرزا صائب را شاه تکلیف شراب کرد. مرزا ابا نمود. فرمود، چرا نمیخوری؟ التماس کرد که مزیل عقلست. قبول نیفتاد و مبالغه از حد برد. چون مرزا شراب خورد و بدمست شد، دلِ شب از بزمش برآورد. صبح که مرزا حاضر گشت، گفت، بسیار از آب بد برآمدی. آدم اینهمه خم تنک نمی باشد. گفت عرض کرده بودم که شراب مزیل عقل است. گفتا، مگر من نخورده بودم؟ گفت، سرت گردم، بحث در ازالۀ عقل

found one liver that had its paired heart missing. His countenance clouded, and he glared at his steward. That man was
quite witty; he immediately said, "No fault of mine, sir. And
the butchers are equally innocent. That happens to be the
liver of Mirza 'Heartless.'"[102]

(22) Alavi Khan was a great physician—in fact, his fame   298
does not need my endorsement.[103] He had a boon companion
named Mir Ma'sum. Once the mir arrived rather late. Alavi
Khan asked, "Mir Ma'sum, where were you?" "I went for a
walk outside the city," the mir replied. "And what did you
see there?" the khan asked. "Graves," the mir said. "There
were graves as far as I could see. And on each the headstone
said: 'By the grace of Alavi Khan Sahib.'" The khan said,
"Won't you ever stop jesting?" The mir replied, "Do not take
it badly. Be grateful. For, by God's grace, I discovered that
my master's hand had 'blessed' many more people than the
hand of his late father."

(23) Once, in the Pavilion of Pleasure, the shah asked   299
Mirza Sa'ib to have some wine. When the mirza declined, the
shah asked for his reason. "It takes away one's intelligence,"
replied the mirza. The shah didn't accept that and pressed
him even more. Finally the mirza gave in, but became so
drunk that by midnight, he had to be removed from the gathering. Next morning, when he again came to the court, the
shah said to him, "You made quite a mess of yourself last
night. One shouldn't be so shallow when it comes to holding one's liquor." The mirza said, "I had humbly told you
that wine takes away one's intelligence." The shah retorted,
"But I drank too, didn't I?" "May I die for you, sir," the
mirza replied. "But my reasoning concerned losing one's

میرفت. تو خود عقل نداشتی.

۳۰۰ (۲۴) امیرخان انجام امیر کلانی بود. طلاقت لسانی و نستعلیق
گوئی او مشهور است. سلیقۀ درستی داشت. برادرش را دایم
الخمر و سرشار میگفتند. چون کار نادرستیش برسوائی کشید و
باین رسید، روبروی خودش طلبید و گفت که ای خانه خراب،
کدام مردآدمی در خانۀ خود برای تفنن طبعیت این عمل نمی
کند لیکن نه باین رسوائی.

۳۰۱ (۲۵) شخصی زنی شریفه نام در خانۀخود نگهداشته بود. روزی
در نشه شراب با ظریفی اوصاف پدر خود نقل میکرد. آنعزیز باو
شوخی داشت. گفت، محامد والد شریف چه میگوئی، حکایت او
پس سر شد. بیچاره مرد و رفت. اکنون از خصایل والدۀ شریفه
بگو که بر روی کار است.

۳۰۲ (۲۶) چمیلی پلاو بخانۀ اعظم خان کلان خوب پخته میشد. آن
اینست که روغن را در گلهای یاسمن دو سه روز نگاه میداشتند
تا بو میگرفت و بهمان روغن پلاو می پختند. بوی خوشی میداد.
برهان الملک تعریف آن طعام شنیده فرمایش کرد. آنعزیز طیار
نموده دو سه قاب برای او فرستاد. خورد و حظی بسیار برداشته
بظرافت گفت، این قاب پلاو نیست، مرقد مبارک حضرت نظام
الدین اولیاست. چون بر مزار شریف آن بزرگوار گلهای مذکور
چمن چمن آوردۀ زایران میافشاندند آن مرقد برنگ خرمن گل

318

intelligence, and you already possessed none."

(24) Amir Khan "Anjam" was a grand noble, still remembered for his eloquence and highly elegant speech. He lived a life of propriety, but his brother was reported to be a drunkard. When the word of it spread and reached Amir Khan, he summoned his brother and said to him, "Oh you 'Ruin of the House,' who doesn't drink a little at home to enliven the spirit—but none does to such discredit."

(25) A certain man had taken as his mistress a woman named Sharifa—the feminine form of *sharīf*, i.e., "noble." One day when he had had too much to drink the man started enumerating to a certain wit all the wonderful attributes of his own father. The wit, who could be bold with him, said, "Why sing the praises of your *sharīf* father? His is a tale of yore. The poor man passed on long ago. Tell me instead the fine qualities of your *sharīfa* mother who is still going strong."

(26) They used to prepare a fine jasmine pilaf at the house of A'zam Khan Sr.[104] They would put jasmine flowers in some oil and let it sit for a few days so it would absorb the fragrance. Then they would use the oil to cook the rice, which gave it a fine aroma. Burhan-ul-Mulk heard its praise and made a request to Azam Khan Sr., who then had some prepared and sent over in several big platters. Burhan-ul-Mulk ate it with relish, then remarked in a jocular vein, "It's not a platter of pilaf; it's the blessed grave of Hazrat Nizamuddin Auliya." The remark was greatly enjoyed, for people in fact used to bring jasmine flowers in great quantities to cover that revered person's grave. It would then look like a heap of flowers, and their fragrance would transport passersby

300

301

302

319

بنظر می آمد و بوی خوش بمشام آینده و رونده از دور می رسید،
این سخن لطف بهم رسانید.

۳۰۳ (۲۷) شخصی پیش مرزاجانجانان مظهر آمد و گفت که باد
برآورده ام. ظریفی پرسید [از] کجا؟.ایشان گفتند،از جای که بر
می آید.

۳۰۴ (۲۸) روزی احمدعلی خان نام مصاحب برهان الملک شلوار
کمخاب پوشیده آمد. نواب دید و پاخوانی کرد. آنعزیز تر آمد.
مصاحب دیگر که نامش از خاطر من رفته است گفت که در عالم
شراب شب غلط کرده است.

۳۰۵ (۲۹) لهجهٔ عراقیان است هر الفی که بعد از آن نون می آید آن
الف را بواو بدل کرده میخوانند، مثل آن و کمان و جان و جهان.
و اینکه کجلافیان هر الف را بواو بدل میکنند غلط فاحش است.
صفدرمحمد خان که از عراق بود روزی برای مجرای محمد شاه
رفت. پادشاه، نظر بر انکه بعضی الفاظ اینقسم در لهجهٔ ایشان
بقباحت منجر میشوند، مخاطبش نموده این مصراع شیخ سعدی
بر زبان راند: «ای مرغ سحر عشق ز پروانه بیاموز.» خان مذ کور
در حال بتهه سخن رسیده گفت، بلی، «کون سوخته را جون شد
و آواز نیامد.»

۳۰۶ (۳۰) یکی خان مسطور بخانهٔ قزلباش خان آمد و مهمان شد. او
خانه آنسوی شهر مشرف به نهر داشت. ساکنان محلات آنطرف

even at some distance.

(27) A visitor came to Mirza Mazhar Jan-e Janan and said, "A chance wind brings me here." "From where?" asked a wit who was present. The mirza interjected, "From the place wind breaks out of."[105] *Mughal sarcasm*   303

(28) Once Ahmad 'Ali Khan, a courtier of Nawab Burhan-ul-Mulk, put on a *shalwār* of brocade and came to the court. The nawab noticed this and made some caustic comments about the unmanly trousers. The khan was terribly embarrassed. Another courtier, whose name slips my mind, remarked, "He must have confused his own pair with someone else's during last night's drinking party."   304

gender norms in terms of dress

(29) In the Iraqi pronunciation, every *alif* before a *nūn* is changed into a *wāw*,[106] for example in such words as *ān*, *kamān*, *jān*, *jahān*. However, the fools who put on airs and change every *alif* into a *wāw*, they make a shameful mistake. Anyway, once Safdar Muhammad Khan, who was from Iraq, went to pay his respects to Muhammad Shah. The emperor, recalling that certain words get terribly distorted in the Iraqi manner, looked toward him and recited the line from Sa'di, "*ai murgh-e sahar 'ishq za parwāna biyāmūz.*" The khan immediately grasped what the emperor had in mind and responded, "Indeed, '*kun sokhta ra jun shud-o awāz niyāmad.*'"[107]   305

(30) Once the abovementioned Safdar Muhammad Khan was a guest at the house of Qizilbash Khan Umid. The latter lived at the far side of the city, close to the canal. The people of the neighborhood used to throw their garbage there, and a big pile had formed behind his house. When the two sat down to eat, a breeze heavy with stench blew in from that   306

اکثر قاذورات را در آنجا می انداختند. چنانچه قریب دیوار خانه اش مزیله زار شده بود. وقت طعام بادی ازان سو آمد که کاروان بوی بدی در دربار داشت. مهمان بیدماغ شد و گفت، امروز عجب آش در کاسه است. میزبان که سخن رس رس مقرری بود گفت، در خانه هرچه مهمان هرکه.

(۳۱) محمد حسین کلیم که ریخته را بطرز شعر مرزا بیدل میگفت روزی پیش اسدیار خان بخشی نواب بهادر که طبع شوخی داشت اشعار بارد خود بسیار خواند. او بیدماغ شد و مرا مخاطب ساخت که دوش خواب عجبی دیده ام. گفتم، چطور است؟ گفت، دیده ام که در جناب مرتضوی حاضرم و فقیری بر دروازه شور میکند. اشارتی بمن کردند یعنی برو و ببین. رفتم و دیدم فقیری دبنگی لنگوته بندی چوب کلانی بر دوش گذاشته ایستاده است. گفتم که ای بیجگر، باین تن و توش ترا که زده است که متصل می نالی. گفتا که من بیدلم، کلیم نام ریخته گوی هر روز از دیوان من دوصد مضمون می دزدد و بعبارت پوچ بسته بنام خود میخواند. این معنی سوهان روح منست. خدا را باّن بیدرد بگوئید که از دیوان من دست بردارد. گفتم که برو، من او را معقول خواهم کرد. کلیم بیچاره تر آمد و رفت.

(۳۲) ملا فرج الله شوشتری وارد شاهجهان آباد شد. اینجا طنطنهٔ اشعار میان ناصرعلی شنید و مشتاق گردید. روزی جهت

۳۰۷

۳۰۸

shrewdness

direction. The guest, much displeased, remarked, "Must be some special soup today." The host, well known for his perspicacity, responded, "Nothing special for your sake, for what we have is yours anyway."

(31) Muhammad Husain "Kalim" wrote *rekhta* verses in 307
the style of Mirza 'Abdul Qadir Bedil's Persian.[108] Once he attended upon Asad Yar Khan, the Bakhshi of Nawab Bahadur and a jocular person, and recited too many of his insipid verses. The nawab, becoming irritated, turned to me and said, "Yesterday I had a strange dream." "How so?" I asked. He replied, "I saw that I was in the presence of Imam 'Ali, the most revered one, and there was some beggar making much noise at the door. I was commanded to go and check, and found standing there a robust fakir, dressed in a loincloth and carrying a heavy staff against his shoulder. I said to him, "You poltroon! You're so big and hefty, and yet you cry so. Who beat you up?" He replied, "I'm Bedil. There is a *rekhta* poet named Kalim who every day steals from my collection a couple of hundred verses, recasts them in his own mediocre words, and then presents them as his own. It causes me great anguish. Please, for God's sake, ask that heartless person to keep his hands off my collection." "You may go now," I then told him, "I'll make sure that fellow sees the light." Poor Kalim felt so abashed, he immediately got up and left.

plagiarism in Mughal India

(32) Mulla Farajullah Shustari arrived in Shahjahanabad. 308
Here he heard the fame of Miyan Nasir 'Ali's poetry.[109] Eager to meet him, he visited him one day. Nasir 'Ali asked, "And what name do you bear?" The mulla replied, "Farajullah." Nasir 'Ali smiled inwardly, but on the outside he remained silent and thoughtful. When the mulla saw that no conversa-

ملاقات او رفت. پرسید که چه نام داری. گفت، فرج الله. خنده
زیرلبی کرد و سر بجیب تفکر برد. چون ملا دید که سر حرف وا
نمی شود دانسته گفت که اگر از اسم شریف هم اطلاع بخشند
بعید از مهربانی نخواهد بود. سر بر کرد و گفت، ذکرالله. ملا
بسیار بیمزه شد و گفت، لعنت الله.

(۳۳) روزی ناصرعلی شاگرد مرزا بیدل را دید و پرسید که مرزا ۳۰۹
چه می کند. گفت، درین ایام «چارعنصر» مینویسد. گفت، پیام
من خواهی رساند که چرا وقت عزیز را ضایع میکنی، فرداست که
این چارعنصر خراب اند، مفت آنها که پنجروزه عمر را دریابند.

(۳۴) مرزا بیدل لفظ «النوید» را در شعرخود آورد. حکیم شیخ ۳۱۰
حسین شهرت بخانهٔ او رفته اعتراض کرد که نوید لفظ فارسی است،
بر او آوردن الف لام بطور الفاظ عربی چه معنی دارد. مرزا قصیدهٔ
استادی بخاطر داشت که در صدر هر بیت آن لفظ معرف باللام
بود چنانچه مصرعی ازان بیاد من هم مانده است، «النوید آفتاب
عالمتاب». شخصی را مخاطب کرده خواند. حکیم حیران شد و
برو درماند. چون ساکتش یافت گفت، حکیم صاحب، پیش شاعر
حکیم و پیش حکیم شاعر، پیش هیچ هر دو و پیش هر دو هیچ.

(۳۵) سفیهی با ایرانی مغلی صحبت گرم نموده خواست که ۳۱۱
معتقدخویش کند. شروع بمناقب بزرگان چشت کرد و گفت،
کمال خواجه معین الدین مشهور است، حال خواجه قطب

tion was about to start, he deliberately said, "It would be very nice of you if you would kindly let me know your name too." Nasir 'Ali raised his head and replied, "Zikrullah." The mulla was incensed, and said, "May God's curse be on you!"[110]

some pun I don't understand

(33) One day, running into a disciple of Mirza Bedil, Nasir 'Ali asked him, "What is the mirza doing these days?" "Writing *The Four Elements*."[111] Nasir 'Ali said, "Give him this message from me: 'Why waste your time? Any day now these four elements that we are made of will disintegrate. Better that you made some sense of the proverbial five days of life.'" *a cage for literature and art over science*

309

(34) Mirza Bedil used the word *al-nawed* in one of his verses. Hakim Shaikh Husain Shuhrat went to him and raised an objection: since *nawed* was Persian, how could Bedil add an *alif* and *lām* to it as was done with Arabic words? The mirza knew an ode by some master in which, at the beginning of every verse, the same word occurred in that very form. One hemistich of it has stuck in my memory too: *al-nawed āftāb-e 'ālamtāb*.[112] The mirza turned to someone else who was present and recited the entire ode. The hakim was astounded; he could say nothing. Noting his silence, the mirza said, "Hakim Sahib, before poets, you're a physician, and before physicians, a poet. Before neither, you're both, and before both, neither."

310

(35) A silly fool was enthusiastically talking to a Mughal from Iran, desirous of converting the latter to his own beliefs. He began by praising the Chishti saints, "The perfection of Khwaja Mu'inuddin is renowned; and Khwaja Qutbuddin is still talked about. The incredible deeds of Shaikh Fariduddin are beyond numbers; and the miracles of Shaikh

311

325

الدین مذکور است، خرق عادات شیخ فرید از حد شمار افزون،
کرامتهای نظام الدین از حیز بیان بیرون. چون ازینقسم بسیار
چاوید، بیدماغ شد و گفت، کسی هست که این قرمساق تذکرة
الاولیاً را بردارد؟

(۳۶) ظریفی زن خانگی طلبید و تکلیف شرابش نمود. آن کس
فراخ برای نمود عصمت و اظهار عفت خودش خشن شد و گفت،
مگر زن شما هم شراب میخورد. ظریف گفت، اگر بطور شما جای
میرود چرا نمیخورد.

(۳۷) روزی شاه عباس بیدماغ بود. حاجبان کسی را برای مجرا
نمیگذاشتند. عنایت گل که مسخره قالب بود ترسان ترسان رفت
و دید که شاه چوبی در دست دارد و بر خیابان نشسته زمین
میکاود. پرسید، بلاگردانت شوم چه میکاری. بخشونت گفت
[کیر]. گفتا که آهسته بگو که حرم نزدیکست. مبادا خدمهٔ محل
بشنوند و از بیخ بردارند. شاه خندید و آن بیدماغی رفع شد.

(۳۸) روزی شاه در شاه نشین مست شراب بود و استفراغ کرد.
عنایت گل که پائین آن می نشست همه بر سر او افتاد. چشم ببالا
کرد. شاه گفت، چه می بینی، قی سرت کردم. گفتا، بلی، بر روم
ریدی. اگرچه قیصر بصاد است لیکن لطف از شرکت تلفظ بهم
رسید و لطیفه شد.

۳۱۲

۳۱۳

۳۱۴

bored by the guys historical prattling on

Nizamuddin cannot be encompassed in words." When he went on prattling that way, the Mughal became angry and said, "Is there anyone here who will throw out for me this pimp of a *Tazkirat-ul-Auliya*?"[113]

(36) A witty person once sent for a *khānagī*,[114] and when she came asked her to share some wine. That cunt of a woman, wanting to display her pretensions to chastity and genteelness, irritably said, "I guess your wife drinks too." The wit replied, "Sure. Wouldn't she if she went around like you?"

sex work in mughal India

312

(37) One day Shah 'Abbas was in a foul mood, and the door-keepers were not letting anyone into his presence. 'Inayat Gul the clown, however, crept in, trembling with fear. He found the shah squatting on a garden path, holding a stick in his hand with which he was scratching the ground. Inayat said, "May your misfortunes instead fall upon me, but what are you sowing?" "My cock," the shah barked. "Not so loud," said 'Inayat. "The maids in the harem might hear you and pull it out by the root." The shah burst into laughter, and his anger disappeared.

313

vulgar humor

(38) Once, having had too much to drink, the shah, seated on the royal platform, threw up. The vomit fell on 'Inayat Gul's head, as he always sat below him. 'Inayat looked up. The shah said, "What are you looking at? *qay sarat kardam.*" Inayat replied, "Indeed, *bar rūm ridi.*" Although *qaisar* is written with a *swād* while *sar* is written with a *sīn*, the fun here is in their homophony.[115]

314

↳ how does humor translate?

(۳۹) روزی شاه بعنایت گفت که دلم سادهٔ ناگاده میخواهد. ۳۱۵
رفت و زنکه آورد. گفت، مردکه، من امردی را طلبداشته بودم تو
زنکه آوردی. گفتا که این هر دو دارد. گفت، دل من میخواست
که با خایهٔ او بازی کنم. گفتا، هرچه کردنست باین زن بکن، و
برای بازی خایهٔ من بگیر.

(۴۰) روزی مرتضی خان میرتزک بخانهٔ برهان الملک رفت و ۳۱۶
خبز خورد. بعد طعام دست شستن بتکلف آغاز کرد. سه چار بار
آرد نخود گرفت و دو سه بار کنجارهٔ سائیدهٔ خوشبو. گفت، ای
مرتضی خان این همه دست بمبالغه شستن چه معنی دارد. مگر
بخانهٔ من گه پخته بودند.

(۴۱) ایرانی پیش والی توران رفت. او پرسید که چه مذهب ۳۱۷
داری؟ جواب نداد. گفتند، چرا سکوت کردهٔ. گفتا که میرسید،
اگر اعتراف بتشیع مینمایم والی بیدماغ میشود وگر بسنّی گری
اقرار میکنم میپرسد دُمت کو. حیرانم که چه بگویم.

(۴۲) لوطی در چشمهٔ مسجدی با کوچک ابدال خود اغلام ۳۱۸
میکرد. ناگاه باران بشدت آمد. بازاریان پناه بمسجد بردند. گفت
که ای زنجلبان، اینجا جا کجاست. نمی بینید که آدم بالای آدم
افتاده است.

(۴۳) قاضی جای از هزار جای پس آورده دختری داشت. روزی ۳۱۹
آن دختر بصحرا رفت و دستخوش لوطی شد. تاب کلهٔ سخت

[handwritten margin note: was child prostitution normal]

(39) Once the shah said to 'Inayat, "I lust for a nice virgin 315
boy." Inayat went out and returned with a short little woman.
"You wretch," the shah said, "I asked for a tender youth, but
you bring me a puny woman." Inayat said, "She has 'both.'"
The shah said, "But I wanted to play with the boy's balls."
"Do the 'doing' with her," 'Inayat rejoindered. "And for
'playing,' grab my balls." *[handwritten: wow]*

[handwritten margin note: what does this mean?]

(40) Once Murtaza Khan, the Mir Tuzuk, was visiting with 316
Burhan-ul-Mulk, and they had something to eat. Afterward,
he started washing his hands rather elaborately, using several
kinds of cleansing agents. The host said, "Murtaza Khan,
why this incredible cleansing of hands? Was it shit they
prepared in my kitchen?" *[handwritten: — rules of hospitality]*

(41) An Irani went before the king of Turan. The latter 317
asked him, "What sect of Islam do you belong to?" The Irani
didn't give an answer. Someone asked him, "Why have you
fallen silent?" The Irani replied, "Do not ask. If I confess
that I'm a Shia, the king will get mad. And if I declare I'm a
Sunni, he will immediately ask, 'But where is your tail?' I'm
in a quandary what to say." *[handwritten: — was Sunni/Shia divide that prevalent??]*

(42) A rogue was busy fucking his young companion inside 318
the gateway of a mosque. Suddenly it began to pour, and the
market people rushed in to take shelter from the rain. The
fellow said, "Hey, pimps, there's no room here. Can't you
see we are already one on top of the other?" *[handwritten: — to what extent is all of this true??]*

(43) The *qāzī* of some godforsaken place had a daughter. 319
One day, while out in the woods, she was grabbed by a lusty
fellow. Unable to bear his battering, she cried out, "Hey, this
cunt is of a *qāzī's* daughter, not some rustic's you grabbed
in the woods." Since the rake hadn't had a woman for some

او نیاورده فریاد برآورد که مرا مگر از صحراجسته‌ٔ، نمیدانی که
این کس دختر قاضی است. چون لوطی از مدّتی جماع نکرده بود
زود منزل شد و گذاشت. وقتی که بخانه آمد قاضی پرسید که تا
اینوقت کجا بودی. گفت مرا لوطی گرفته برده بود. طاقت ضربت
جماع او نیاورده نام حضرت گرفتم، باری دست برداشت. قاضی
دیوث ریش را بدست گرفته گفت که ای ریش، ای ریش، تو در
خانه و هیبت تو در صحرا.

۳۲۰ (۴۴) تورانی با خواجه سرای اغلام کرد.آن پس دریده و پیش
بریده از ملای پرسید، کسی که این عمل کنانیده باشد چه طور
پاک شود. ملا گفت که حج کند. رفت و حاجی شده آمد. روزی
بهمان کوبنده‌ٔ خود برخورد. او باشتیاق تمامش در بر کشید و
باز نهاد. بکمال بیدماغی از انجا برآمد. شخصی پرسید که حاجی
سبب بیدماغی چیست. گفت، چه میپرسی، زن قحبه باز برای
حج فرستاد.

۳۲۱ (۴۵) بهورن زن فاحشه بود و بصاحب سلیقگی شهرت داشت.
یکی بمرزا جانجانان مظهر گفت فرستاد که دل برای ملاقات می
طپد لیکن حیف که شما چاریاری اید. من این مذهب را اختیار
نمیتوانم کرد. چاریاری شدن عیب زنان است. ایشان به تکلف
جواب او گفتند که مگر اثناعشری شدن هنر است.

۳۲۲ (۴۶) نوربائی زن فاسقه است و بلسانی زبانزد عالم. یکی پسرش

time, he was done in a moment and let go of her. When she reached home, the *qāzī* asked, "What took you so long?" She replied, "A nasty fellow caught hold of me. But when I couldn't bear his ramming and called out your name, he let go of me right away." That cuckold of a *qāzī* smoothed his beard with much satisfaction and said, "Ah, my beard, my wonderful beard! You're here at home, but you strike terror out in the woods!" *— the father wasn't at all concerned what his daughter was raped ???*

(44) A Turani fucked a eunuch. That "trimmed-in-the-front and cracked-in-the-back" fellow went to a mulla and asked, "If someone has this sort of thing done to him, how should he purify himself?" The mulla said, "He should perform the hajj." The eunuch did so, and returned a hajji. One day he ran into that same batterer of yore, who eagerly grabbed him and rammed it into him again. When the eunuch came out, he looked highly irritated. Someone asked, "Hajji, why are you so angry?" He replied, "Why ask? That cuckold is sending me on another hajj." [320]

(45) Bhuran was a woman of pleasure; she was also known for her elegant ways and manners. Once she sent the following message to Mirza Mazhar Jan-e Janan: "My heart longs to meet you. But you're a 'lover of four' and I can't be the same. Being a lover of four is not good for a woman." He sent back an equally polite reply, "Yes, perhaps it is more virtuous to be a 'twelver.'"[116] [321]

(46) Nur Bai was a woman of pleasure, and known to everyone for her eloquence. Once her son was sitting in Amir Khan's assembly. Someone asked about him. Amir Khan said, "I'm amazed that you do not know him. He is the darling child of the world."[117] [322]

پیش امیرخان نشسته بود. شخصی متحفص احوال او شد. گفت
که این نور چشم عالم است، عجب که شما نمیدانید.

(۴۷) میرزا رضی دانش مصاحب داراشکوه بود. روزی او و ٣٢٣
شهزاده برای دیدن فقیری رفت. آن دبنگ بسخن درآمد که ای
بابا داراشکوه، وقتی که در میان پیغمبر و شاه مدار جنگ واقع
شد شما چند ساله بودید. شاهزاده بجانب مرزای مذکور دید و
گفت که قطع نظر از کمالات دیگر حضرت تاریخ دان بی بدل
اند.

(۴۸) عبدالرحمان نام ملحدی در صحن قدمگاه پیغمبر علیه ٣٢٤
الصلوة اکثر نشسته می ماند. از بداعتقادیش مردمان باو خوش
نداشتند. شاه گلشن که درویش خالی از کمالات نبود، سعادت
زیارت حاصل نموده میرفت. آن ملحد آواز داد. درویش ملتفت
نشد. خشن شد و گفت که ای گلشن، من ترا آدمی میدانستم تو
خر برآمدی. درویش گفت، اگر همه عقاید شما همین قسم برآیند
جای افسوس است.

(۴۹) سفیهی پیش سید حسن رسول نما آمد و گفت مرا راه ٣٢٥
خدا بنمائید. فرمود که این راه ها مگر خاله صاحب شما درست
کرده باشند.

(۵۰) ملا محمد سعید اشرف استاد زیب النسا دختر عالم گیر ٣٢٦
بود، کمال شوخی داشت. بیگم برای خدمت او کنیزی فرستاد.

(47) Mirza Razi Danish was a courtier to Prince Dara Shukoh. One day, he and the prince went to visit with a fakir. The latter, a shamelessly irrepressible fellow, started prattling, and said, "Dara Shukoh, my child, you must have been only a child when the battle between the Prophet and Shah Madar took place." The prince turned to the mirza and said, "Never mind his other amazing attributes; our revered master is obviously a matchless historian." 323

(48) An atheist named 'Abdur Rahman used to sit in the courtyard of the building that contains the footprint of the Prophet, may peace be upon him. People abhorred the man because of his beliefs. Once Shah Gulshan,[118] a perfect saint, was coming out after having obtained the blessed sight of the relic. The atheist called out his name to gain his attention, but the shah ignored him. The atheist said, "Gulshan, I had believed you were a man, but you turned out to be an ass." The dervish replied, "How sad indeed it would be if all your beliefs turn out that way." 324

(49) A foolish man came to Sayyid Hasan the "Prophet shower,"[119] and said, "Show me the road to God." He retorted, "You think your dear auntie laid out these roads?" 325

(50) Mulla Muhammad Sa'id Ashraf was the tutor of Zebunnisa Begum, the daughter of the Emperor Aurangzeb 'Alamgir. The begum sent him a maid to serve him. Then one day she asked, "Mulla, how is the maid?" He said, "Why ask, she's wonderful. But she doesn't know *gharbila*." "What is *gharbila*?" the begum asked. He exclaimed, "How sad! The begum doesn't know either!" The word *gharbila* means "the coquetry and ways that women engage in during sexual intercourse." 326

روزی پرسید که ملا، کنیز چه طور است. گفت، چه پرسیدنست،
لیکن غربیله نمیداند. بیگم گفت، غربیله چه معنی دارد. گفت،
وای که بیگم هم نمیداند. غربیله بمعنی ناز و اصولی که زنان در
جماع می آرند می آید.

(۵۱) روزی به بیگم گفته فرستاد که دل سنبوسهٔ بیسن
میخواهد. بیگم گفت که به پیغام راست نمی آید. لطف این
لطیفه آنست که چون لفظ سن از سنبوسه دور کنند بوسه میماند
و بیسن آرد نخود را میگویند که ازان اقسام طعام و شیرینی پخته
می شود.

(۵۲) شخصی با مغلی بی علم آشنا شد. یکی پرسید که صدغتین
انچه دریافته می شود عربی است، در فارسی چه می گویند.
چون آن کج پلاسی نمیدانست با بیدماغی گفت که در ولایت ما
صدغتین نمی باشد.

(۵۳) هندی سفیهی با مغل ایرانی اختلاط شروع کرد و پرسید
که در ولایت شما گندم هم می شود. او بیدماغ نشسته بود؛
گفت، نه. گفت، برنج خوب پیدا میشود. گفت، نه. گفت، روغن
زرد بهم میرسد. گفت، نه. متعجب شد و گفت، پس انجا چه چیز
میخورند؟ گفت، چه چیز میخورند؟ گه میخورند و بس.

(۵۴) در خانهٔ افغانی شادی اتفاق افتاد. قوم و قبیلهٔ او جمع
آمد. مغنیان و زنان رقاص را طلب داشت. مقرر بود که هر کسی

۳۲۷

۳۲۸

۳۲۹

۳۳۰

funny play on words

(51) One day the same mulla sent word to the begum, 327
"My heart longs for *sanbosa-e besan*." The begum replied,
"It can't be conveyed through words." The fun of this joke
lies in this: when one removes *san* from *sanbosa*, one gets
bosa. And *besan* is the name for chickpea flour, from which
many kinds of foods and sweets are made.[120]

(52) A certain man befriended an ignorant Mughal. Once 328
the man said to the Mughal, "The word *sudghatain*, as we
know, is Arabic. What is it in Persian?" Since that boastful
ignoramus didn't know, he irritably said, "In our country we
do not have *sudghatain*."[121] lol

(53) A foolish Indian, trying to be familiar with an Irani, 329
asked him, "Do they have wheat in your country?" The Irani,
who was already fed up with him, replied, "No." "Is there
much rice there?" "No." "Can you get clarified butter?"
"No." The Indian was astounded and asked, "Then what
do they eat there?" "What do they eat there?" the Irani
retorted. "They eat shit, that's all."

(54) There was a celebration at an Afghan's house, and 330
his clan and family had assembled. Musicians and dancing
girls were also summoned, and it was expected that every
guest would give the entertainers something according to
his ability. It so happened that in that gathering no one gave
even a penny. After the party broke up, the host sat greatly
perturbed, wondering how he was going to pay the musicians. A witty woman from among them came to him and
said, "Khan Sahib, why be so worried? Our reward is no problem. Give it, if you wish, or do not. You had a happy occasion
at your house, and so we came. But listen, do not ever go into
a battle relying on these brothers of yours."

موافق استعداد بارباب نشاط چیزی بدهد. اتفاقاً در آن صحبت کسی خرمهره نداد. چون مجلس بشکست صاحب خانه متردد نشست، یعنی در فکر انعام آنها افتاد. زن ظریفه پیش آمد و گفت، خانصاحب، اینهمه تشویش برای چه. انعام ما سهل است، بدهید ندهید. در خانهٔ شما بزم عیش بود. آمده حاضر شدیم. لیکن باعتماد این برادران در رزم نخواهید رفت.

۳۳۱ (۵۵) شخصی بدقیافه پیش ظریفی آمد و نشست. از بدقیافگی بیمزه شد و از راه ظرافت گفت که شما را قوت منفعله هم هست؟ آن مردکه فهمید که قوت منفعله شاید نام کتابی است. گفتا، بنده چه که والد شریف و جد بزرگوار هم نداشتند، اگرچه کتابهای بسیار جمع کرده بودند.

۳۳۲ «هو المستعان». من هیچ مدان این چند فقره از زور طبعیت نگاشتم و بر جریدهٔ عالم گذاشتم. غرضکه نام این نسخه «ذکر میر» کرده ام و در تالیف این رنج بی پایان برده ام، بر این امید که شاید بدست صاحبدلی درآید و او در حق من دعای خیر مینماید.

مسمی باسمی شد ای باهنر
که این نسخه گردد بعالم سمر
ز تاریخ آگه شـــوی بیـــگمان
فزائی عدد بست و هفت اَر بران

(55) A person whose looks bespoke his ignorance came   331
to a man of intelligence and wit. The latter, displeased by
his foolishness, asked him in jest, "Do you have *quwwat-e
munfaʿila?*"—i.e., any sense of shame. That base fellow
thought that it was perhaps the name of some book; he
replied, "What, me? Even my revered father and grandfather
didn't have it—though they had huge collections of books."

lots of making fun of uneducated people

"And we seek help from God alone." I, this ignorant person,   332
wrote down these few phrases aided by my inherent nature
and left them to remain as my memento in the register of
this world—in short, I have named it *Zikr-e Mīr,* and I have
endured endless hardship in its preparation—with the hope
that if it reaches the hands of someone with a heart, he would
pray for my benefit.

> *This book has been given a name, my talented friend,*
> *that should make it a tale heard around the world.*
> *And you will doubtless learn its completion's date*
> *if you will add seven and twenty to its name.*[122]

NOTES TO THE TRANSLATION

1   The Qur'an, *passim*. All translations from the Qur'an are mine.
     Mir also quotes lines of poetry, often his own. These are identified,
     whenever possible, within the translation.
2   The Qur'an, 24:35.
3   The point of a reed pen is split in the middle in order for it to retain
     ink.
4   *Takhallus* (*Takhalluṣ*), the name Urdu poets choose to include in
     their verse for identification.
5   Commandant of a local unit of the imperial army, e.g., in a fort or
     a city.
6   "'Ali, the God-fearing one." His actual name was Muhammad 'Ali,
     as Mir reports later.
7   Mu'awiya, the first Umayyad caliph. His son, Yazid, is condemned
     by all Muslims for causing the martyrdom of Imam Husain, but
     Mu'awiya himself is not. Though he is condemned by Shias, ordi-
     nary Sunnis give him respect. Apparently, Mir's father, a Sunni,
     had adopted beliefs similar to the Shias but was still uncertain how
     he was to look upon Mu'awiya.
8   "Master of the seraglio," always a eunuch.
9   A senior Mughal grandee, his name was Khwaja Muhammad
     'Asim. He helped Mir after Muhammad 'Ali passed away. The first
     title indicates he was "the noble above all nobles."
10   Mir implies that his father covered the distance of three days in
     half the time.
11   Khizr or Khizar, a legendary figure, is immortal but remains hidden
     from human sight except when he appears to those who are lost
     and guides them to safety.
12   The Qur'an, 47:38.
13   *Jawān-e 'Azīz:* "Noble youth" or "Dear youth."
14   A medieval Central Asian habit for a lover was to brand his hand
     or arm as a sign of his slave-like devotion to his beloved.
15   Muslims are traditionally supposed to have formed into seven-
     ty-two separate sects, only one of which, according to a Hadith of
     the Prophet, is on the right path.
16   Literally, "The moon would not make haste," which makes little

sense except perhaps as a metaphor for the passage of time. The verb used by Mir here was likely chosen to rhyme with the verb in the previous sentence.

17   A *hadīth-e qudsī*, i.e., an extra-Qur'anic divine revelation to the prophet Muhammad. Though of questionable authenticity, such sayings are particular favorites of Sufis.

18   Nusrat Yar Khan reportedly died in Delhi in 1722.

19   Starting here, Mir uses the word *rū*, "face," singly or in compounds fifteen times in subsequent sentences. I could only partly indicate the repetition.

20   I have retained Mir's "error" in the Persian text but translated it as he intended. The phrase he wished to use, according to Arzu's *Charāgh-e Hidāyat,* is: *barg-bed.*

21   Tipcat, like the Indian game of *gillī-ḍanḍā,* is played with two sticks, one of which, very small and pointed at both ends, is called "tipcat pussy."

22   A sixteenth-century Iranian poet.

23   Mir's word is *takhta* (a wooden board). The reference is to the practice of Christians in many Ottoman lands of beating on a log called a simandron instead of ringing bells—if the latter was prohibited—to call the devout to prayers.

24   The binary opposition describes two kinds of learning: the former refers to the "transmitted" knowledge of the Qur'an and the Hadith, while the latter includes the "rational" sciences such as mathematics and astronomy. For the Sufis, the heart was also the seat of *'aql* or intellect, but what the latter implied was closer to pragmatism than intellectualism. In other words, Mir's father asked Amanullah to be conventional in word and appearance, but a Sufi pragmatist in private and unbeknownst to the general population.

25   It echoes a Hadith popular among the Sufis: the Prophet reportedly said, "Die, before you die." In other words, one must cut off all worldly ties before death cuts them for us.

26   The name of the city, reportedly in Mazandran near the faraway Caspian Sea, also literally means "blue-dressed."

27   The ritual of remembrance and prayers performed on the third day after the death.

28   'Aziz Murda, "Someone who lost a dear one."

29   This is the same sobriquet that Mir's "uncle" uses for another youth earlier.

30 Three hundred was a considerably large number for books in one man's private possession at the time. Mir's father could have been a dealer in books.

31 Most scholars estimate that Mir's father died in early 1734, and certainly no later than early 1735.

32 Arzu is believed to have been Mir's stepmother's brother.

33 I use here a feminine gender reference, but there is no specifically feminine attribute or epithet used by Mir. Persian of course has no grammatical gender, while Urdu does.

34 It could have been a book consisting of excerpts of prose and poetry written out in diverse hands. There is strong reason to believe that Mir did learn professional calligraphy early in his youth.

35 Elsewhere, Mir describes him as "an affable man, mild in manners and given to brevity in speech. There was the sweetness of a dervish about him ... and his verse was not devoid of pleasure. He was very friendly with me." Mir Sa'adat 'Ali reportedly died in Delhi sometime before 1751.

36 'Imad-ul-Mulk, whose name was Shihabuddin, was at the time only sixteen!

37 The well-known treatise on rhetorics by Taftazani (d. 1390).

38 Though the title is identical, this Samsam-ud-Daula should not be confused with Mir's first benefactor or his family.

39 *Dīwān* of *khālisa* and *tan,* comptroller of the crown lands—the lands reserved for the royal treasury and directly controlled—and the Jagirs—the lands assigned to various nobles. Nagar Mal's elevation took place after September 1757.

40 Mir clearly wrote this while employed by Raja Nagar Mal, for in an earlier book he had disparaged him.

41 *Salātin,* pl. of *Sultān*—the male children of the House of Timur. The reigning Mughal monarch usually kept all possible surviving claimants to the throne confined to their quarters, for ambitious nobles used the same for their own purposes.

42 In fact, less than six lunar years.

43 At Kunjpura. The subsequent battle occurred on December 24, 1759.

44 The Old City refers to the urban sprawl outside the walled city that had existed for a few centuries, and where much of New Delhi now stands.

45 In this and the subsequent ten sentences, Mir uses eight unusual

idioms based on the word *dast*, "hand."

46 Presently known as Aligarh.

47 The word Mir uses, *'alūfa*, generally means a soldier's stipend or wages. Earlier, when Mir served Nawab Bahadur, he was listed as a soldier but was excused from keeping a horse and performing related duties. In other words, though chiefly esteemed for his poetry, Mir, for "bureaucratic" purposes, was like any low-rank member of his patron's soldiery.

48 The Master, in such contexts, means 'Umar Khayyam, but this *rubā'ī* is not found in the present definitive editions of Khayyam's works.

49 Made with the dust of Karbala in Iraq, where Imam Husain was martyred.

50 Sectarian sentiments were high at the time. One reason for the failure of Shah 'Alam's second campaign was a bloody riot involving the Sunni Rohillas of Najib-ud-Daula and the Shia soldiers in Shuja-ud-Daula's army.

51 Azimabad is now known as Patna.

52 Present tense in the original.

53 Present tense in the original.

54 Nawal Singh was Suraj Mal's third son, as Mir indicates correctly later.

55 Present tense in the original. Sometime between February and July 1771.

56 A neighborhood near Humayun's tomb in present-day New Delhi.

57 Monsieur [René] Madec, a French mercenary.

58 Present tense in the original; January 1773.

59 Present tense in the original.

60 Present and future tenses in the original. Probably written in January 1773.

61 Another possible reading would have the emperor take the money from Durrani in exchange for Husamuddin Khan.

62 Present tense in the original. Probably written in June 1773. The personal remarks that follow also use the present tense and were written at the same time. Accounts of subsequent historical events were added later.

63 In the final text, prepared ten years later, Mir informs us that he eventually had all his teeth taken out. That one brief sentence is not included in the Persian text here.

64 End of Narrative A (c. March 1773), composed in Delhi. The

remaining historical account was written in Lucknow, much of it perforce based on hearsay; consequently, there is some chronological confusion in Mir's account of a few incidents.

65 April 1774. This gushing and chronologically out of place mention of Shuja-ud-Daula, compared to Mir's earlier biting comments about him, indicates how Mir prepared the new text for presentation to Asaf-ud-Daula, Shuja's heir and Mir's patron.

66 Mir, however, did write a long panegyric in honor of Shah 'Alam, which he must have presented personally on some occasion.

67 Present tense in the original. The events described here happened in Lucknow in the summer of 1776. Mukhtar-ud-Daula was killed by the eunuch general Basant 'Ali Khan, who in turn was killed by the nawab to hide his own role in the first murder. Sarfaraz-ud-Daula Hasan Raza Khan was the nawab's third and final prime minister. Though decent and generous, he was also described as almost illiterate.

68 Now begins the historical narrative as continued in "Narrative B."

69 Present tense in the original.

70 The *firangī* in question was Antoine Louis Henri Polier, a French-Swiss engineer/adventurer.

71 Warren Hastings, who came to Lucknow in March 1784.

72 Mir wishes to indicate that the governor general honored the nawab by marching out one stage from his own camp to meet him.

73 In this section describing the governor general's visit, Mir has used rhymed prose, lists of foods and items of luxury, and unusual words in a bravura performance reminiscent of story literature. The translation makes no attempt to reproduce the effect.

74 The entire Gangetic plain was in the grip of a horrible famine at the time, and the city of Lucknow must have been filled with the stench of the dead and the dying. Mir makes no mention of the famine.

75 A better idea of the actual situation may be gained from what the "splendid guest" wrote to his wife from Lucknow on August 13, 1784: "The Roads and Streets have been for some Months covered with emaciated Wretches who have flocked from all Quarters to the Capital for Subsistence ... It pains me to go abroad to hear the Cries, and see such Spectacles of human Misery ... This Calamity is not the Effect of One Season. The three last Years have all failed, and almost universally from the Border of Bengal, which had also its Share, to the Lands which extend beyond

Lahore." Grier 1905: 300.

76 Hastings reached Lucknow on March 27 and started back on August 27, 1784. Mir was referring to the lunar months.

77 Present tense in the original. Jawan Bakht returned to Lucknow after Hastings's departure (October 22, 1784), but a few months later went back to Benares, where he died in 1788.

78 *Mukhammas* are poems with stanzas of five lines each. The nawab took each couplet of Mir's *ghazal* and expanded its original contents in assorted ways by adding three more lines.

79 *Zamīn* is the particular combination of a *ghazal's* meter and rhyme scheme.

80 Ghulam Qadir's occupation of Delhi lasted from the middle of July till the beginning of October 1788.

81 Present tense in the original. Mir's historical narrative ends here. Though he lived for another twenty-one years, he made no further additions.

82 I have been less literal in my translation of the jokes, and also added numbers to make referencing easier.

83 Since books by both the scholars were prescribed at Islamic seminaries, there was, in popular belief, a kind of rivalry between them. The mulla used the final phrase of a verse in the Qur'an (78:40) in a punning manner, while the mir responded by putting the phrase in its actual context: the dismay of the unbelievers on the Day of Judgment.

84 The great Sufi poet Jalaluddin Rumi and his friend and mentor, Sadruddin Qunavi.

85 A proverbial hemistich, implying: "I'm still greater than you."

86 Mulla Muhammad Baqir Majlisi (d. 1698) was an eminent Shia scholar of the Safavid age in Iran.

87 *Lūtī*, a man of vulgar and obscene habits; a sodomite; a shameless and good-for-nothing fellow.

88 Afzaluddin Khaqani (d. 1199), a Persian poet famous for his panegyrics.

89 "'Imad, the Wild." "Lur" refers to the people of Lorestan, a province in Iran, who were stereotyped as foolish and wild.

90 Shamsuddin Muhammad Juvaini (d. 1284?), the eminent minister and historian of the Mongol king Abaqa Khan s/o Hulagu.

91 Auhaduddin Anvari (d. 1189?), famous for his panegyrics and *ghazals*.

92 According to Mir, "A *fāzil* (*fāẓil*) tree is any tree by the roadside that is regarded by common people to be an abode of the jinns, and upon which they then cast pieces of cloth and strings. In India they call it *pīr gudaṛiya* [or the patchwork-robed saint]."

93 Mirza Muhammad 'Ali Sa'ib (d. 1669) of Tabriz, a Persian poet who spent several years in India before going back to Iran to be the poet laureate of Shah 'Abbas II.

94 In the coffee shops of Iran and India in the past people used to sit lined up against the walls.

95 Originally from Iraq, this particular sayyid clan settled in Barha (presently in Muzaffarnagar district). First mentioned in history as brave and reckless soldiers in Akbar's army, the sayyids of Barha reached the zenith of political power in the second decade of the eighteenth century when two brothers, Sayyid Hasan 'Ali 'Abdullah Khan and Sayyid Husain 'Ali, briefly became the "king makers" at Delhi. Both were widely hated for their cruelty and lust for power.

96 *Sūra* 109 of the Qur'an, the same as in the joke about Rumi above. It is one of the first *sūras* that any Muslim child is taught to read.

97 *Jahālat*, "ignorance," implies a mixture of foolishness and obstinacy. Abu Jahl, "Father of Ignorance," was the epithet of one of the worst enemies of the prophet Muhammad. Naming a child after him would be an act of total imbecility.

98 *Alif*, the first letter of the Arabic alphabet, has no additional diacritic. The word *alif*, using the same reference, means "stark."

99 In other words, verses that were not about "abstract" thoughts but referred to imagined "incidents" and "objects."

100 Literally, "Let it not be *makhfī*," but idiomatically, "Let it be known that..." It was a phrase conventionally used at the beginning of most ordinary communications. The word itself means "hidden."

101 Shuhrat, an Arab from Bahrain, came to India during Aurangzeb's time and joined the service of Prince A'zam Shah. Though he was dead by the time Mir reached Delhi, Shuhrat's fame as a physician and as a jovial person lasted long after him.

102 Mirza "Heartless," Mirza 'Abdul Qadir "Bedil" (1644–1720), one of the finest Indo-Persian poets. His *takhallus*, Bedil, literally means "without a heart."

103 Originally from Shiraz, the learned physician spent most of his life in Delhi, where he died at the age of 84 in c. 1750.

104 A'zam Khan and Burhan-ul-Mulk Sa'adat Khan were eminent

nobles during the reign of Muhammad Shah (ruled 1719–1748).

105 An eminent Naqshbandi Sufi and scholar, mentor to many of the Urdu poets of the eighteenth century.

106 An *a* before an *n* is changed into a *u*.

107 Sa'di's couplet translates: "Oh nightingale singing at dawn, learn Love from the moth. // Inflamed, it was totally consumed but never made a sound." In the Iraqi pronunciation, *kān soḵẖta*, "that inflamed one," became *kūn soḵẖta*, "that anus-inflamed one."

108 Muhammad Husain "Kalim" was a noted Urdu poet of his time; his particular predilection is recorded by other writers too. Kalim was married to Mir's sister, and his son married Mir's daughter. Mir speaks of him more kindly elsewhere.

109 Nasir 'Ali Sirhindi (d. 1696) was a major Persian poet of India, mostly known for his *ghazals*.

110 The joke lies in the written forms—*frj* and *ẕkr*—of the two words that have been transcribed here as "Faraj" and "Zikr," "comfort" and "remembrance," respectively. Since short vowels are not indicated in the script, the other readings, insinuated by Nasir 'Ali, would be *farj* and *ẕakar*, "vagina" and "penis" respectively.

111 *Chahār 'Unṣur*, a major work by Bedil, a kind of intellectual/Sufi autobiography in prose and verse.

112 "Greetings, Sun, you who light up the world."

113 *Taẕkirat al-Auliyā*, a famous biographical dictionary of eminent Sufis by Fariduddin 'Attar (d. 1220?).

114 A woman who takes lovers for money but outwardly lives like an ordinary housewife.

115 The shah, trying to be witty, said words that could be heard to mean either "I vomited on your head" or "I made you the Caesar." 'Inayat, not one to be easily fooled, responded with words that could equally mean either "You shat on my face" or "You shat on the Byzantine."

116 "Lover of four," i.e., a Sunni—he honors the first four caliphs. "Twelver," i.e., a Shia—she reveres the twelve imams.

117 Literally, "light of the world's eyes" [*nūr-e chashm-e 'ālam*]. The phrase echoes the mother's name; it also idiomatically means "the progeny of the world."

118 Shah Sa'dullah "Gulshan" was a well-known Naqshbandi Sufi at the time of Muhammad Shah; he was also a mentor to many of the earliest Urdu poets.

119 Sayyid Hasan "Rasul Numa" (d. 1692?). His title refers to the legend that he could make anyone have a vision of the Prophet in a dream. His tomb is on Panch Kuiyan Road near Cannaught Place, New Delhi. His shrine and the shrine of the Prophet's footprint were major centers of devotion in the eighteenth century.

120 *Sanbosa,* present-day *samosa,* is a popular savory snack. The poet puns on the word *besan,* implying that it should be read as *be-san,* "without *san.*" So when he asks the princess for a *be-san sanbosa,* he is in fact asking for a *bosa,* i.e., a kiss.

121 The Arabic word *ṣudghatain* means "temple," i.e., the flat part of the head next to the ear.

122 The numerical value of *Ẕikr-e Mīr* is 1170. Adding twenty-seven will give A. H. 1197 (December 7, 1782–November 26, 1783).

HISTORICAL PERSONAGES

The following notes provide brief biographical information concerning some of the more prominent historical figures that Mir mentions. First listed are the Mughal emperors in the chronological order of their succession; then follow others in the alphabetical order of their names.

Mughal Emperors

MUHAMMAD SHAH. Mughal emperor, ruled 1719–1748. He succeeded to the throne at the age of seventeen and only as the arbitrary choice of two powerful nobles, the Sayyid Brothers. In popular imagination he is known as a debauch and a worthless king, and his reign is better known for the pillage of Delhi in 1739 at the hands of the Iranian invader, Nadir Shah.

AHMAD SHAH. Mughal emperor, ruled 1748–1754. He succeeded his father, Muhammad Shah, at the age of twenty-one. He had no administrative or military experience; consequently, he depended entirely on the advice of his mother, Udham Bai, and her favorite, the eunuch Jawid Khan. After Jawid Khan's assassination, the emperor's vazirs, first Safdar Jang and then 'Imad-ul-Mulk, dominated state affairs. Eventually 'Imad-ul-Mulk deposed and blinded Ahmad Shah, replacing him with a person of his choosing.

'ALAMGIR II. Mughal emperor, ruled 1754–1759. He was the son of Emperor Jahandar Shah (1712–1713) and a first cousin of Muhammad Shah. He was fifty-five years old when 'Imad-ul-Mulk pulled him out of virtual captivity and placed him on the throne while retaining all powers. Eventually 'Imad-ul-Mulk, driven by his own ambitions, also had him killed. During his brief reign, Delhi underwent another pillage, this time at the hands of the Afghan marauder, Ahmad Shah 'Abdali.

SHAH JAHAN III. Mughal emperor, ruled 1759–1760. He was randomly chosen by 'Imad-ul-Mulk from among a host of likely claimants, but then 'Imad-ul-Mulk himself lost out to the Marathas, and Shah Jahan III was sent back to captivity before a year was over. The Maratha commander, Sadashiv Bhau, confirmed Shah 'Alam II's

349

succession to the throne and appointed the latter's eldest son, Prince Jawan Bakht Jahandar Shah, as the heir and viceroy until his father's return to Delhi.

SHAH 'ALAM II. Mughal emperor, ruled 1759–1806. Born in 1729, he was the son of 'Alamgir II. The father and son, like most Mughal *salātīn* (princes), had lived as virtual captives in the Red Fort until 'Imad-ul-Mulk chose the father to be the new emperor. The son received the titles of Ali Gauhar and Shah 'Alam, and began to participate in matters of state. When 'Imad-ul-Mulk plotted an attempt on his life in 1758, Shah 'Alam fled eastward. The next fourteen years were spent in seeking support against his enemies at Delhi, combined with a couple of unsuccessful attempts with Shuja-ud-Daula of Avadh to regain control of the lost eastern territories of the original Mughal Empire. In 1759 he was in Bihar when he received the news of his father's murder; he then declared himself the new emperor: Shah 'Alam II. After the crushing loss at Buxar in 1764, Shah 'Alam became a dependent of the East India Company and lived at Allahabad. In January 1772, with the help of the Marathas, he returned to Delhi. In 1788, he suffered terribly at the hands of the Rohilla marauder, Ghulam Qadir. He was still on the throne when the British took Delhi in 1803 and made him again their grateful pensioner. He died in 1806. Shah 'Alam's *takhallus* in poetry was Aftab (The Sun). Besides writing poetry in Urdu and Persian, he also composed verses in Braj for musical settings, and even a short romance in Urdu prose.

Other Key Persons

'ABDALI, AHMAD SHAH (1722?–1772). An Afghan of the 'Abdali tribe, he became the king of all Afghans in 1747. He invaded northern India eight times, maintaining an uneasy control of the Punjab and a similar dominance over Delhi and its environs for much of the time. The critical event in that regard was the so-called Third Battle of Panipat in 1761, when 'Abdali, with the help of Najib-ud-Daula, Shuja-ud-Daula, and various Rohilla chieftains, routed the combined forces of the Marathas who then controlled Delhi. The Sikhs, however, continually challenged his authority in the Punjab and came to dominance themselves after 'Abdali's last campaign in 1767.

ARZU, SIRAJUDDIN 'ALI KHAN (1687?–1756). Arzu spent his early years in Gwalior, Mathura, and Agra, and after reaching maturity joined the imperial service like his father. He also continued his studies with different scholars. In 1719, Arzu moved to Delhi, where he eventually obtained the patronage of a major noble, Motaman-ud-Daula Ishaq Khan, a great favorite of Muhammad Shah. Arzu remained attached to him and his family for the rest of his own life, eventually moving to Lucknow with Ishaq Khan's sons. Though he died at Lucknow, Arzu's body was later brought to Delhi and buried there. Prodigious in learning, Arzu, through his poetic, literary-critical, and linguistic writings and personal interaction, deeply influenced two generations of poets and writers in Delhi. He also championed Indian writers of Persian against the attacks of visiting Iranian literati. Arzu's keen interest in linguistics is evident in his three lexicographical works, one of which, *Charāgh-e Hidāyat,* was extensively exploited by Mir in both *Faiẓ-e Mīr* and *Ẓikr-e Mīr.*

ASAF-UD-DAULA (1749–1797). His name was Mirza Yahya, and he was the eldest son of Shuja-ud-Daula and Bahu Begum, the sister of Mutaman-ud-Daula Ishaq Khan. Asaf succeeded his father as ruler of Awadh in 1775, more as a vassal of the English than of the emperor, whose vazir he nominally was. Soon after, he permanently shifted his capital from Faizabad to Lucknow. Most chronicles describe Asaf as willful and erratic in behavior, corpulent in physique, and much given to pleasure and luxury. His popular reputation, however, celebrates his exemplary generosity. His continuing fame rests on the beauty and excellence of the religious buildings he constructed in Lucknow. He used Anjam as his *takhallus,* and a small volume of his Urdu verse has survived.

GHULAM QADIR KHAN (d. 1789). He was the son of Zabita Khan and grandson of Najib-ud-Daula. After the latter's death, Zabita Khan was the regent in Delhi until Shah 'Alam's return, at which time Zabita Khan lost his eminence due to court intrigues—his fort of Ghausgarh was plundered by the Maratha and royal armies, and his wives and children were held prisoner for some time. Ghulam Qadir, then a young boy, was forcibly emasculated. Succeeding his father in 1785, Ghulam Qadir quickly exploited court rivalries and gained much power. In July 1788, he occupied Delhi, plundered the citadel, and inflicted immense suffering on the royal family. Shah 'Alam II was blinded, the princes were flogged, and the princesses were brutalized, while being denied food and water for days—to force them to disclose their hidden wealth. After two months, the Marathas relieved the city, and Ghulam Qadir fled, only to be hunted down and held captive at Mathura, where he was blinded and mutilated until he died.

HASTINGS, WARREN (1732–1818). Born poor but genteel, Hastings joined the service of the East Indian Company and came to Calcutta in 1750. By 1761 he was a member of the Bengal Council, and a few years later he returned home a very rich man. He again came to India in 1769, and in 1773 he was appointed the first governor-general of the British dominions in India. After an eventful career of three terms that were full of major successes and controversies, Hastings resigned in 1785 and returned to England for good. Three years later he was impeached by Parliament on twenty charges, including personal corruption, neglect of duty, and oppression and maltreatment of Indian nobility. The trial lasted seven years but ended in full acquittal.

HOLKAR, MALHAR RAO (1693–1766). Despite being born in one of the lowest castes among the Marathas, Holkar rose to be a major figure in Maratha history. After being raised by an uncle who had a small estate, he joined the royal Maratha army and rose rapidly in its ranks, simultaneously gaining large properties. Together with his Sindhia rivals, Ranoji and Mahadji, Holkar played a major role in subjugating various Rajput and Jat kingdoms and expanding Maratha control northward to Delhi and beyond.

'IMAD-UL-MULK (1736–1800). Born Shihabuddin, he was the grandson of Nizam-ul-Mulk Asaf Jah, the founder of the ruling dynasty of Hyderabad and the most prominent member of the Turani or Turk faction at Delhi. 'Imad was in Delhi when his father died in Aurangabad. Fearing confiscation of his father's property, 'Imad sought protection from Safdar Jang, the vazir of Emperor Ahmad Shah and the leader of the rival Irani faction. Safdar Jang interceded on his behalf and had him appointed—at the age of sixteen—the paymaster general of the imperial army, with the titles of 'Imad-ul-Mulk Ghaziuddin Khan Firuz Jang. Extremely ambitious and ruthless, 'Imad soon conspired against his benefactor. By June 1754, with the help of the Marathas, he had forced Safdar Jang out of Delhi, deposed and blinded Ahmad Shah, placed a puppet Emperor 'Alamgir II on the throne—only to have him murdered five years later—and had himself declared the vazir of the realm. The rise of the Rohillas and the defeat of the Marathas by Ahmad Shah 'Abdali put an end to 'Imad's ambitions. He first sought shelter with the Jats, moving from place to place, then settled down at Baoni, near Kalpi. He wrote some poetry in Urdu and used Nizam as his *takhallus*.

JAWID KHAN (d. 1752). A eunuch, he had been the assistant superintendent of Emperor Muhammad Shah's harem and an intimate of Udham Bai, Muhammad Shah's favorite consort and the mother of Emperor Ahmad Shah. With the latter's accession to the throne, Jawid Khan, who was then close to fifty, rapidly rose in rank. He received the unprecedented title of Nawab Bahadur and came to wield all real power, despite the fact that he was illiterate and had no previous experience of either administrative or military duty. Safdar Jang, the new vazir, after suffering several humiliations at his hands, conspired against him and had him assassinated.

JUGAL KISHORE. Possibly a member of the bardic caste of Bhats, he gained favor with Alivardi Khan Mahabat Jang, the governor of Bengal, who appointed him his *vakil* or representative at the court of Muhammad Shah. Jugal Kishore lived in great luxury; the extravaganza of his son's wedding was long remembered in Delhi. In 1739, Nadir Shah's soldiers, by Jugal Kishore's own account, robbed him of movable property worth 20,000,000 rupees, while the shah further extorted from him 4,000 gold coins, 124,000 silver rupees, and 8 elephants. In return he was assigned the job of collecting levees from the eminent Hindus of the city. Jugal Kishore was close to Safdar Jang, and his death in a suspicious accident sometime before 1759 could have been due to those ties. His *takhallus* was Sarvat, but his poetry has not survived.

MAHADJI SINDHIA (d. 1794). He was the successor to Ranoji Sindhia (d. 1750), the founder of the ruling family of Gwalior and a high-ranking commander under the Maratha king, Baji Rao I. Mahadji Sindhia played a major role in the northward expansion of Maratha power. He was badly wounded in the 1761 debacle at Panipat but continued to dominate the political and military scene for a long time. He escorted Shah 'Alam II back to Delhi and continued to support him during the subsequent conflicts between the various factions at the court. In 1784, Shah 'Alam conferred on Mahadji the rank of *wakīl-e muṭlaq* (regent plenipotentiary), which formally established a tie between Mahadji and the emperor independent of the Maratha king, the Peshwa, and also entitled him to the fruits of any success he then obtained in the field. When Ghulam Qadir occupied Delhi and blinded the emperor, it was again Mahadji who came to the rescue.

In 1782 Mahadji helped resolve the five-year-long conflict between the Marathas and the English. The rivalry between the Holkars of Indore and the Sindhias of Gwalior was a major factor in the political history of the Rajputs, the Jats, and the later Mughals.

NAGAR MAL (d. 1774). Emperor Muhammad Shah's comptroller of the crown lands was a Khatri named Raja Bakht Mal, who had an employee named Chaj Mal Khatri, a native of Noshehra, in Punjab. Nagar Mal was Chaj Mal's son and came to Delhi to join his father when he was fourteen. He found favor with Bakht Mal and obtained a minor position under him. After Bakht Mal's death, his son, Jiwan Mal, succeeded him, but was removed from the position by Nadir Shah. Eventually the job went to Nagar Mal. In 1748, Ahmad Shah appointed Nagar Mal the comptroller of gifted lands (*dīwān-e tan*) and placed the crown lands under the control of Najm-ud-Daula Ishaq Khan. When the latter died in 1750, the position again went to Nagar Mal. 'Imad-ul-Mulk at first plotted against Nagar Mal, but soon the two reconciled. In return for his help against Safdar Jang, Nagar Mal further received near the end of 1757 the titles of maharaja and 'umdat-ul-mulk from 'Alamgir II. The emperor's son, the future Shah 'Alam II, later accused Nagar Mal of misappropriating the revenues of the crown territories and "despoiling the treasury." Nagar Mal seems to have played many a mediating role during the period under review. Some are mentioned by Mir, but others are not—for example, the meeting arranged by the raja between Najib-ud-Daula and Suraj Mal at Dankaur in the third week of November 1761. Apparently Mir did not always accompany the raja on his trips. Nagar Mal's personal estate was in Rewari, Haryana.

NAJAF KHAN (1737-1782). He was born in Mashhad, Iran, where his ancestors had been hereditary custodians at the tomb of Imam Riza. His sister married Mirza Muhsin Khan, Muhammad Shah's ambassador at the Iranian court, who brought him along to Delhi and raised him. Najaf Khan chose the career of a soldier of fortune and served Qasim Ali Khan of Bengal, only to abandon him later and raise his own expertly trained forces in Bundelkhand whose services were sought by the local Bundela chiefs. Eventually he threw in his lot with the British. His role in various campaigns resulted in his accompanying the Emperor Shah 'Alam II to Delhi in 1772. As the commander of imperial armies, he conducted successful campaigns against the Jats and the Rohillas, but once appointed as the emperor's regent plenipotentiary, he settled down to a life of luxury in Delhi that soon led to dissolution and death.

NAJIB-UD-DAULA (d. 1770). An Afghan of the Umar Khel clan, he started as an ordinary soldier in the army of Ali Muhammad Khan, the Rohilla chief, but made rapid progress, gained contingents of his own, and married the niece of Ali Muhammad Khan. For helping 'Imad-ul-Mulk against Safdar Jang, he received the title Najib-ud-Daula and was also made the commandant of Saharanpur. In 1757 Ahmad Shah 'Abdali made Najib the paymaster general of the realm. That, however, brought him into conflict with 'Imad-ul-Mulk, forcing him to retire to his estate. After the latter had Emperor 'Alamgir II killed, Shah 'Alam declared himself the new emperor and appointed Najib his regent. After 'Abdali's decisive victory over the Marathas in 1761, Najib became the virtual ruler at Delhi as the emperor's regent plenipotentiary, and by all accounts ably managed his affairs.

SAFDAR JANG (1708?-1754). His name was Mirza Muqim. At the age of fifteen, his mother's brother, Sa'adat Khan Burhan-ul-Mulk, the governor of Avadh under Muhammad Shah, invited him from Nishapur to India. Burhan-ul-Mulk gave him his daughter in marriage and had him appointed his deputy. When Nadir Shah invaded India in 1739, Burhan-ul-Mulk betrayed Muhammad Shah for his own gain; he, however, died while the shah was still in Delhi, leaving behind no son. Safdar Jang, who was in Avadh, offered 20,000,000 rupees to the shah and was elevated to his uncle's position. Muhammad Shah confirmed the appointment and conferred on him the title Safdar Jang. Like his uncle, Safdar Jang busied himself with the affairs and intrigues at Delhi and succeeded in becoming the vazir under Emperor Ahmad Shah in 1748. Five years later, Safdar Jang was out-intrigued by 'Imad-ul-Mulk and had to retire to Avadh, where he died a year later. His remains were brought to Delhi and buried there. Shuja-ud-Daula, his son and successor, built the tomb that is still a landmark in Delhi.

SAMSAM-UD-DAULA. (1672?-1739). Member of a Central Asian Naqshbandi Sufi family settled at Agra. His name was Khwaja Muhammad 'Asim. He rose in rank and power with the rise of Emperor Farrukh Siyar (1713-1719), whose tutor he had been. During Muhammad Shah's reign, he was one of his three highest-ranking nobles and held the position of the paymaster general of the realm. He is described as priding himself on his Indian birth and ways—for example, he used to practice yoga and was more at home in Urdu than in Persian; his delight at Mir's droll comment on "pen case" could be indicative of his view of courtly Persian. As a person, Samsam is described as generous and faithful but also somewhat vain—the latter tendency probably cost him his life on the battlefield. A later Samsam-ud-Daula mentioned in the text was a man of lesser worth.

SHUJA-UD-DAULA (1732–1775). Named at birth Mirza Jalaluddin, he received his title from Emperor Ahmad Shah during the heyday of his own father, Safdar Jang, whom he replaced as the governor of Avadh after the latter's death in 1754. Later, Shah 'Alam II, while still in exile, made him his vazir. In 1761, Shuja-ud-Daula sided with Ahmad Shah 'Abdali at Panipat, but lost out to Najib-ud-Daula in the final control of Delhi. After the defeat at Buxar, Shuja-ud-Daula lost most of his hard-earned eastern territories to the British; the only further gain he could make was westward, at the cost of the Rohillas. He was the last independent ruler of Avadh. Contemporary accounts describe him as an able administrator and a brave general but also condemn him for excess and dissoluteness.

SURAJ MAL (1707?–1763). He was the adopted son of Badan Singh, the first Jat leader to create a nation out of a people whose previous prominent occupation had been banditry on the imperial highway from Delhi to Agra. From an early age, Suraj Mal shared the burden of work with Badan Singh in all matters. Together they constructed a number of fortified cities and luxurious palaces, and shrewdly used the rivalries between Jaipur and Mewar, as well as the conflicting ambitions of the factions at the Mughal court, to expand Jat territory and power while keeping at bay their most powerful antagonists, the Marathas. After Badan Singh's death in 1756, Suraj Mal dominated the scene for seven more years, managing even to get the better of Ahmad Shah 'Abdali. His generosity of spirit is evident from the protection he provided to 'Imad-ul-Mulk, his erstwhile enemy. In fact, during the worst days of trouble in Delhi, thousands of its people of every rank and religion found shelter in his forts at Kumher, Dig, and Bharatpur.

GLOSSARY

AKBARABAD Agra. The name Akbarabad was given to it by Shahjahan, Emperor Akbar's grandson

bakhshī paymaster in the Mughal imperial administration

chādar a sheet of cloth

dīwān in the context of the Mughal administration, a revenue minister or the head of a revenue department; in the context of poetry, a collection of verse

doab (*do-āb*) any area lying between two rivers; here, the stretch of land in north India between the rivers Ganga and Jamuna

fakir (*faqīr*) an unworldly person. Also used to refer to oneself as an expression of humility

faujdār commandant of a body of soldiers assigned to maintain law and order in specific areas, such as a fort or a town

firangī a European. From "Frank"

ghazal a short lyrical poem with a specific rhyme and meter structure

ḥalwā a sweet dish made from clarified butter, flour, and sugar

'ishā the final prayer of the day, performed a couple of hours after sunset

JAT (*jāṭ*) name of a tribally identified group of people, now mostly in western Uttar Pradesh, northeastern Rajasthan, and Haryana

KAABA the "House of God" at Mecca that Muslims circumvent during the hajj

khāliṣa crown lands, the revenues of which were earmarked for the royal family

khān-e sāmān the chief steward; master of the imperial household

khwāja sarā master of the seraglio, who was always a eunuch; a eunuch

kuroh a measure of distance, roughly equivalent to two kilometers

lungī a wraparound cloth for the lower body

lūṭī a lewd person; a sodomite

maghrib the prayer time just after sunset; lit. west

MARATHA (*Marāṭhā*) name of a cohort of people of western and central India—present-day Maharashtra—consisting of several ethnically identified groups

maṣnawī a narrative poem consisting of rhymed couplets in certain preferred meters

mīr bakhshī paymaster general of both the civil and military establishments under the Mughals

nāẓim administrator; head of a province

nāẓir officer assigned to supervise the administration of a city or fort

rekhta an earlier name for Urdu; also earlier referred to the poetry written in that language

ROHILLA (*rohīla*) a group of Afghan origin settled in western Uttar Pradesh, in the region named Rohilkhand after them

SHAHJAHANABAD (*shāhjahānābād*) the walled city built by Emperor Shahjahan at Delhi

shaikh chief; mentor; a Sufi master

suba (*ṣūba*) province

subedar (*ṣūbedār*) chief of the province

tahajjud the nonobligatory prayers that devout Muslims perform sometime after midnight

takhallus (*takhalluṣ*) the name Urdu and Persian poets added to their given names—often a part of the original name—to use in the "signature" verse of any composition, which usually became the name they were most known by

takiya the habitat of any otherworldly person or fakir

tan the imperial department that managed the pay or estate (in lieu of pay) assigned to nobles

tazkira a biographical dictionary; a biography

vazir (*wazīr*) prime minister; minister

zamīndār landholders who were not themselves tillers of the land

BIBLIOGRAPHY

Editions and Translations

Mir, Mir Taqi. 1928. *Ẕikr-e Mīr*. Edited by Abdul Haq. Aurangabad: Anjuman-e Taraqqi-e Urdu.

———. 1929. *Faiẓ-e Mīr*. Edited by Syed Masud Hasan Rizvi Adib. Lucknow: Anjuman-e Urdu.

———. 1982. *Kulliyāt-e Mīr*. Edited by Kalb-e ʿAli Khan Faʾiq. 6 vols. Lahore: Majlis-e Taraqqi-e Adab.

———.1984. *Nikāt-al-Shuʿarā*. Edited by Mahmud Ilahi. Lucknow: Uttar Pradesh Urdu Academy.

Mir, Mir Taqi. 1996. *Mīr kī Āpbītī*. Translated by Nisar Ahmad Faruqi. Delhi: Anjuman-e Taraqqi-e Urdu. Original edition, 1957. (Urdu)

———.1999. *Zikr-i Mir: The Autobiography of the Eighteenth-Century Mughal Poet: Mir Muhammad Taqi 'Mir.'* Translated by C. M. Naim. New Delhi: Oxford University Press.

Other Sources

Arzu, Sirajuddin ʿAli Khan. 1970. *Charāgh-e Hidāyat*. Bombay: Ali Bhai Sharaf Ali.

Azad, Muhammad Husain. 1917. *Āb-e Ḥayāt*. Lahore: Azad Book Depot.

Grier, Sydney C., ed. 1905. *The Letters of Warren Hastings to His Wife*. Edinburgh: William Blackwood Sons.

Heber, Reginald D. D. 1843. *Narrative of a Journey Through the Upper Provinces of India from Calcutta to Bombay, 1824–1825*. 2 vols. London: John Murray.

Jalibi, Jamil. 1983. *Muhammad Taqī Mīr*. Delhi: Educational Publishing House.

Khan, Dargah Quli. 1993. *Muraqqaʿ-e Dihlī*. Edited by Khaliq Anjum. New Delhi: Khaliq Anjum.

Mushafi, Ghulam Hamdani. 2012. *ʿIqd-e Ṣuraiyā*. Edited by Shahabuddin Saqib. Aligarh: Shahabuddin Saqib.

Rashid, Sh. Abdur. 1978. *History of the Muslims of Indo-Pakistan Sub-Continent*. Lahore: Research Society of Pakistan.

Sarkar, Jadunath. 1964. *Fall of the Mughal Empire*. Vol. 1. 3rd ed. Calcutta:

M. C. Sarkar Sons.

———. 1966. *Fall of the Mughal Empire.* Vol. 2. 3rd ed. Calcutta: M. C. Sarkar Sons.

———. 1964. *Fall of the Mughal Empire.* Vol. 3. 3rd ed. Calcutta: Orient Longman.

———. 1972. *Fall of the Mughal Empire.* Vol. 4. Calcutta: Orient Longman.

INDEX

Abaqa Khan, King, 344n90
'Abbas II, Shah, 313, 327, 345n93
'Abdali Durrani, Ahmad Shah
157, 165, 223, 227, 350; Lahore
attacked by, 135, 151; Delhi
plundered by, 169
'Abdul Ahad Khan, Majd-ud-
Daula: as *dīwān* or revenue
minister, 251, 255, 279; *firangīs*
and, 291; imprisoned, 291, 297;
Najaf Khan and, 263, 271, 273;
Raja of Patiala and, 263, 265;
relatives of, 253, 269; Shafi
and, 279, 281, 283
'Abdul 'Aziz 'Izzat, Shaikh, 19
Abdul Haq, Maulvi, xvii, xxi
'Abdul Majid Khan, 251
'Abdul Qadir "Bedil," Mirza, 317,
323, 325, 345n102
'Abdur Rahman, 333
Āb-e Ḥayāt, ix
Abhay Singh of Jodhpur, 139
Abu Jahl, 313, 345n97
Abul Barkat Khan, 269
Abul Fath, 117
Abul Qasim Khan, 253, 269
Adam, 5
Afghans, 137, 143, 171, 199, 201,
335
Afrasiyab Khan, 279, 281, 283,
291, 293; as Amir-ul-Umara,
285
Afzaluddin Khaqani, 344n88
Agra, vii–viii, xi. *See also*
Akbarabad

Ahmad 'Ali Khan, 321
Ahmad Beg Hamadani, 281, 283,
285
Ahmad Beg, 111. *See also* Jawan-e
'Aziz
Ahmad Khan Bangash, 153, 155,
177, 223
Ahmad Khan, brother of Qa'im
Khan, 141
Ahmad Shah, Emperor, 135, 137,
143, 149, 349
Ahmedabad, 7
Ajmer, 137, 139
Akbar, Emperor, 345n95
Akbarabad, 23, 25, 151, 247,
291; Ahmad Beg Hamadani
holds, 281, 283; Alamganj
neighborhood in, 115;
Asadullah in, 101; fort in,
203, 261, 297, 299; Idgah of,
45; 'Imad-ul-Mulk in, 151,
153; Jats control, 261; Jawahir
Singh in, 227, 231; Marathas
in, 177, 297, 299; Mir "belongs
to," xi; Mir's family or family
graves in, 7, 29, 115, 203, 229;
Mir returns to, 203, 229;
Mirza Isma'il in, 297, 299,
301; Najaf Khan in, 261, 263,
269; poets of, 203; route to
Shahjahanabad from, 203. *See
also* Agra
'Alamgir II, Emperor, xiii, 149,
151, 349; murdered, 161, 163,
165

361

Nawab, 141, 143, 149, 277, 317
Ishar Singh, 135
Islam, 91, 211, 329, 344n83
Isma'il Beg, Mirza, 297, 299, 301
I'timad-ud-Daula, Qamaruddin
    Khan, Vazir-ul-Mamalik, 135,
    145

Jacob, 11
Ja'far, Mir, 133
Jahan Khan, 157, 175
Jaipur, 231, 237, 245
Jai Singh (mace bearer), 155
Jai Singh, Raja, 135, 179, 229
Jamuna, 147, 161, 175, 231, 235;
    Faridabad crossing, 243; forts
    near, 177; Mir visits, 205;
    Panipat crossing, 165, 187
Janko, 161
Jats: battles or conflicts of, 233,
    235, 257, 259, 261, 263; chiefs
    or nobles, viii, 223, 241, 257,
    259; forts of, xviii, 257, 261,
    303; places controlled by, 255,
    257, 261; soldiers or army of,
    xiii, 243, 257, 259
Jawahir Singh, 209, 217, 229;
    Delhi besieged by, 223; killed,
    231; Marathas attack, 225, 227
Jawan Bakht Jahandar Shah,
    Prince, 175, 199, 291, 344n77
Jawan-e 'Aziz, 45, 339n13
Jawan-e 'Aziz, Ahmad Beg, 111,
    113, 115
Jawid Khan, Nawab Bahadur,
    137, 141, 143, 323, 342n47, 353
Jesus, 21
Jhansi, 245
Jiya Ram, 233

Jodhpur, 139
Jugal Kishore, Raja, 149, 155, 179,
    353

Kaaba, 95, 111, 113
Kabud Jama, 97, 99, 101
Kalim, Muhammad Husain, 323,
    346n108
Kalimullah Akbarabadi, Shah, 9
Kaman, 179, 237
Kara, 265
Karbala, 342n49
Karnal, 165
Kashmir, 269
Katra Miranpur, 267n
Khafshan Namud, 19
Khan-e Saman, 183
Khaqani, Hakim Afzaluddin,
    307, 344n88
Kheri Singh, 233
Khizr, 27, 339n11
Khizri Gate, 303
Khundsar, 307
Khurasan, 307
Khwaja Ghalib, 157
Kishori, 261
Kol, 175
Kumher: fort at, xviii, 233, 261;
    Mir and Raja Nagar Mal in, xi,
    xvi, xviii, 179, 187, 189
Kunjpura, 87n, 341n43

Lahore, 17, 137, 159, 199, 201,
    344n75; Durranis attack, 135,
    151, 157
Lahori Gate, 247
Latafat 'Ali Khan, 281–283
Lorestan, 344n89
Lucknow, 285, 343n67, 343n71,

344n76; famine in, 343nn74–
75; Jawan Bakht in, 291,
293, 344n77; Mir in, viii–ix,
xiii, xviii, 277, 279, 343n64;
nawab's palace in, 287

Madec, René, 243, 342n57
Madho Singh of Jaipur, Raja, 229,
231, 237
Mahadji Sindhia, 239, 245, 295,
297, 303, 353
Maha Narain, 143
Mahram Khan, 9
Maidan Garhi, 257
Majma'-al-Nafā'is, xvi
Makhfi, Makhfiya-e Rashti, 315
Malhar Rao Holkar. *See* Holkar,
Malhar Rao
Marathas: in Akbarabad, 177,
247, 297, 299, 301; at battle of
Barari Ghat, 167; at battle of
Kunjpura, 187; battle tactics
of, 189; chieftains of, 147, 157,
165, 175, 185, 223, 235, 239,
241, 245, 301; in Delhi, 153,
167, 185, 235, 239, 245, 247,
295, 297, 303; *firangīs* and,
225; Ghulam Qadir and, 299,
301, 303; 'Imad-ul-Mulk and,
147, 161, 175, 185; Jawahir
Singh and Sikhs fight, 225,
227; looting by, xiii, 147, 153,
231, 243; Muhammad Beg
Hamadani or Mirza Isma'il
and, 293, 297, 299, 301; Naval
Singh and, 233, 235; Raja
Nagar Mal and, 153, 185;
Rajputs and, 231; Shah 'Abdali
Durrani and, 157, 159, 165, 167,

175, 177, 187, 189, 191, 193, 227;
Shah 'Alam II and, xiii, 159,
239, 241, 243, 245, 247, 249,
291, 295, 297, 299, 301, 303
Ma'sum, Mir, 317
Mathura, 153, 233
Maulana Rum. *See* Rumi,
Jalaluddin
Mazhar Jan-e Janan, Mirza, 321,
331
Mewat, 175
Mir, Mir Muhammad Taqi: in
Akbarabad, viii, 203, 205, 207,
229; birth or family of, vii–ix,
xiv–xv, 7, 119, 123, 127, 145,
183, 341nn31–32, 346n108;
death of, ix; in Delhi, viii, xii,
xviii, 125, 127, 143, 169, 173,
179, 195, 197, 199, 237, 269,
275, 343n64; in Dig, xviii; as
diplomat, xvi, 237; on hunting
trips, x, 293, 295; ghazals by,
vii, 279, 295, 344n78; health
or teeth of, 253, 255, 342n63;
Ihsanullah visited by, 47,
55; in Kaman, 179, 237; in
Kumher, xviii, 179, 187, 189;
in Lucknow, viii–ix, xviii, 277,
279, 343n64; *masnawi* by, vii;
oeuvre of, vii, ix; patrons of,
viii, xvi, xix, 125, 127, 135, 141,
143, 145, 155, 157, 179, 181,
183, 189, 223, 237, 239, 241,
251, 253, 269, 277, 279, 295,
342n47, 343n65; Persian works
by, x, xviii; religious views of,
xiv; studies of, viii, 37, 131, 133,
143, 341n34; *takhallus* of, vii,
xi, 7; "uncle" Amanullah and,

37, 47, 73, 107; Urdu works
by, vii, ix, xviii, 133. *See also*
Zikr-e Mīr
Moses, 77, 79
Muʻawiya, 9, 338n7
Muʻinuddin Chishti, Khwaja,
139, 327
Muʻin-ul-Mulk, 135, 137, 151, 159
Mughals, 221, 327, 335;
emperors, xii, 251, 341n41,
349–50; Marathas and, 243,
245, 247, 249; officials, viii, ix,
339n9
Muhammad, the Prophet, vii, 19,
61, 313, 333, 340n17, 340n25,
345n97
Muhammad ʻAli, vii–viii, xii,
119, 125, 339n6; advises Mir,
11, 15, 109, 119, 121; Ahmad
Beg meets, 111; Amanullah
meets, 31; Asadullah visits,
97, 99, 101, 103; in Bayana, 23;
death and burial of, 121, 123,
339n9, 341n31; in Delhi, 19;
as dervish, xiv, 9, 21, 27, 29,
39, 73; inheritance of books
from, 119, 341n30; known as
ʻAli-e Muttaqi, 9, 29, 43, 47,
55, 73, 101; known as ʻAziz
Murda, 107, 109, 115, 340n28;
in Lahore, 17; returns to
Akbarabad, 25
Muhammad Ashraf, 307
Muhammad ʻAsim, Khwaja. *See*
Samsam-ud-Daula
Muhammad Baʼith, 115
Muhammad Baqir Majlisi,
Mulla, 307, 344n86
Muhammad Basit, Khwaja, 125

Muhammad Beg Hamadani, 293,
297
Muhammad Hasan, Hafiz, viii,
119, 121, 123
Muhammad Khan Bangash, 141
Muhammad Razi, Mir, viii, 123,
141
Muhammad Saʻid Ashraf, Mulla,
333
Muhammad Shah, Emperor, xii,
127, 135, 137, 317, 321, 349;
nobles during reign of, 145,
149, 346n104
Muhammad Taqi, viii
Mukhtar-ud-Daula, 271, 343n67
Muraqqaʻ-e Dihlī, xii
Murtaza Khan, 329
Muslims, 11, 91, 95, 203, 339n7,
339n15, 345n96. *See also* Shias;
Sufis; Sunnis
Mutawwal, 143
Muzaffar Jang, 277

Nadir Shah, xii, 127
Nagar Mal, Raja, 161, 211, 217,
235, 251, 354; goes to Kaman,
235–237; Marathas and, 153,
177; Mir leaves service of, xvi,
237, 239; as Mir's patron, viii,
xvi, xviii, 155, 157, 179, 187,
189, 341n40; Najib-ud-Daula
and, 217; promoted, 149, 151,
341n39; shah summons, 193;
sons of, 155, 157, 183, 237, 239;
Suraj Mal and, 151, 169, 185,
187, 203, 211
Najabat Khan Rohilla, 187
Najaf Khan, Zulfiqar-ud-Daula,
354; ʻAbdul Ahad Khan

339nn1–2, 340n24, 344n83, 345n96
Qutbuddin Bakhtiyar Kaki, Khwaja, 255, 327
Qutbuddin Khan, 253

Raghunath Rao, 227
Rajputs, 229, 231, 297
Ranjit Singh, 233, 259, 261
Rao Ratan Singh, 231
"Rasul Numa," Sayyid Hasan, 333, 347n119
Remembrances. See *Zikr-e Mīr*
Ri'ayat Khan, 135, 137, 139
Rohillas, 141, 145, 153, 215; Delhi attacked by, xiii, 167, 169, 171; Hafiz Rahmat Khan leads, 265, 267, 269; Marathas defeat, 303; as Sunnis, 342n50
Rumi, Jalaluddin, 305, 344n84, 345n96

Sa'adat 'Ali, Mir, 133, 340n35
Sa'adat 'Ali Khan, Nawab, ix
Sadashiv Rao Bhau. *See* Bhau, Sadashiv Rao
Sadat Khan, Zulfiqar Jang, 137, 143
Sa'di, 321, 346n107
Sadruddin Qunavi, Shaikh, 305, 344n84
Sa'duddin Khan, 151, 183, 253
Safdar Jang, 141, 143, 147, 153, 179, 354; Ahmad Shah and, 135, 137; becomes vazir, 137; death of, 149
Safdar Muhammad Khan, 321, 323
Saharanpur, 153, 243, 299

Sahiba, 159, 165
Sa'ib, Mirza Muhammad 'Ali, 311, 315, 317, 345n93
Sakar Tal, 235
Salam, 143
Salar Jang, Nawab, 277, 279
Samad Khan, 183, 187
Sambhar, 139
Samsam-ud-Daula, 147, 149, 341n38
Samsam-ud-Daula, Khwaja Muhammad 'Asim, 21, 125, 339n9, 355
Sarai Arab, 239
Sarfaraz-ud-Daula Hasan Raza Khan, 270, 343n67
Sarkar Begum, 209
Sattar Quli Khan Kashmiri, 139, 159
Sauda, Mirza Muhammad Rafi', xvi
Sayyid Sharif, Mir, 305
Shahabad, 223
Shah 'Alam II, Emperor, xiii, 159, 199, 203, 209, 342n50, 350; 'Abdul Ahad Khan and, 255, 263, 283; Azimabad attacked by, 219; blinded, 301, 303; in Battle of Buxar, 221; finances of, 221, 239, 245, 247, 251, 255, 265, 297, 303; *firangīs* and, 159, 219, 221, 281; Ghulam Qadir and, 299, 301, 303; Mir and, 269, 343n66; Marathas or Mahadji Sindhia and, 239, 241, 243, 295, 297, 303; Najaf Khan and, 255, 263, 275
Shahdara, 303
Shah Jahan, Emperor, 9

ABOUT THE BOOK

Murty Classical Library of India volumes are designed by Rathna Ramanathan and Guglielmo Rossi. Informed by the history of the Indic book and drawing inspiration from polyphonic classical music, the series design is based on the idea of "unity in diversity," celebrating the individuality of each language while bringing them together within a cohesive visual identity.

The Persian text of this book is set in Nassim, an award-winning, versatile typeface designed by Titus Nemeth. Befitting its use in a new edition of classical literature, the type's contemporary design incorporates elements derived from Islamic manuscript practice.

The English text is set in Antwerp, designed by Henrik Kubel from A2-TYPE and chosen for its versatility and balance with the Indic typography. The design is a free-spirited amalgamation and interpretation of the archives of type at the Museum Plantin-Moretus in Antwerp.

All the fonts commissioned for the Murty Classical Library of India will be made available, free of charge, for non-commercial use. For more information about the typography and design of the series, please visit *http://www.hup.harvard.edu/mcli*.

Printed by Replika Press, Sonipat, India.

Topic Ideas

- qualities of Sufi aescetism
- importance of dialouge and <u>religious</u>
★ <u>debate</u> in Sufi tradition

- father-son relationship (not much)
- treatment of "mental illness" or
  "madness" in the Mughal period
- male admiration of other men